Praise for Every Ounce of Courage

"In Every Ounce of Courage Ms. Besa-Quirino has woven memoir, history, and culinary narrative into an engrossing account of her mother's remarkable life. I was as absorbed by Quirino's suspenseful telling of her mother's fearlessness in Japanese-occupied Manila during WWII as I was enchanted by her depictions of family life in the Philippine provinces post-war. And, I was made very hungry by her memories of the mouthwatering dishes that Ms. Quirino's mother lovingly made for her family."

—Robyn Eckhardt, Food Writer, and Author, Istanbul And Beyond

"Book is heart wrenching. A daughter's loving homage to her mother through the prism of family recipes that were handed down through several generations. More than that, it is a daughter's discovery of a courageous and selfless woman who saved the lives of countless prisoners-of-war during World War II in the Philippines."

—Cecilia I. Gaerlan, Founder & Executive Director, Bataan Legacy Historical Society

"This book is a treasury of family lore, a fond look back at a lost world. It is a human and humane encounter with greatness and kindness, the two necessarily sustaining each other; and it is a compendium of delights for the senses which is what all good food and the discussion of good food can be and should be. A labor of love, it will kindle in all who read it, a love, in return, for what it means to be a Filipino and belong to a family—the extended kind we Filipinos all uphold and defend."

—Manuel L. Quezon III, Columnist, The Philippine Daily Inquirer

"This book is as warm and comforting as a home-cooked meal at a family table. I savored every intimate morsel of these well-told and beautiful stories."

—Ben Montgomery, author of New York Times bestselling Grandma Gatewood's Walk

"Woven in between her family's stories is a mouthwatering description of Filipino food and recipes. I had such a unique experience reading Every Ounce of Courage. I was riveted, moved and inspired, and at the same time, I was hungry for dishes from my home country. I loved every page/bite."

—Bren Bataclan, Author of Fe, A Traumatized Son's Graphic Memoir

"Only a writer, such as Elizabeth Ann Quirino, can bring to life true stories from different generations with remarkable vividness and veracity. Any food or historical nonfiction enthusiast will find Every Ounce of Courage *a gem of a book."*

—Jacqueline Chio-Lauri, Picture Book Biographer and Anthologist, Author, Editor of The New Filipino Kitchen: Stories & Recipes from around the Globe

"Elizabeth Ann Quirino aims a sharp lens on World War II in the Philippines, centering the women and 'Godmothers' in wartime stories that typically have only had men as heroes."

—Elena Buensallido Mangahas, Filipino American National Historical Society, Lifetime Member and Museum Docent

"Growing up in Tarlac, and connections with Manila and Silay, Besa-Quirino takes us onto a culinary journey that is both heartfelt and profound. Opening past wounds of the second World War is key to the purging of the physical and mental anguish caused by COVID-19. During the pandemic, Besa-Quirino was undaunted and focused, cooking and baking her mother's recipes, channeling her mother's bravery, and wrote the accompanying essays and recipes as a form of defiance against the silent enemy that loomed over us for two and a half years. Deliverance through sheer reflection, because food and mothers are sources of joy, comfort, and strength, especially during times of adversity."

—Ige Ramos, Food Writer and Book Designer

"In this loving tribute and meticulously researched biography of her mother, a daughter brings together pieces from others' memoirs, letters, and diaries, where her mother is described as 'Joan of Arc' by a POW, and artifacts, such as two Medals of Freedom from the US government for assisting American POWs during World War II, as well as the writer's memories. Her mother is not only a war hero, but a visionary in the kitchen, each dish cooked with love and imbued with the history of the women who made these recipes. Read this memoir if you want to learn about what life was like for one family during the early 20th century in Philippines, if you want to know what World War II in the Philippines was like from the perspective of a Filipina trying to do her part, if you like food writing, if you are interested in mothers and daughters, and if you are inspired to read about a woman who is brought from the margins of others' stories to the center of her own book."

—Grace Talusan, Author, The Body Papers

"In this beautifully crafted memoir, Elizabeth Ann Quirino amazingly combines and weaves together the gustatory and the historical."
—Desiree Ann C. Benipayo, VP, Research and Education Philippine World War II Memorial Foundation

"That we get not just an amazing story of an incredible woman's courage, but also the precious family recipes that go with it, is worth its weight in gold! This book is a gift to all who read it."
—Joey de Larrazabal, Food Writer, Recipe Developer, 80 Breakfasts

As she uncovers her mother's story, Elizabeth Ann shows us how food is the thread that binds us together, revealing how Lulu is not just a heroine to her family but to the equally courageous American and Filipino POWs who owe her their lives. What a beautifully written and inspiring memoir!
—Liren-Legaspi, Baker, Writer and Founder, Kitchen Confidante, Author, Meat to the Side: A Plant-Forward Guide to Bringing Balance to Your Plate

In Every Ounce of Courage, *renowned journalist and cookbook author Elizabeth Ann Besa-Quirino shares the astounding story of her mother, Lulu Reyes Besa, whose lifetime of bravery and resilience included saving the lives of countless Filipino and American POW's during World War II. This moving saga follows Lulu's family through four generations, from her childhood and wartime in Manila, to marriage and raising her family in Tarlac Province; through seasons of prosperity and survival, harmony and discord, joy and heartbreak. Fueled by her deep faith and generous heart, Lulu nourishes her community as well as her family from her kitchen and her table, as a parent, volunteer, and faithful friend. The author's evocative descriptions of Lulu's extraordinary cooking kept me hungry as I read. Thankfully, she has included an array of irresistible recipes, from Tito Willie's beloved Beef Pochero to Dad's favorite Pan de Sal and her own signature Mango Jam."*
—Nancie McDermott, Cookbook Author, Food Writer, Cooking Teacher

"Three generations of mother and daughter relationships joined by love and the passion for food and its preparation come alive in the narratives and invite the reader to savor their recipes and experience life's joys, sadness, and the bittersweet."
—Edwin Lozada, President, Philippine American Writers and Artists Association (PAWA)

Every Ounce *of* Courage

A daughter's reflections on her mother's bravery

Elizabeth Ann Besa-Quirino

A memoir with Filipino recipes

For information, address Besa-Quirino LLC at info@ebquirino.com.
18 Edward Drive, Flanders, New Jersey 07836, USA

Author: Elizabeth Ann Besa-Quirino
Cover Design: Tim Quirino
Book Interior Design: Barbara Scott Goodman
Photographs from the Besa-Quirino LLC Library
Author's Photo: Fordyce Studio, New Jersey, USA

Paperback ISBN: 979-8-9875550-0-2
Ebook ISBN : 979-8-9875550-1-9
Library of Congress Control Number : 2023910061

CONTENTS

Chapter 1

I Will Never Be as Brave as My Mother

Lulu Reyes, pre-World War II. Manila 1941.

y the second month of lockdowns during a global pandemic, life was beginning to feel so uncertain.

The world seemed to come to a screeching halt in mid-March 2020 when a dangerous new respiratory disease called COVID-19 began an unstoppable sweep around the globe. Thousands of people in America and around the world were dying each day as schools, offices, stores, salons, restaurants—daily activities and services that we normally take for granted—were shut down. My husband Elpi and I, as well as our neighbors, coworkers and friends, were essentially confined to our own homes under a statewide stay-at-home order.

None of us had any idea how long our lives would have to remain in a holding pattern. We could only hope to wait out this deadly novel coronavirus that was spreading so quickly and straining hospitals to breaking point with seriously ill patients. It was surreal and very scary.

To take my mind off the situation, I bought so much flour and yeast from our local supermarket that the cashier jokingly asked through her mask if I intended to open a bakery. I thought I needed to bake simply to pass the time, but deep down I really needed it to calm my fears and anxieties about COVID-19.

On this particular day, I decided to bake ensaymadas. Making the buttery, cheesy brioche-like pastry requires time, patience and attention, which is exactly why I wanted to make them. But they also remind me of my mother, Lulu, and thoughts of her always seem to calm me down.

"Your Lola Nena baked the best ensaymadas," Mom declared when she saw my first attempt. "She would be so proud of these ensaymadas you baked today!"

I remember the warm feeling of basking in her pride and knowing that her happiness was my happiness, too. I was a teenager when I taught myself how to make ensaymadas with guidance from a typewritten recipe passed down to Mom from my grandmother. As she perfected her recipe with each baking, Lola Nena had embellished the margins of the now-yellowed and creased sheet of paper with annotations in her fine handwriting. Reading the revisions and instructions in her graceful script was as close as I could get to learning by her side.

As I kneaded and rolled the supple dough, I thought back to a night more than twenty years before, to another time I was making ensaymadas and a late-night call unexpectedly linked my present with my mother's past.

. . . .

It was around midnight then and my kitchen and dining room were filled with the aroma of freshly baked sweet bread. I don't recall why I was baking at such a late hour, only that I had just carefully laid out a dozen fluffy buns on the dining table and was sprinkling grated queso de bola over them when the telephone rang. The sound was jarring in the quiet of the night. I wanted to let the machine take the message, but a gut feeling told me it was important. Nobody calls at such an hour unless something has happened, I thought to myself.

Still, I hesitated to interrupt my baking ritual; besides, my hands were greasy from handling the buttery rolls. But the shrill ringing was insistent. Finally, the answering machine kicked in, and an elderly male voice came over the speaker as the caller began to leave a message.

"Hello, my name is Robert Dow. I want to make sure I have the correct number. Are you the daughter of Lulu Reyes? If you are, I am calling to thank your mother…"

I nearly slipped on the kitchen floor as I dashed to pick up the phone, grabbing the handset from the wall with butter-slicked fingers.

"Hello!" I said, out of breath but relieved I caught the caller. "This is Betty Ann. Yes, I'm the daughter of Lulu Reyes Besa."

The voice on the other end of the line, no longer amplified by a machine, was softer and tinged with an emotion I didn't yet understand.

"Are you Lulu's daughter? She saved my life," he announced unexpectedly. "I have been searching for your mother for over fifty years."

With the wireless handset gripped in one hand, I reached with the other into a nearby drawer for a pen and a notepad, and then sat down at the kitchen table.

"I found you through your mother's good friend, Nini Quezon," he explained, pronouncing the surname "Kay-son." "I'm Robert Dow. You can call me Bob."

My mother had never spoken of anyone named Robert Dow, but at the mention of my godmother Nini Quezon Avanceña, one of her dearest longtime friends, I felt reassured this call was not some kind of prank.

"Your mother saved my life when I was a POW," he

repeated, and I could hear a tremor of emotion in his voice.

"Because of her, I have had a wonderful life."

He spoke slowly but I still scribbled quickly, eager to capture each word as he began to talk about the woman I thought I knew as well as I knew myself.

More than fifty years ago, Bob was Corporal Robert J. Dow, one of thousands of American prisoners of war in Japanese-occupied Philippines during World War II. Like many of his fellow captured soldiers, Bob suffered miserably through inhumane conditions inside Japanese POW camps and might have succumbed to the ordeal if it were not for my mother.

"Do you even know the dangers she went through to save our lives? She saved so many American soldiers."

I was astounded by what I was hearing. My parents were married several years after WWII had ended, and they led very quiet lives in the province of Tarlac, where I was raised. They rarely talked to me and my younger sister, Isabel, about the gut-wrenching atrocities my mother witnessed in Manila throughout the war. I knew Mom as a loving and nurturing person, but she had never before mentioned the American and Filipino soldiers she apparently saved. The revelations during my phone conversation with Bob on that night in 1999 were mind-blowing. It took me days—no, years—to fully process.

Now, as the deadliest pandemic in a century was ravaging the world, I was baking ensaymadas again and remembering the night that Bob Dow—retired US Army and WWII veteran, recipient of a Bronze Star and a Purple Heart—reached out to me so that he could thank my mother.

In the years since that phone call, I never stopped thinking of the heartrending war stories Bob shared or how his five-decades-long search for my mother in the Philippines instead led him to me in my suburban New Jersey home. In my heart, it actually felt like a sign sent by my mother that it was time to tell her story.

. . . .

My friends had long urged me to write about my mother's life, and yet I always hesitated. To be honest, I was afraid it would be too bittersweet to sift through the archives of my memories for those times we spent together, talking and cooking and experiencing family moments both joyous and somber, only to remember how much I still miss her. I was afraid that whatever I wrote would not do justice to the beautiful life that Lulu Reyes Besa had lived.

But as I brushed melted butter on the ensaymadas and showered a confetti of grated cheese on top, I realized if I didn't write her story, who would? If I could tell people about how she found the courage to face every trial and tribulation life threw at her, then maybe it could inspire another to do the same. Even if it helped just one person, one family or one community to weather an adversity, my mom would have wanted it. She was like that. She lived every day of her life to make a difference in someone else's.

As it turned out, the COVID-19 lockdowns gave me the gift of time to cook her recipes again, to prepare the traditional, slow-cooked dishes that went all the way back to my grandmother and even my great-grandmother. And so I gathered all of my mother's timeless recipes, and I cooked and baked each one for the next fifteen months.

With each recipe, the recollections of time spent with Mom sprang forward, as vivid as if they had happened just a short while ago. Every time I cooked, it was as if she were looking over my shoulder, whispering guidance and encouragement. The rituals of cooking—assembling the ingredients, choosing the right pot or pan or utensils, putting on an apron—gave me strength to face each uncertain day of our pandemic reality. Every ingredient and step in the recipe, every whiff of aroma that filled the kitchen, every single day of cooking and baking, evoked memories embedded deeply in my heart.

As I researched for this memoir, poring over newspaper clippings, recalling stories from family and friends, and scrutinizing faded photographs, a more detailed portrait of my mother emerged. I felt new wonderment and admiration for the vibrant, remarkable woman that she was, and I wondered if I could ever be as brave or as courageous as her.

By learning more about her heroic war efforts and revisiting her old recipes during the COVID-19 pandemic, I gained a clearer perspective of my own life. As I try to live my ordinary life in this anxious and uncertain era, I look to my mother's extraordinary life to draw comfort from the dishes she taught me to make, to find my own source of courage through her example, and to discover a purpose in sharing the story of the singular, exceptional Lulu Reyes Besa.

Chapter 2

The First Love Story:
Nena and Ponciano

1912

The kusinera gently dropped each plump dumpling into a simmering cauldron of clear chicken broth, careful not to let the liquid splash out onto the fire. She was preparing pancit Molo, a savory soup full of wontons stuffed with pork, and it required a fair amount of skill as the raw meat mixture inside needed to cook all the way through before the delicate dough encasing it overcooked and fell apart. She gave the pot a gentle stir, setting the wontons to bob in a languid swirl of broth.

The enticing aroma of pancit Molo, pungent and heady with the scent of garlic, onions and scallions, drifted from the kitchen into the living room where Nena sat by a large bay window, absentmindedly combing her long hair. She knew it meant lunch was almost ready, and she gazed out the window as she waited to be called to the table.

Luz Jugo y Seraller, fondly known as Nena, was just fifteen years old. As the only daughter of the late Dr. Simplicio Jugo y Vidal and his wife, Juana, the pretty teenager was pampered by her protective, conservative family.

Her father had studied medicine at the Universidad Central de Madrid and was a contemporary of Jose Rizal and Juan Luna, who were also scholars in Spain at the same time. It was in Madrid where he met and fell in love with a beautiful Spanish lady named Juana Seraller, whose wealthy father was sufficiently impressed by the Filipino medical student that he offered to finance the remainder of his studies when political turmoil between the Philippines, Spain and the United

States threatened to cut off his funding. The young couple married shortly after meeting and initially settled in Spain. But after the tragic deaths of their first two infants, they decided on a new start in Simplicio's native land.

Although he was a doctor by profession, Don Simplicio was appointed as the first governor of Capiz province in 1901 by future US President William Howard Taft, then Governor-General of the Philippines. During his two-year tenure, he gained widespread respect for using his own money to help fund construction of provincial government buildings. When he died in 1910, he left his widow and their three children with sufficient means to maintain a comfortable, privileged life. The family continued to live in the ancestral home that stood across from the plazuela of Capiz town, and Doña Juana ensured that Nena and her brothers Juancho and Rafael were well-educated and fluent in Spanish and English as well as the regional language Ilonggo.

Nena had the delicate features of a mestiza: a fair complexion, beautiful large brown eyes and glossy mahogany tresses that reached nearly to the floor. The latter was the reason she was seated by the open window facing the town's public square, running a simple comb through her just-washed hair and hoping the cool, late morning breeze would quickly dry the damp strands.

At that same moment, a gifted young lawyer named Ponciano Reyes was standing across the street, staring up at the Jugo family house. In his early twenties and recently returned from studying in the United States as a pensionado, or government-sponsored scholar, he had been appointed to the chief provincial prosecutor's office, known as the fiscal, and located in the Capiz town hall. He was strolling around the plaza while on a break when he caught sight of the winsome young lady combing her lustrous hair by the window of a stately house.

Ponciano instantly fell in love.

According to the norms of Philippine polite society in the early 1900s, a young unmarried woman first had to be formally introduced to a prospective suitor by an older relative or friend of the family before any courtship could begin. But Ponciano paid no mind to the customs of appropriateness. His heart was beating fast. Heedless of the conservative rules that dictated social manners, he sprinted across the street, unable to resist the need to find out immediately who the lovely girl was and perhaps to meet her.

The loud knocking at the door reverberated through the house. In the sala, Nena stopped what she was doing. From where she sat, she could hear the voices, if not the conversation, of a young gentleman and the housemaid who had answered the knock.

Nena peeked around the doorway to take a surreptitious look at the visitor. She saw that he was handsome and well-dressed, and she knew instinctively he had come to meet her. Suddenly conscious of her appearance and too shy to meet a stranger, even one as attractive as the young man at the front door, she ran to her bedroom to avoid an introduction. In her rush, she left behind the dainty slippers she had taken off when she sat by the window.

The wispy aroma of pancit Molo lingered in the air

as Ponciano was led into the room that Nena had only just vacated. He looked toward the window seat and spotted the abandoned slippers on the floor. Imagining the lovely figure whose delicate feet had been wearing such elegant footwear, he was even more smitten.

In her bedroom, Nena nervously fidgeted with the comb in her hand. Her curiosity was great but her uncertainty was even greater. Who was the young man? Was he really there to see her? As if reading her mind, one of the housemaids tapped on the door. "Señorita, your mother is asking you to come and meet the guest."

Nena turned to face the standing mirror in her room. She gathered her now-dry hair in a satin ribbon, smoothed down a few wrinkles in her dress and slipped her feet into a pair of shoes. Straightening her shoulders, she opened the door and stepped out to meet her first suitor.

....

Christmas 1918

Ponciano and Nena married soon after she turned sixteen years old. Their first child, a daughter, was born on October 31, 1913 in Jaro, Iloilo, where Ponciano had been transferred the previous year after being named fiscal of Iloilo. They christened her Lourdes and gave her the nickname Lulu.

By 1918, Nena was twenty-one years old and the busy mother of three—Lulu and the boys Roberto and Guillermo, whom their parents called Bobby and Willie. Her husband, meanwhile, had established a stellar reputation in the Philippine judiciary. Four years earlier, Ponciano had received a prestigious appointment as assistant department attorney in the Department of Mindanao and Sulu and was promoted to legal head just eight months later. As his star rose ever higher, he moved his young family all the way to Manila and into a house in the Malate district to be closer to the national offices of the Department of Justice.

Then, in 1917, he was named a judge of the Court of First Instance of Zamboanga for the Sixth District. This latest appointment in Zamboanga required him to hold court in the far southern island of Mindanao, but with Nena pregnant with their fourth child, he did not want to uproot his family again. Instead, he chose to travel every week between Manila and Zamboanga by inter-island ferry.

On Christmas Eve 1918, five-year-old Lulu was tasked with making sure her toddler brothers did not go near the Christmas tree, which she had helped to decorate, or play with the gifts underneath, which she had helped to wrap. Already aware of her responsibilities as a big sister, the little girl loved her rambunctious brothers dearly, and it was never a chore to watch over them.

In the kitchen, Nena busied herself preparing the family's Noche Buena dinner. She liked to make the Spanish-Filipino recipes her mother, Juana, had taught her, such as callos, paella and relleno, and desserts like canonigo. Appetizing aromas filled the kitchen and distracted her from the rain and wind whipping against the windows.

A typhoon signal had been raised in Manila, yet Ponciano was preparing to journey back to Zamboanga that night.

Luz "Nena" Jugo and Ponciano Reyes Sr. on their wedding day. 1912

Nena begged him to cancel his trip due to the weather, but he was committed to his work. There were pending cases he wanted to close out before the New Year, and he was considering the many families awaiting judgments who would be affected by a judicial delay. So, after promising his beloved Nena he would be back to spend the rest of the holidays with her and the children, he left the house on Christmas Eve and boarded the steamship SS *Quantico* at the port of Manila.

The following day was Christmas and that evening Nena was again in the kitchen, watching over a simmering pot of fragrant pancit Molo—one of Ponciano's favorites—while Lulu, Bobby and Willie played with their newly opened presents in the sala as holiday music from the phonograph filled the air. The doorbell sounded, and Nena went to answer the front door.

Lulu was curious about who had come by, but she couldn't see the person Mama was talking to. She looked up from her toys as her mother walked back into the living room, reading a piece of paper in her hand, but was startled when Nena suddenly slumped to the floor in front of the Christmas tree as wrenching sobs shook her body. Her cries of grief alarmed the two boys, who turned in distress to their sister. Lulu didn't know what was wrong. She quickly got up from where she and her brothers were playing and ran to their mother, trying to wrap her arms around her distraught parent.

"Mama, porque estas llorando?" she asked worriedly. *Mama, why are you crying?*

"Tu Papa. No va venir mas. Se murio," Nena sobbed. *Your father. He isn't coming anymore. He died.*

Bobby and Willie were still too young to comprehend what was happening, but Lulu understood: Papa was not coming home again.

The slow-moving typhoon that seemed to be skirting past the eastern side of the Philippine archipelago had suddenly and inexplicably made a sharp, almost 90-degree turn directly into the central islands where the SS *Quantico* was sailing south toward Zamboanga. Approximately eighteen hours after leaving Manila port, the inter-island steamer was violently driven onto the rocks of Tablas Island by powerful storm winds. Twenty-one of the seventy-two passengers and crew on board were lost, including Ponciano. Eyewitnesses later reported that Judge Reyes had been swept from the deck of the stricken steamship by a large wave and drowned in the rolling waters of the Romblon Pass.

The tragic loss of such a young man and brilliant legal mind shocked his peers and colleagues. As Judge Jose C. Abreu later wrote of his friend:

When a man dies of the type of Ponciano Reyes who proved himself to be a good citizen both in public and private life… the sentiment of sorrow is universal. It ceases to be a mere family sorrow, and becomes the object of national mourning.[1]

But on Christmas night, to his wife and children, Ponciano's death was purely the most agonizing of family sorrow. Lulu hugged her sobbing mother and her little brothers. For the first time in her five-year-old life, she knew she had to be

1 Abreu, n.p.

brave and strong for Mama, her brothers and the baby sibling who was yet to be born.

She looked up from where they huddled in a tight embrace. Through the doorway of the kitchen, she could see the large pot of pancit Molo on the stove, now forgotten. The broth overflowed the sides, hissing as it spilled onto the heat and sending acrid steam billowing up toward the ceiling. It was Papa's favorite soup, and he would never again share it with them.

Chapter 3

Little Lulu

For years, I was curious about my grandfather and the circumstances surrounding his untimely death. I knew that he died in the early morning hours of Christmas Day, but Mom had left out all the tragic details. As the long days of the pandemic finally gave me time to search online for stories about Lolo Ponciano, I found an article from the *Manila Times,* dated December 28, 1918. Beneath the headline announcing the wreck of the SS *Quantico* was the subheading, "Judge Reyes among victims on Quantico."

My heart beat faster as I read the account. I felt as if my mother was somehow nearby as I learned more about her beloved papa.

The emerging details began to fill out what little I knew about Lolo Ponciano. I learned that he was the first Filipino permitted to practice law in the state of California, and that in addition to having been appointed as a judge, he was also serving as a director of the national census for the year he died. More somberly, the article also told of how Frank Carpenter, the American governor of the Department of Mindanao and Sulu who had personally brought him in to join that office, refused at first to believe his friend was dead without seeing his body. It was a testament to how highly regarded he was among his colleagues.

I was fixated by the news clipping, reading it several times as unanswerable questions swirled in my head. Did Lolo Ponciano really have to leave for Zamboanga that night? Why didn't he listen to Lola Nena's entreaties not to travel during a typhoon? If only he waited for the storm to pass, he could have enjoyed so many more Christmases with his family. It was clear, however, that my grandfather honored his duty to his country above all.

Absorbing the story in the midst of pandemic anxieties, I felt a lump in my throat and a heaviness inside of me. My fears were nothing compared to the depth of grief my grandmother, mother and uncles experienced on that Christmas night. But I gained a better understanding of their immeasurable pain and loss, and I felt a sense of comfort mixed with pride knowing that my grandfather—not yet thirty years old at the time of his death—had led a full life and had accomplished more than many lawyers could hope for in a career only a decade long. Even more, my admiration for Mom and Lola Nena intensified as I realized how much bravery, courage and resilience they demonstrated in the years following the family's tragedy.

. . . .

Little Lulu grew up fast after the night her father died. She was only five years old when it happened but old enough to know she had to be brave like Papa to help Mama and her brothers.

The Christmases that followed were difficult for Nena. Every year during the holidays, Lulu would pray that Mama wouldn't be so sad this time around. She knew her mother cried all night on Christmas Eve because no matter how hard Nena tried to muffle the sound of her sobs, it pierced through the wall between their bedrooms.

Lulu tried to be particularly helpful during the holidays. One year, Nena couldn't hold back her tears until bedtime, and Lulu found her crying quietly in the kitchen as she prepared the family's Noche Buena meal.

"Mama, te voy a ayudar," Lulu offered. *Mama, I'll help you.*

"Estoy cocinando relleno. Acabo de limpiar la gallina," Nena replied reassuringly as she wiped away her tears. *I'm cooking relleno. I just finished cleaning the chicken.*

Lulu stood on a step stool to reach the kitchen counter and took over mixing the stuffing for the relleno. Using a large spoon, she stirred the chopped onions, celery and raisins into the ground pork that was already in a large bowl. Mama added a dash of soy sauce and handed the salt and pepper shakers to her daughter to season the mixture.

Lulu then soaked slices of white bread, called pan Americano, in a cup of milk, squishing the torn pieces with her small hands to moisten them, just as Mama taught her. When the bread had soaked up all the milk, she added it to the pork mixture.

Mama chopped some piquant Spanish chorizos and tossed them into the bowl as well. The robust aroma of chorizo reminded Lulu this was a holiday dish, so she took up the large spoon with renewed enthusiasm and put all her attention and energy into mixing the stuffing well.

They stuffed the deboned chicken together with Nena showing Lulu how to neatly spoon the filling into the boneless bird until it was plump. As the relleno baked in the oven, they savored the luscious aroma that slowly filled the kitchen.

Lulu went to the sala to see what mischief Bobby, Willie and Ponciano Jr. were up to. She had to keep them away from the Christmas tree as the gleeful brothers liked to shake each brightly wrapped gift a little too vigorously to guess what was inside.

Poncy, as he was affectionately called, was the baby of the family and named for the father he would never meet. His birth only a few months after Ponciano Sr.'s death had brought the family joy during a time of heartache. He was proving to be the naughtiest of the three boys, but Nena and especially Lulu indulged his impish nature.

Lulu watched her brothers play and listened to their laughter. It helped lighten her heart as she watched Mama bring out the special holiday plates and set the dinner table for six.

There would always be a setting and an empty chair at the Christmas table for Papa.

....

As roast goose or baked ham are traditional Christmas fare in the West, so is chicken relleno for Pasko in the Philippines. While I finished stuffing a whole boneless chicken for our Christmas dinner, I thought of how my mom and Lola Nena prepared this same dish for many a holiday, and how I've continued the family tradition in my own home in America.

The process of making chicken relleno is laborious, starting with removing the bones from the chicken. Nowadays, an online search will yield tips, tricks and shortcuts, but there is really no easy way. My mom knew how to debone a chicken expertly so that it maintained its original chicken shape. She tried to teach me and I learned grudgingly, but it will never be one of my favorite things to do.

"If you can't debone the chicken yourself, look for a butcher to do it for you," Mom once advised me with obvious practicality.

"Or I don't have to debone the chicken at all," I countered, trying not to sound too sassy. "A shortcut would be to stuff the whole roast chicken with the bones in."

She laughed, but I think she secretly approved of my easier method.

Before I placed the properly deboned and now-stuffed bird into the oven, I stepped back to admire it resting on my wooden chopping board. The relleno was generously plumped with a richly seasoned stuffing of ground pork and beef, Spanish chorizos, raisins, chopped carrots and onions, sweet peas and sweet pickles, a little grated cheese, and some sliced hard-boiled eggs. Later, I would baste the chicken skin with melted butter so it would turn a golden brown during its long, slow roasting.

I always know I've made a perfect chicken relleno when the immense amount of filling doesn't spill out and the roasted bird holds its shape the moment I slice into it straight out of the oven. The chicken and its meaty filling will have become one.

Each scrumptious slice should be packed with a medley of tastes: a flavorsome meatiness, the sweetness of raisins and a hint of pleasant sourness from pickles. I usually serve my relleno with a thick brown gravy made from scratch with the pan drippings—my head spins just thinking about the deliciousness!

Nena Jugo Reyes with teenaged daughter, Lulu.

My mother's recipe for chicken relleno is not quite the same as the one she taught me because I tweaked it when making it for the people in my life whom I love. When my sons Tim and Constante were little, for instance, they liked to argue over who got to the eggs first. In order to avoid any fights, I made sure to add an even number of egg slices so that each of them could get an equal share. My husband, Elpi, on the other hand, loves raisins, so I always add a little more for him.

Although Christmas came with painful memories for my mother and grandmother, cooking traditional holiday dishes like chicken relleno served as a balm, and they were determined not to let the sorrow of loss dim the joy of the season for others.

Mom and Lola Nena taught me that food, whether for the holidays or for every day, is made out of love and served with love.

Chapter 4

A Summer in Paris

$\mathcal{E}$lpi and I moved to the United States several years after my mom passed away. She did not live to see us get married, but I am so grateful she got to know him well before she died the year before our wedding in 1982. In fact, Mom knew even before I did that Elpi was the man for me.

I was back home in Tarlac on Christmas break from college. The morning after a party with some high school classmates, my younger sister, Isabel, poked her head into the room to wake me. "You got a phone call while you were asleep . . . an Elpi Quirino?" she announced.

I was perplexed. He was the son of Mom's personal physician Dr. Constante D. Quirino, and we had been class-mates from kindergarten to second grade. Although he was at a different school from the third grade onward, Elpi and I were still considered "batchmates," or part of the same gradu-ating class year, because the all-girls Holy Spirit Academy and the all-boys Don Bosco Academy were twin institutions. We regularly came into each other's orbit whenever we attended sports and other school events at both campuses. Even so, we were more acquaintances than friends and had exchanged only a few sentences during the party the night before. Why would he be calling? Isabel shrugged. "Oh, he said he's returning some records, so he asked if he can come by this afternoon."

My confusion deepened: I had brought brownies, not re-cords, to the get-together. Nevertheless, Elpi and three friends came over later that afternoon. While I served them a merien-da of freshly baked brownies and scoops of mango ice cream, which they devoured in the sala reserved for guests, Dad read

newspapers in the family room, trying to look simultaneous-
ly stern and indifferent while keeping an eagle eye on the
male visitors. Mom came downstairs to say hello and be her
charming self, but she followed me into the kitchen when I
went to slice some more chocolate squares. Nodding toward
Elpi, she asked, "Who's the tall one?"

"He's Dr. Quirino's son," I replied, oblivious to the
knowing smile on her face.

I almost dropped the Pyrex dish when she declared with
a twinkle in her eye, "You both don't know it yet, but you're
already in love with each other. You're going to marry that
one."

....

Mom wasn't clairvoyant; she simply knew me better than
I knew myself.

Had she still been alive when Elpi and I were making
plans to emigrate from the Philippines, I might have found
it impossible to leave her and the special closeness we shared.
Ironically, Mom once revealed to me a similar reason for why
she married at a later age: she could not bear to leave her
own mama behind, alone in the house where she raised four
children on her own.

I never knew my grandmother, and I'm sad about that.
Lola Nena died just a couple of years before I was born. I
often wish we had met and touched hearts in her lifetime. I
know that she was a powerhouse in the kitchen, and I would
have reveled in learning from her all the classic Filipino and
Spanish dishes she had learned from her mother, Juana. I

would have loved to see her in the flesh, especially after seeing many photos of her dressed resplendently in elegant ternos and ball gowns, her cascades of wavy, dark brown hair that had so enthralled a smitten young lawyer named Ponciano, pinned into fashionable updos. Although she was gone by the time I came along, the stories I heard from my mother left no doubt her bond with her only daughter Lulu was unbreakable.

After Lolo Ponciano's early death, Lola Nena and Mom were inseparable, and their relationship shaped my mother's life. She would tell me about my grandmother's strength and tenacity during those early years, of how she never gave up despite the difficulties she faced as a young widowed mother. To her, nothing was impossible and everything was possible.

According to Mom, they always cooked together, a ritual they both cherished. Telling stories, sharing life lessons, and teaching and learning recipes and cooking techniques enlivened what could have been a routine chore.

Many years later, Mom would recreate the same loving experiences with me. We had our own moments while cooking together. One time, we were making adobo, and as the heady aroma of garlic and vinegar permeated the kitchen, she began telling me about a long-ago trip to Paris and another pot of adobo in another kitchen.

....

1924

Nena and her four children arrived in Paris during the warm summer months of 1924. The First World War had ended six years before, and the city was in the midst of "les années folles," or the crazy years—a glorious time of economic, social and artistic blossoming, akin to the Roaring Twenties in America. The city hosted the Summer Olympics that year, and favorable currency exchange rates attracted increasing numbers of foreign visitors lured by the reasonably low cost of food and accommodations that prevailed through most of the decade.

It was also an important epoch for French fashion as Paris' s already lofty reputation as the capital of couture reached new heights with the emergence of such legendary designers as Coco Chanel, Jeanne Lanvin and Jean Patou, who revolutionized women's fashion by transforming silhouettes and introducing fragrances that would become iconic. *(The classic perfume Joy de Patou was my grandmother's favorite, and later my mom also wore it well into the 1980s.)*

This was the exciting era and environment in which the Reyes family arrived. Lulu was eleven years old and very much the mothering older sister to nine-year-old Bobby, seven-year-old Willie and Poncy, who had just turned six years old. Nena chose for their lodgings an apartment building centrally located in one of the more family-friendly arrondissements. Their rented apartment was ideal for a few weeks' stay—a home away from home where she could cook and do laundry in between exploring the city with the children.

The family of five spent their days walking along narrow laneways, through charming squares and gorgeous parks bursting with people taking promenades down meandering paths. They marveled at the Cathedral of Notre Dame, then strolled across the Petit Pont to wander around the center of

Parisian café culture in the 6th arrondissement and to browse among the stacks of books at the original Shakespeare and Company bookshop, where F. Scott Fitzgerald, James Joyce and Gertrude Stein were regular patrons.

("You might have been sipping coffee or eating a croissant next to some famous artist or writer—Hemingway might have been enjoying his food and wine next to you!" I gushed as Mom narrated the story and smiled at my excitement.)

For a fleeting, impetuous moment, Nena contemplated moving to this vibrant city, far away from her relatives in the Philippines. After the loss of Ponciano and then the passing of her widowed mother, Juana, within the last few years, she couldn't quite banish the feelings of loneliness and sadness. Perhaps Paris could lift her spirits—she felt a sense of rejuvenation in this city.

One afternoon, Nena decided to cook Filipino adobo for the children. She bought fresh chicken from a local butcher, a bottle of French vinegar and other requisite ingredients such as garlic, bay leaves and pepper, all of which she tossed into a heavy stockpot. The stew simmered for nearly half an hour as the powerfully pungent aromas of vinegar and garlic whirled around the tiny kitchen and their small living quarters. Fragrant steamed rice stayed warm in another cauldron on the burner next to the adobo.

The daytime temperatures during a Parisian summer could be stifling inside a small apartment, so Nena kept the windows open all the time.

"Lu, open the windows wider, please. It's too hot in here," she asked her daughter.

A sudden, loud banging at the door startled mother and daughter, and the boys looked up from where they sat on the sofa. Nena rushed to open the door as Lulu gathered her brothers to stand by their mama. Lulu felt apprehensive at the insistent knocking. She held her mother's arm protectively, as if to reassure her—and herself—that everything was going to be alright.

Nena slowly opened the door and peered up at a tall, burly man. "Yes?"

The stranger began yelling at her in French well beyond Nena's tourist-level grasp of the language, and she could barely understand what was being said. A woman from an adjacent apartment joined the one-sided conversation as other neighbors came out to stand in the hallway and watch the drama unfold.

"Your cooking smells bad," the neighbor translated in accented English.

"What smells bad?" asked Nena, confused as to why these folks were so irate.

"Your cooking. Very bad smell," the neighbor repeated. "Throw away. We all smell it. Up in the apartments." As if to emphasize the point, she pinched her nostrils and grimaced while pointing toward the upper floors.

Realizing that her fellow residents were repulsed by the smell of the adobo she was cooking, an acutely embarrassed and dejected Nena fought back tears as she closed the door and walked back into the kitchen. She turned off the stove and spooned the adobo and rice into small bowls. If she threw it away, as her neighbors demanded, what else would they have to eat?

Lulu, Poncy, Willie, Bobby and their mother, Nena Reyes.

Nena had lost her appetite, and the familiar and heart-warming meal she had prepared could provide no comfort.

Lulu wished she could say something to ease the distress so plain on Mama's face. Thinking back to the scene at the door, she trembled, partly from anxiety caused by the neighbors' raised voices and partly from anger at their arrogance and snobbery toward her mother. It was clear to her what they thought of her family—strangers from a foreign land who cooked malodorous food.

The upsetting conversation made Nena realize that she and her children really had no place among the people in this building or in this city they had come to love. Their time here had been, for the most part, lovely and recuperative, but it was not home. She made a decision right then and there: Paris had been a welcome respite, but it was time to return to where they belonged.

"Hijos, ya vamos.Vamos ya a volver a Manila." *Let's go, children. Let's go back home to Manila.*

. . . .

My mother used to say, "You can cook adobo anywhere in the world, and if you know how, you will never be hungry." I've passed along her words to my sons Tim and Constante, but having this backstory gives it a deeper meaning.

She told me the story many times, yet no matter how many years had passed since it happened, I could tell the memory continued to sting. Nowadays, adobo is cooked and eaten with great enjoyment all over the world, and its native history and multitudes of variation have made it a culinary emblem of the Philippines and of Filipinos. A century ago, however, the world was a different place.

What would have happened if Lola Nena had made a sweet dessert instead of a vinegary, garlicky stew? An elegant dish with honeyed flavors instead of a common dish full of bold aromas? She knew how to make canonigo very well, for instance. Canonigo is a sophisticated dessert of airy meringue drizzled with caramel and floating on a rich custard sauce. In fact, canonigo bears a close resemblance to a French confection called île flottante, or floating island. Though it's a popular treat in the Philippines, it is usually found in fine restaurants and hotels or served in exclusive clubhouses. Its presumed Spanish origins have bestowed a certain European cachet and many Filipinos consider it sosyal, or elite.

I imagined what the scenario might have been if Lola Nena made canonigo in their little Parisian rental: instead of irate neighbors banging on the door, demanding to throw out food, she might have knocked on their doors, inviting them over to share a dessert. She would have spooned sweetened custard sauce onto dainty dishes and placed a delicate cloud of meringue on top of each, the pristine white garnished with trickles of golden caramel, and perhaps her neighbors would have been delighted to be served such an exquisite treat.

How strange to think the choice of dishes you make in the kitchen could influence the direction of your life. If they hadn't felt ostracized, perhaps Lola Nena and her children would have stayed in France and become Parisians. But if they had stayed, then my mother and father would never have met and fallen in love, and my sister and I would not be here. It is a sad irony that in order for me to be here, writing these words, my grandmother and her children had to experience such a bitter taste of bigotry.

In the end, bigger things were meant for Lola Nena, Mom and her brothers in the Philippines, and in the coming years they would all find their individual strengths of character as they shared both the joys and the heartaches of family and life.

Chapter 5

The House on Indiana Street

As the COVID pandemic raced across America and the world, I tuned out the stress by cooking and baking more than at any other time in my life, never mind that it was just me and Elpi at home. I made recipes meant for gatherings such as my mother's beef morcon, which she used to make on the mornings my parents, sister and I traveled by car from Tarlac to spend the weekend at my grandmother's home in Malate, Manila.

She showed me how to lay a large, thin cut of skirt steak flat on a cutting board and arrange julienned ham, carrots, onions and pickles lengthwise in the center of the meat. She would then dot it with butter before carefully rolling the beef on its long edge and securing it with twine. While a sweet tomato sauce simmered in a stockpot, she would quickly sear the meat roll in a skillet. Finally, she would place the morcon in the tomato sauce to finish cooking through.

Recipes such as this will always remind me of Lola Nena's house, of the stories Mom used to tell about the luncheons, dinner parties and other gatherings that she and Lola Nena used to hold there, and of the Sunday suppers we shared when our family visited every weekend. It was the home she loved with all her heart, and my treasured memories of it as a place of warmth and happiness helped me through the worst of my worries and fears during the pandemic.

....

During my childhood in the 1960s, my family would make the three-hour drive from our home in Tarlac to my grandmother's house in Malate every weekend. Mom would prepare several dishes to take with us, and because food spoiled quickly in our tropical climate, she would wake up very early in the morning to cook before we left. A cooler holding containers of chicken and pork adobo, beef morcon, lumpiang ubod, paksiw na bangus and fresh fruit from my father's orchards filled the trunk of our Oldsmobile as we set out on the highway toward Manila. On occasion, we even brought a cavan of newly milled Milagrosa rice from Dad's first harvest of the season.

I can recall vividly the crunching sound of car tires rolling over gravel as we arrived at Lola Nena's compound and passed between the iron gates garlanded by blooming bougainvillea. As we drove up the brick-lined driveway, the sight of verdant grounds shaded by tall acacia trees was a refreshing welcome after the long, hot drive from the province.

Lola Nena's home as I remember it was actually the second one to stand in its spot: the original house built by her and Lolo Ponciano was destroyed in the Battle of Manila during World War II. The rebuilt post-war structure was a two-story confluence of Asian, American and Spanish architectural styles with a white façade trimmed in green and decorative ironwork grilles fronting large bay windows. I often scampered onto the built-in benches inside and peered out the windows to check if my weekend playmates—the children of my grandmother's tenant-neighbors—were outside in the common yard. If they were, I would dash out to play with them all day.

The interior of the house featured imposing cement columns separating a spacious and airy living room from the dining room on the ground floor. Further back, the kitchen was a large, functional area where there always seemed to be a pot bubbling or a pan sizzling on the stove. A door led outside to the back of the house and into a garden with a cemented veranda which, according to Mom, often transformed into a dance floor during the many parties and festivities hosted by Lola Nena in years past.

My grandmother's house became so much like our second home that by the age of four, I knew the address by heart. "1632 Indiana Street, Malate, Manila," I would proudly recite when prompted.

Sadly, the address and the house to which it belonged no longer exist today. The street was renamed some time during the late 1970s to Pilar Hidalgo Lim Street, after the noted feminist, educator, and co-founder of the Philippine Girl Scouts, and though the number remains, it now belongs to a bleak, low-rise office building surrounded by barbed wire. The brutalist cement structure is a far cry from the cherished family home that once stood there—the home where my mother grew up and which she loved immensely.

....

1917–1941

Lulu was about four years old when Ponciano Sr. and Nena moved their family from Iloilo province to Manila, to be closer to his work with the Philippine judiciary. The young parents chose to make their home in Malate near Intramurous, the city's old walled district and historic seat of government.

The area was developed shortly after the turn of the 20th

century by an American, Henry M. Jones, on a large swathe of reclaimed saltmarsh along Manila Bay. With the neighboring district of Ermita to its north, Malate was one of the country's very first residential subdivisions, where prominent Americans and affluent Spanish and mestizo families lived in spacious homes on streets named after US states.

The young couple acquired a 2,500-square meter property on Indiana Street, large enough to build three houses and a small apartment building. Ponciano was not only gifted in matters of law but also financially astute. He saw an opportunity to establish a steady income through rental properties that would provide for the family, no matter what happened in the future. His decision proved to be prescient.

After Ponciano's tragic early death, Nena found strength in her resolve that with every new day came new strength. She chose to remain in Malate to raise their four children, supporting them with the revenue from the rental units in the compound and her late husband's government pension, which was posthumously granted to his family in 1935. Raised in a prominent and affluent family, Nena had learned what was considered at the time the most appropriate skill set for a young lady, namely household management. But she was also an adroit seamstress, thanks to her mother's early tutelage, and she used this practical skill to supplement the rental income by sewing for clients drawn from among her wide circle of friends and their families. As Mama's young helper, Lulu was tasked with preparing snacks for the numerous visitors who came to the house for fittings or to order new outfits for the next ball or soirée.

Lulu, Bobby, Willie and Poncy spent an idyllic childhood in the Manila of the 1920s and '30s. During the weekday, they walked a short distance to school on streets shaded by mature acacia trees and past the gracious homes of local elites. On the weekend, Nena would take them to Ermita to visit quaint shops and restaurants, or if they fancied a ride, she would bring them on one of the city's electric streetcars, called the tranvia, to Luneta Park where they could enjoy a treat from food carts serving hotdogs, hamburgers and fresh fruit juices. Sometimes, the five of them would just sit on the grassy esplanade between palm tree-lined Dewey Boulevard[2] and Manila Bay, listening to the waves splash on the rocky seawall, feeling the cool sea breeze kiss their cheeks and watching as the day ended with a spectacular, incomparable sunset.

The house on Indiana Street was more than just a structure or a dwelling for the family. It was a sanctuary of love, affection and acceptance, and it was often filled with two of the most important things in life: friends and food. Nena loved to cook and entertain, and she passed that love to Lulu. Together, they hosted numerous gatherings from small dinners to formal parties over the following years.

As Lulu grew into a lovely, graceful young woman, she attracted a circle of friends from among the finest families of Manila as well as those from Iloilo and Bacolod, which were the epicenters of high society in the Visayas region where her mother's family tree was rooted. Although Nena never remarried and had not lived in Capiz since she and Ponciano

---

2 Renamed Roxas Boulevard in the 60's, in honor of the 5th president of the Philippines Manuel Roxas

moved to Manila, she retained her social status as the daughter of a former provincial governor and noted physician, and as the widow of a highly respected attorney and judge. Her old money background provided her beautiful young daughter the genteel pedigree to help open the doors to the country's highest social echelons.

From her first appearance in 1932 in an announcement for her nineteenth birthday, Lulu became a regular fixture in Manila's society pages for several years. Sifting through the archives of *La Vanguardia,* the influential Spanish-language newspaper in Manila, one could practically trace Lulu's carefree young life as a socialite in the accounts of lavish dinner dances and refined luncheons she attended, and in photographs of her dressed in exquisite ballgowns and fashionable day suits and dresses.

There was no doubt she was a beauty—she was named among "the most beautiful and distinguished girls of Manila society" in 1934—but she was also very popular among her peers and was even nominated for the title of Most Popular Woman in the Philippines in 1935.

Lulu counted among her good friends the sisters Aurora "Baby" and Zeneida "Nini" Quezon, the daughters of Manuel Quezon, the second President of the Philippines; Helena Benitez, a future Philippine senator and the daughter of Filipino statesman Conrado Benitez; and many other daughters and wives from the most prominent business and political families with names such as Roxas, Osmeña, Pamintuan, Araneta and Diokno.

Rarely was a party or ball held in the city and covered

by the press in which Miss Reyes did not appear in photos of the event or was not mentioned in the coverage. There she was smiling gaily at a dinner held by Pacita Roxas, from a distinguished old family in Lipa, Batangas; at an Alice in Wonderland–themed soirée thrown by Lucy Pamintuan, a celebrated society belle; or modeling in a fashion show, resplendent in sequins and satins. And Lulu wasn't always just a guest—she and Nena often hosted their friends for birthday gatherings and despedidas (going-away parties) at the house on Indiana Street, where she honed her hostessing and cooking skills.

Early on, though, Lulu proved herself to be more than just a pretty social butterfly. Within a couple of years of her public debut in Manila's society pages, she was no longer simply attending events and gatherings, she was also organizing them. And rather than being a passive member of social-civic clubs, she became active in their leadership. Over the succeeding years, she served as treasurer of the elite Smiles Club, president of the Rho Alpha (another well-known socio-civic group), and auxiliary treasurer and then vice president of the exclusive Kahirup Society, comprised of the children of upper-crust Visayan society and named after the Bisaya word for "togetherness."

Just a year after being accepted into Kahirup in 1933, twenty-year-old Lulu was already organizing their dances, including the prestigious Rigodon de Honor—the grandest ball in the Bacolod/Visayas society calendar held annually at the elegant Manila Hotel. More than just putting together an evening of entertainment for the elite, however, she turned the occasion into a charity event, reflecting a growing desire to use her social privilege in the service of social responsibility.

As the years passed and her friends and fellow socialites began appearing in the society columns for engagement news, followed by wedding coverage and then birth announcements, Lulu turned toward a more public-spirited focus. She became increasingly involved in philanthropic causes as her social conscience and religious faith drew her toward a deeper calling. "What more can I do?" she asked herself. She had plentiful resources and connections—why not use them for a greater good?

The society pages bore witness to her new trajectory: whereas a few years before she had been snapped wearing a sassy majorette costume for a Smiles Club musical revue, now she was appearing in photos smartly dressed in a Red Cross uniform as a volunteer at the organization's canteens serving meals to the community and members of the armed forces. She still enjoyed membership in Smiles Club, Kahirup and other social groups, but she had also joined the Teresitas, a group formed in devotion to Saint Thérèse of Lisieux, with whom she went on religious retreats to a nearby Carmelite convent and for whom she eventually served as president for a few years. And by 1940, she was instrumental in helping philanthropist and educator Josefa Llanes Escoda establish the Girl Scouts of the Philippines, along with Helena Benitez and other good friends from Manila society.

Her desire to do meaningful work was driven largely by her religious devotion. Lulu's piety seemed innate and was further nurtured since childhood by her mother, whose own steadfast faith had helped her weather the challenges of widowhood and single motherhood. As in many Filipino homes, Nena kept an altar—a credenza on which she displayed several hand-carved and painted figures of saints placed inside bell jars—where the family could pray the rosary. They also attended Mass regularly at their local parish church, Our Lady of Remedies (known simply as Malate Church), not just every Sunday but also on all Holy Days of Obligation in the Catholic liturgy.

For Lulu, the months of May and October were especially meaningful for veneration—the former as the month of the Blessed Virgin Mary and the latter as the month of the Holy Rosary as well as her birth month. Years later, when she had a family of her own, she continued to pray the rosary after supper every night. She also developed a long-lasting friendship with Father Forbes J. Monaghan, an Irish American Jesuit priest and the pastor of Malate Church who became her confessor.

Rather than just living a life of privileged frivolity, Lulu turned her focus and energy toward compassionate social causes. She learned how to leverage her advantages for the benefit of others in need, creating a network of contacts to organize philanthropic projects and to charm funds and favors from donors. Little did she know, however, that every soft skill she acquired and every humanitarian instinct she honed as a socialite would soon become critical, life-saving skills; and that many of the people she called friends and mentors would become her comrades in a dangerous fight for the lives of others, as the dark and destructive clouds of war loomed over the Philippines and the world.

Lulu Reyes Besa with daughter Elizabeth Ann. Malate, Manila.

Chapter 6

The Search for Willie

1964

The combination of hunger, boredom and unchecked curiosity was guaranteed to get a certain six-year-old into trouble.

During one of our weekend visits to the house on Indiana Street, the traditional Sunday lunch of beef pochero was taking longer than usual to prepare, or so it seemed to me. Impatient and unsupervised, I began to wander around the house, peeking into closets, rummaging through cupboards and poking into any spaces that looked like they might be hiding something of interest.

Although Lola Nena had passed away nearly ten years before, my mom and uncles had left her home furnished the same as it had always been, including one room where she kept a heavy wood credenza that had long served as the family altar. Arrayed on top were hand-carved wooden religious figures called santos, depicting the Holy Family and an assortment of saints. Some were dressed in elaborate miniature vestments while others sported fading shades of paint, and all looked suitably serene. However, I wasn't as interested in the small statues as I was in the drawers they guarded below. This was where Mom kept family photo albums and other important files, and I was not allowed to go through them. Her warnings rang in my head, but a sense of mischief goaded by a vivid imagination (was there a secret treasure map inside, or maybe a skeleton waiting to spring out suddenly?) overpowered any obedience—after all, there was no one in the room to see.

As I opened one heavy drawer with some effort, a musty smell swirled out like a mildewed genie popping out of a bottle. I nervously reached inside, half-expecting a bony hand to grab at my own, and pulled out a packet of old family photographs. I sat cross-legged on the floor to sift through faded pictures of unknown people and places. A buzz of familiarity made me stop at one black and white image of a young man posing proudly in a plain uniform and wearing a rounded helmet[3] with a broad brim. I had to peer at the photo closely before I vaguely recognized the figure as my Tito Willie, Mom's middle brother. He had died about two years before, and I missed him very much.

As I studied the picture and wondered why my uncle was dressed the way he was, Mom came into the room in search of me. Seeing the open drawer, the photos in my hands and the flush of guilt creeping over my cheeks, she briskly gathered them up, returned them to their place and shut the compartment with finality. She then turned to me and spoke in a calm but unmistakably stern tone.

"Do not touch these. Do not open these drawers again."

Chastened, I obediently followed her out of the room to join the rest of the family for Sunday lunch.

. . . .

April 9, 1942

It was just after lunch and the Reyes family gathered

3 Many years later, I learned that this particular helmet was called a guinit and was made of pressed coconut husk fibers. Although steel helmets were standard military headgear by World War II, most Filipino soldiers were issued these locally made helmets that offered protection from the sun but not from deadly projectiles.

around the radio in the living room. Lulu sat with Mama Nena as Bobby fidgeted with the dials and Poncy and Helen, Willie's wife, waited tensely. News from Bataan had progressively worsened since Good Friday six days before, as the Imperial Japanese Army bombarded American and Filipino defensive lines with relentless air and artillery fire throughout the Easter weekend, and the besieged defenders were driven further back by a fierce assault from enemy infantry supported by tanks. The family tried to remain optimistic, but they feared the worst for the young men who were fighting—especially one dearest to them.

Many Filipinos thought the war would be over in less than six months. It was now four months since the Japanese launched an invasion of the Philippines just hours after their surprise attack on Pearl Harbor in December. They were confident the Americans, led by the greatly respected General Douglas MacArthur, would protect the country and defeat the invaders. But as Japanese forces continued to advance on Manila, General MacArthur had evacuated from Corregidor to Australia in early March, promising to return and leaving behind 90,000 American and Filipino troops to take defensive positions on the Bataan Peninsula. Among them was Lulu's middle brother Guillermo, known affectionately as Willie.

Willie was just a little over a year old when Ponciano Reyes Sr. perished during the Christmas Typhoon of 1918. He barely remembered his father, but as he grew up, he hoped to follow in his footsteps and pursue a career in law.

Now in his mid-twenties, he was of average height and build, and shared with his two brothers the handsome mestizo

Helen and Willie Reyes in happier times. Manila 1941.

features inherited from Mama Nena's side of the family. His demeanor could be serious and thoughtful one moment and then easygoing and fun-loving the next. In other words, he split the difference in personalities between the reserved and quiet Bobby, who was two years older, and the more mischievous and gregarious Poncy, who was two years younger.

Willie was the first of the Reyes siblings to marry, after he met a lovely, half-American girl named Helen Moreno.

They wed in September 1941, but scarcely three months later, the Japanese invasion of the Philippines began. Without hesitation, he left his bride in the care of his family in Malate and volunteered for the Philippine Scouts, a special unit of the US Army comprised of American and Filipino soldiers who were fighting on the front lines in Bataan and Corregidor.

From the day Willie enlisted, his wife, mother and siblings fervently prayed for his safety. They followed all the news on the radio in anxious hopes of gleaning where he might be fighting, and their worry for him only intensified with the reports of General MacArthur's withdrawal from Corregidor and of Allied losses on the battlefield.

Lulu was as determined as Willie to do her part for the country. She had been volunteering at canteens run by the Philippine branch of the American National Red Cross[4] since her late teens, and had joined Baby and Nini Quezon, the daughters of President Manuel Quezon, in collecting donations for Christmas care packages intended for soldiers just weeks after the Japanese invasion began. She also served with the Volunteer Social Aid Committee (VSAC), whose members were known as the Girls in Blue for their distinctive blue and white uniforms. The group had been formed by her good friend Helena Benitez, and its membership included many of

---

4 President Manuel Quezon (1942–44) wanted to create an independent Philippine Red Cross (PRC), but the Commonwealth of the Philippines was not a signatory to the Geneva Conventions. During the Japanese occupation, a puppet PRC was created to provide aid to POW and internment camps. Today's PRC was formally chartered in 1947 by President Manuel Roxas (1946–48), after the Philippines had gained independence and finally able to sign the Geneva Conventions as a sovereign state.

the women with whom she had attended dinner parties and formal balls just a few carefree years before.

Months before the start of the war in the Pacific in December 1941, Lulu serendipitously joined the newly organized Chaplains Aid Association, where her natural leadership qualities and adept networking skills quickly made her indispensable. Composed of young society ladies, the association had been formed by Father Edwin Ronan, CP, as a kind of civilian support branch of the Philippine Army's Chaplains Service, which trained clergymen of different faiths to provide spiritual support for soldiers. The group's original mandate was mainly to provide military personnel with recreational social activities, such as picnics and dances, but as the war intensified, the association's focus shifted dramatically to providing civilians and soldiers on the front lines with critical supplies such as food, clothing and medicine.

On this Thursday afternoon, however, Lulu joined the rest of the family to listen intently to the latest radio dispatch from the Voice of Freedom, which was being broadcast from a makeshift station in the Malinta Tunnel complex beneath Corregidor. The announcer, 3rd Lieutenant Norman Reyes, gravely intoned a brief introduction before speaking the words no one wanted to hear:

Bataan has fallen.

The Philippine-American troops on this war-ravaged and bloodstained peninsula have laid down their arms. With heads bloody but unbowed, they have yielded to the superior force and numbers of the enemy.[5]

5 Lopez, n.p.

The announcement left the family stunned, silent and unmoving, until Mama Nena let out a guttural cry and collapsed to the floor.

"Mi hijo, mi hijo! Dios mio, mi hijo!" *My son, my son! My God, my son!*

Struggling to keep herself from breaking down as well, Lulu held her sobbing mother. The last time she had seen her parent so bereft and inconsolable was on a Christmas Day nearly twenty-four years ago.

"Mama, no llores, le vamos buscar a Willie," she promised. *Mama, don't cry. We will look for Willie.*

But even as Lulu made the vow, doubt and fear amplified her grief. Where would she start? How would she find him? Was he even still alive?

The subsequent days and weeks were filled with desperate attempts to locate Willie or find some clue regarding his fate. The family heard that approximately 70,000 soldiers who were captured at Bataan were being marched to a prison camp in Tarlac, and they hoped he might be among them. Lulu used all means of communication available, from letters to phone calls to telegrams, to contact everyone on her formidable list of friends and acquaintances, but no one could confirm his whereabouts or even if he had survived the battle.

In the meantime, she threw herself into relief work with the Chaplains Aid Association and other humanitarian groups. Less than a week after the surrender at Bataan, Helena Benitez mobilized the Girls in Blue after receiving an emotional phone call from Josefa Llanes Escoda, a prominent Manila social worker and activist, who had just witnessed the brutal treatment and distressing condition of captive soldiers as they arrived in San Fernando, Pampanga on their forced march to Tarlac.

The VSAC volunteers, including Lulu, wasted no time gathering any relief supplies they could find or solicit. Pharmacists gave whatever they could spare from their already depleted stores of medicine. At the Bureau of Plant Industry, the country's pre-eminent food scientist and pharmaceutical chemist Maria Orosa[6] provided them with energy-rich concentrated juice powder made from the native citrus calamansi and muscovado sugar. The Girls distributed the much-needed supplies to various prisons and internment camps that the Japanese had swiftly established in and around Manila.

Lulu soon realized her involvement with relief organizations would be her best hope of finding Willie: humanitarian aid workers were the only civilians allowed to enter the camps and interact with any prisoners. Knowing she was unlikely to be allowed to visit among the military internees, Lulu figured the Jesuit mission and the Chaplains Aid Association presented a perfect opportunity to talk to imprisoned clerics who were permitted to hold religious services and minister to the POWs. They would be her eyes and ears in the search for her brother.

---

6 During the war, Maria Orosa also invented Soyalac, a soybean-based powdered drink, and vitamin B1-rich rice cookies called Darak that helped prevent beriberi; both products are credited with saving the lives of thousands of POWs and civilians suffering from malnutrition. Equally notable are her invention of the palayok clay oven and the staple Philippine condiment, banana ketchup. She served as an officer with a guerrilla group smuggling supplies into Japanese prison camps and was killed during an American bombing raid after refusing to abandon her post during the Battle of Manila.

....

May 1942

Willie struggled to open his eyes. The chills and fever that wracked his body during each malaria attack left him exhausted and only just strong enough to prop himself up. Even if he had more strength, there was little room to move inside the bamboo and thatched-roof barracks. Men were crammed onto long, platform-like bunks with only woven palm-leaf mats called banig providing any kind of cushion. Those who could not find space on these makeshift beds instead sat or lay on the floor.

More than a month had passed since he and over 60,000 of his fellow Filipino and American soldiers had reached Camp O'Donnell, a former Philippine Army training facility turned POW camp, after being forced on a torturous 65-mile trek from Bataan to Capas, Tarlac. The acts of inhumanity unleashed by the Japanese Army against its unarmed captives during those ten days in April would later earn the hellish journey the name Bataan Death March.

The Japanese considered American troops cowardly and dishonorable for surrendering and therefore deserving of their contempt. But Filipino soldiers… well, they were not viewed as soldiers at all and barely as fellow human beings. Their treatment at the hands of their captors seemed especially inhumane, such as one account by a surviving Philippine Scout officer, Mariano Villarin, who described how his countrymen were used as living dummies for bayonet practice during the march.

The Imperial Army's brutality also extended to civilians

along the route as Japanese soldiers viciously beat or shot dead any locals, including women, children and the elderly, who dared to show the malnourished and mistreated marchers even the smallest measure of compassion.

By the time Willie and his fellow POWs reached O'Donnell, approximately 10,000 prisoners had died en route, 90% of whom were Filipino. The situation hardly improved for the survivors, who were segregated in different halves of the camp—10,000 Americans in the north sector and 50,000 Filipinos in the south. While the barracks and provisions were not much different in both sections, the sheer number of the latter group amplified the camp's atrocious conditions. Aside from the lack of beds, potable water came from only two taps in the entire prison, forcing most of the Filipino internees to drink fouled water wherever it could be found.

Malaria and dysentery ran rampant among the men who lived practically on top of each other. In the nine months be-tween April 1942 and January 1943 that O'Donnell operated as a POW camp, an estimated 1,600 Americans and 26,000 Filipinos died within its confines—a staggering rate equal to 102 dead per day. To the men trapped in this purgatory, the prison came to be known as "Camp O'Death."

Lying ill and helpless in a bunk, Willie didn't want to think of what he had witnessed during the march—of com-rades shot, bayoneted, beheaded or run over by tanks, or dying no less cruelly from starvation, dehydration or exhaustion. He didn't want to recall the sight of women who had been raped and executed along the roadside, or of children being beaten for offering a morsel of food or a sip of water. He didn't want to remember being packed into a boxcar—over a hundred men in a space meant for less than half that number—and waiting hours in unbearable heat, terrified of suffocating and fighting for every breath, before the train started rolling from the rail yard at San Fernando to the terminus in Capas, where they had to march a final nine miles to Camp O'Donnell and into another level of torment. What he wanted was to forget where he was and what was happening all around him.

His best friend. Hector Syquia, also felled by sickness, slept fitfully nearby. He and Hector were close in age and had been each other's best man at their weddings. They had joined the Philippine Scouts together when the Japanese invasion began, fought side by side during the Battle of Bataan, and watched out for each other on the Death March along the dusty, deadly roads to Tarlac. They boosted their morale and will to live by talking to each other about their plans for the future—Willie with Helen and Hector with his wife, Amparo, known affectionately as Ampi. It was all the hope they had left to cling to now.

Weakened by malaria, Willie knew he should try to eat what little food he was given, which was usually a very thin lugaw, or rice soup. On very, very rare occasions, there might be a bite of spoiled camote (sweet potato) or even filaments of shredded carabao meat added to the gruel, but most of the time it was just a flavorless slurry. He thought about the Sunday lunches back at home in Malate, when Mama Nena would often make one of the Spanish-Filipino recipes taught to her by Lola Juana, like his favorite beef pochero.

In his mind's eye, he could see his mother in the kitchen, ladling the still-simmering stew from a pot on the stove and into a large casserole. Each spoonful would be filled with succulent cubes of beef and chunks of spicy Spanish chorizo, quartered potatoes and sliced carrots, green beans and cabbage, and a rich, deeply flavorsome tomato-based gravy. When she brought it out to the dining room, she would set it on the table alongside a salad of roasted, mashed eggplants seasoned with vinegar, garlic and red onions, and an accompaniment of ripe saging saba (plantains), plump and boiled to a pleasantly sweet softness. And after a prayer of thanksgiving, the family would fill their plates with the abundant meal that had been patiently prepared since morning.

The imagined aromas of food and the thought of his loved ones—Helen, Mama Nena, Lulu, Bobby and Poncy—gathered around the table soothed Willie's fears and exhaustion, and he closed his eyes to feast on the memory.

....

In the weeks after the fall of Bataan, Lulu determinedly accessed every prison camp in and around Manila—Los Banos, Bilibid, University of Santo Tomas, Cabanatuan, the Port Area and Camp O'Donnell—as part of relief missions with the Chaplains Aid Association, the Red Cross and the Girls in Blue. Between distributing relief goods and talking to imprisoned clergy, she looked for any sign of Willie. It was nearly two months before she finally received the first hopeful report that he was being held in O'Donnell, which was soon confirmed via an exhaustive list of names, patiently compiled by Josefa Escoda, of the thousands of Filipino POWs at the camp.

Returning to Capas with the Red Cross, Lulu somehow convinced the Japanese guards to permit her entry into the camp to meet with the commanding officer. As she was being escorted toward his office, she caught a glimpse of her brother in one of the barrack-huts now overflowing with POWs. He was emaciated and clearly very ill, but he was alive! She wanted so badly to embrace him and weep with relief, but she had to restrain herself from showing her emotions. She couldn't risk revealing their relationship and raising any suspicion among the Japanese regarding her reasons for being in the camp. Instead, she continued to walk steadfastly toward her meeting with the man in charge of her brother's prison.

On the drive back to Manila, Lulu gave in to her tears. She had convinced the camp commandant to allow her to return with food and medicines for the prisoners, but her thoughts at the moment were entirely on Willie. As she began praying with all her heart for a way to free him, she gripped a rosary made of black, hand-carved wooden beads, which felt warm and comforting as she rubbed them between her fingers. They helped remind her that she was a humble servant of God and that she should put her trust and faith in Him. The truck rode over stretches of rural dirt paths and paved roads damaged by shelling and heavy tanks, but the discomfort of the ride could not shake her focus from her devotion.

In the end (and of absolutely no credit to them), the enemy provided the answer to Lulu's prayers. Japanese authorities announced a "Filipino Sick POWS Release Policy" by which Filipino prisoners in Camp O'Donnell who were suffering serious illnesses would be released beginning June

30, 1942. Eventually, a broader parole policy was also announced for all other captive Filipinos.

It was a gesture of goodwill aimed at pacifying the populace as the Japanese looked toward a long, if not permanent, occupation of the Philippines under what they magnanimously called the Greater East Asia Co-Prosperity Sphere. But several caveats in the policy made it clear the benevolence was only a sheen: POWs from regions not under the control of the Imperial Army or deemed to have active insurgencies remained imprisoned; parolees had to sign an oath not to take up arms as guerrillas before being released to their families or the mayors of their hometowns, who were then held personally responsible for their compliance; and healthy prisoners first had to undergo weeks of what Commodore Ramon Alcaraz, then a young Filipino officer imprisoned in the Malolos prison camp, called "Rejuvination [sic] Training" in a diary of his time as a POW.

The program consisted mainly of daily lectures from Japanese speakers, who struck a conciliatory tone toward the Filipino prisoners at odds with their past treatment. "I noted [they] were careful not to offend the POWs, even referring to us as excellent examples of Malayan soldiery [by] the manner we fought in Bataan," Alcaraz wrote in his war diary, conceding most of his fellow POWs considered the scheme as nothing more than brainwashing and indoctrination.[7]

Due to having contracted malaria, Willie only had to sign the oath before being released from O'Donnell as a medical parolee sometime between June and September 1942.

7 Alcaraz, n.p.

He was far from well, but he was alive and back home in the embrace of his relieved and joyous family.

Though they were happy to be together once again, the Reyeses understood the war was far from over. Willie and Lulu, in particular, knew they could not simply count their blessings, hunker down in safety and hope for the best. He had experienced firsthand the cruelty of the Japanese, especially toward his fellow soldiers and countrymen, and she was an eyewitness to the ongoing brutality against those who remained in captivity. Countless people still suffered under the heel of the Japanese, and brother and sister were ready and determined to continue fighting for them.

....

1943–45

Having seen for herself what POWs endured, Lulu never considered giving up her humanitarian work after Willie returned to the family. Too many young men like her brother remained imprisoned in horrific conditions, and too many wives and mothers like Helen and Nena still waited at home helpless with worry for their husbands and sons.

Lulu had been serving as the president of the Chaplains Aid Association from nearly its inception, working closely with and guided by Father Ronan to organize their activities. But during the first half of 1943, the Catholic priest was arrested by the Japanese and shipped to the Saitama civilian internment camp just outside of Tokyo, Japan. She was now essentially in sole charge of the group.

So month after month, camp after camp, Lulu climbed

into battered old trucks and hauled boxes of relief goods through nerve-wracking military checkpoints to bring aid, comfort and perhaps a glimmer of hope to military and civilian internees. It didn't take long for reports to leak out that the supplies she and her fellow workers tirelessly gathered and delivered rarely made it to the prisoners. Instead, much of the aid packs were appropriated by the Japanese for their own use, particularly food and medicines that might have otherwise helped to mitigate the high number of deaths among camp inmates.

But Lulu, her friends Helena Benitez and Josefa Llanes Escoda, and their humanitarian comrades refused to be discouraged, even if it meant taking greater risks. They continued to truck in whatever supplies were permitted by the Japanese, and they smuggled in as contraband those that were not. Lulu slipped unapproved medicines, such as life-saving malaria pills, to imprisoned priests so they could be distributed surreptitiously during religious services. She delivered money and letters from families and news of the outside world, as well as missives not seen, much less vetted, by camp authorities.

Some of Lulu's activities outside of her relief efforts put her in even more danger of being accused of espionage if she were ever caught—a charge which carried an immediate death sentence. The need to secure permission to deliver supplies to internment camps necessitated frequent interaction with high-ranking Japanese officials, and she secretly leveraged these contacts to collect information which she would then pass on to the underground resistance movement.

Furthermore, the house on Indiana Street had become something of a way station and safehouse for members of the underground resistance. Commodore Alcaraz recounted in his diary a particular episode that occurred shortly before Christmas in 1942. Four months after his release from the Malolos POW camp, he received an unexpected invitation from Lulu, whom he knew socially before the war, to attend a "stag dinner" at the Malate house. The other guests turned out to be members of the Philippine underground, including his former commanding officer Colonel Manolo Enriquez, who was wanted by the Japanese secret police known as the Kempei-tai, and Captain Juan Calvo, a distinguished Spanish aviator turned Philippine guerrilla leader. The dinner had been set up to make contact with Alcaraz, who was conducting his own clandestine resistance activities. The young officer recalled his relief when the evening ended without the Kempei-tai raiding the Reyes home to arrest them, although Lulu assured him that, just in case, she had prepared an escape route… for Colonel Enriquez.

....

Willie was as willing as his sister to put his life at risk for a cause. He had taken an oath not to join armed resistance groups as a condition of his release, and he was an honorable man. But there was no honor in a promise made under extreme duress. With a steadfast resolve, an ironclad purpose and a clear conscience, he once again left his wife, Helen, and his family to rejoin the fight against the Imperial Japanese Army almost as soon as he fully recovered from malaria. The

Japanese did not respect Filipinos as soldiers, but they would learn to dread them as guerrillas.

By 1943, Willie was ensconced with guerrilla forces in Iba, Zambales, about 200 kilometers northwest of Manila. The family occasionally received short letters assuring them he was well, but he couldn't share any details that might offer clues to his location or activities—personal letters were screened, he admitted in one message, in case they were intercepted.

He joined American and Filipino officers, soldiers and civilians who formed armed resistance forces in the areas around Manila and throughout the surrounding mountainous provinces. These bands included the Hunters ROTC, formed by junior Philippine Military Academy cadets who were too young to be commissioned as officers at the outbreak of the war but had decided to stay and fight as a guerrilla group rather than go home as ordered; the Marking Guerrillas, led by Philippine Scout Colonel Marcos "Marking" Augustin, who would help capture the strategically important Ipo Dam toward the end of the war; and the Western Luzon Guerrilla Forces, one of whose founders was a young mechanic with the Philippine Army 31st Infantry Division named Ramon Magsaysay.[8] Under his leadership, the 10,000-strong WLGF routed the Japanese from the Zambales coast in January 1945, allowing the US Army's 38th Division to land without resistance and spearheading the liberation of Zambales, the recapture of the Bataan Peninsula and the rapid American advance toward the liberation of Manila.

8 After the war, Magsaysay entered politics and was elected as the country's 7th president in 1953. He was killed in a plane crash nine months before the end of his term in 1957.

Willie remained with the guerrillas until American forces began closing in on the city in early February 1945, when he returned to Helen, his mother and siblings in Malate. There was finally a glimmer of hope that the nightmare of war would soon end, but they had little inkling of the firestorm that was yet to ignite over their city and home.

Whatever was to come, at least they would face it together as a whole family.

As far as I know, Tito Willie rarely spoke about his experiences during World War II. Most of what I heard about his ordeals came from my mother, and who knows how much she held back. Maybe that was the reason she was so cross when she caught me snooping in the drawer of family files when I was a child. How do you explain to a six-year-old full of curiosity and innocent questions what had happened to the proud young man in the photo she held? Perhaps she felt it was his story to tell, and if he didn't want to share it, then it should be left to rest in the past.

My uncle lived the rest of his life as fully and happily as anyone could ever wish for, and I am in awe of that fact after learning more about what he had endured. I remember him as a loving man who cherished his family and indulged his mischievous little niece, and whose jovial, generous manner never displayed any hint of bitterness, anger or resentment. When I think about Tito Willie with the knowledge of his story adding depth to my memories, it now seems to me he lived not only as a man who was grateful for the years he was granted, but also as a survivor who was living for all those who were lost, like his brothers in arms in Bataan and in

O'Donnell, the innocent civilians caught in the crossfires of war, and his best friend, Hector.

Not too long ago, I came across a letter posted online by the children of Nini Quezon Avanceña, my godmother and one of my mother's dearest and closest friends. The letter received little attention or comment from other readers, who likely couldn't identify the writer—it was signed simply "Willie R." But just as I recognized my uncle in a faded photograph on a long ago Sunday afternoon, I knew who had written the letter. The handwriting, the signature and the tone of words were unmistakably the hand and voice of my Tito Willie.

The letter was addressed to Nini and dated 28 April 1945, around the time Mom, Lola Nena, Tita Helen and my uncles were living in a refugee shelter as they waited to rebuild the house on Indiana Street, which had been leveled during the Battle of Manila more than a month before. Willie's writing was lighthearted and optimistic, recalling happier times before the war, sharing hopeful plans for the future and even teasing Nini over her pigtails, her fondness for reading and the foxhole gossip that she had married some young officer. But there were also somber comments, such as his condolences over the death of her father President Manuel Quezon while exiled overseas, and the terrible but thankfully incorrect reports of her own passing. Then he asked if she were acquainted with Ampi Natividad Syquia and revealed the tragic fate of her husband, Hector.

They had been as close as brothers, sharing both the best and worst moments of their lives side by side. Hector had been released with Willie as medical parolees from Camp O'Donnell, but then the parallel path they had walked together for years suddenly diverged. While my uncle joined guerrilla fighters in Zambales after his recovery from malaria, there was little information about his best friend after their release.

I later learned that Hector finally reunited with Ampi and their infant son, Hector Jr., but their life together was cruelly cut short when he was killed by a Japanese sniper sometime during the Battle of Manila, which raged from February to March 1945. Compounding this tragedy, several other members of his family also became victims of what came to be known as the Panggahasa sa Maynila, or the Rape of Manila: his mother Concepcion Jimenez Syquia, a younger sister named Margarita and his eldest sister, Alicia Syquia Quirino and three of her children, who were slaughtered by Japanese machine gunners as they fled their own home in search of safety at the Syquia family residence.

Writing to Nini just a few months later, Willie's simple, heartfelt description of his friendship with Hector conveyed the closeness between them. One passage in particular expressed his mournful resignation over the unfairness of fate and the death of a young husband, father and friend:

We talked over and over again about his plans for Ampi and his son when they got back here.

It is really sad to think they waited for three years for something beautiful to happen, and when it is just about to happen, death comes in and spoils everything.

I cannot begin to imagine what Tito Willie felt over the loss of such a friend. Perhaps that is why he didn't share his traumas—so that the depravity and death he experienced could not bring grief and sadness to anyone else, even in imagination.

Instead, he shut the memories away deep within himself, like faded photographs kept inside a drawer guarded by saints and angels.

"Someone's Son, Someone's Brother"

illie Reyes and Robert Dow never met or knew about each other, but by a strange twist of fate, they are forever connected by a terrible shared experience and a determined lifeline named Lulu who helped save them both.

Like Willie, who was serving as a Philippine Scout, Corporal Robert Joseph Dow of the American Army Air Forces was captured by the Japanese during the Fall of Bataan and forced to endure the arduous trek now known as the Bataan Death March. He was barely twenty years old, a devout Roman Catholic and a very patriotic young man from Wisconsin who claimed to be two years older than he really was in order to enlist in the Army at the age of fifteen. Like thousands of American and Filipino soldiers, he was unprepared for the brutal physical and mental trials he would endure when the US military command surrendered Bataan to the Imperial Japanese Army in April 1942. It would take decades after the war before Robert could bring himself to record his experiences in a cathartic memoir, *Guest of His Imperial Highness: Memories of a Prisoner of the Japanese.*

....

April 1942

The forced march of 70,000-plus prisoners of war, which would cover sixty-five miles from Mariveles in Bataan to Capas in Tarlac and take nearly ten days, began the day after the surrender of Philippine-American forces on April 9.

By the second day, the long columns of captive soldiers reached a barrio in the town of Orani, still in Bataan province, where the men were jammed into dirty, cramped enclosures with barely enough room to sit down, much less lie down. Starving, thirsty and demoralized, some POWs simply fell asleep standing up, leaning against one another. When they were roused to march again, those who were still able began to walk; the ones who could not get up or walk unassisted were immediately executed by the Japanese guards.

As the searing sun blazed down on the exhausted men trudging along rural dirt roads, Corporal Robert Dow let his mind go blank. He was dazed from the heat and lack of water and food, and his feet seemed to take one shuffling step after another without his conscious control. Sometime in the afternoon, the prisoners were ordered to stop. They sat in the dirt for hours during the hottest part of the day as their captors shouted harsh threats or lectured them in English: Do not fight! We are supreme! They could only listen in vulnerable silence as the guards used their physically exhausted and mentally stressed state to attempt some crude roadside indoctrination.

Within himself, Robert fought back. He believed in the power of prayer, and he fervently prayed to the Lord and his guardian angel while he marched under the relentlessly fiery sun. He willed himself to endure the sweltering heat in order to survive. A terrible hunger gnawed at his stomach, so he thought about all his favorite food, especially his mother's Italian spaghetti and his sister's chocolate cake, and imagined them cooking and baking for the family back home. He clung to those memories as his only hope.

"All I could think of was my mother and father, my sweetheart and life back in the States," he would tell me decades later during one of our many phone conversations. "I wanted to see them again. I told myself I had to get through it."

As each day rolled into the next, the prisoners continued marching, not knowing where they were headed. There were constant harsh commands, more torture and more killing of weakened soldiers who fell by the wayside and couldn't go on.

On the fourth day of captivity, the POWs were finally given their first meal: half a cup of cooked rice. There were no utensils, so they were forced to eat their meager meal with dirty hands. Robert was parched with thirst from the heat and dust from the roads. What little water they had in their canteens at the beginning of the march was long gone, and they were given no more.

At one point, the procession arrived at a cool stream. It seemed like an oasis, and the prisoners, sapped of strength and dizzy from dehydration, rushed to quench their thirst. If any of them questioned why their unforgiving captors allowed them this relief, they soon discovered the answer: the stream was fouled with dead bodies. What the Americans and Filipinos thought was a restorative source of water was instead a repository of corpses. The stream was horrifyingly polluted, but it was all the POWs had to drink after four days of marching. They later suffered the terrible consequences for days as many of the prisoners contracted dysentery after drinking from tainted water sources.

When they reached the province of Pampanga to the north of Bataan, the Japanese took the opportunity to show the local townsfolk what happens to enemy captives. They paraded the POWs—many of whom were barely able to stand, much less walk—in a dismal, humiliating display through the main street of San Fernando town toward the train station. The local residents could only stand on the wayside and watch in horror as the pitiful phalanx of fellow Filipinos and Americans struggled to march by. Any captive who fell out of line was publicly beaten. Many of the towns-folk wept openly over the callous mistreatment of the prison-ers and more than a few bravely tried to give them food and water, but the Japanese viciously thrashed civilians who dared to show any compassion.

By the time Robert and his fellow prisoners arrived at Camp O'Donnell in Capas several days later, he was emaci-ated and ill. He might have come across Willie Reyes at the camp if he had remained there, but a few weeks later at the end of May, he and approximately 6,000 American POWs were transferred sixty-five miles northeast to another camp at Cabanatuan in Nueva Ecija province. The facility was former-ly a training center for the Philippine Army's 91st Division under the US Army Forces in the Far East (USAFFE) and now repurposed specifically to imprison American captives.

The treatment and rations at Cabanatuan were as harsh and meager as those at O'Donnell, and Robert struggled to rally his faith and determination to stay alive as his physical condition deteriorated. He contracted wet beriberi, dysentery and scurvy, which resulted in mouth sores and swollen legs. Despite his poor state, he and other captives were conscript-ed for hard labor and put on a truck headed to Manila. They arrived at the New Bilibid Prison, a penitentiary that replaced an older one built by the Spanish nearly eighty years before, but were soon assigned to the Manila Port Area work detail known as the Yamamoto Butai, meaning "labor battalion" and named for the commander Colonel Yamamoto.

The POWs toiled as stevedores, loading and unloading ships day and night, every day. They sometimes lugged thousands of sacks of sugar and rice, each weighing up to 200 pounds; at other times, they transferred tons of crude rubber formed into extremely heavy square blocks. They labored through sickness, injury, hunger and unpredictable beatings. Loading cargo took all the strength Robert could muster, especially after he contracted malaria and the frequency of the cycle of chills and fever increased. He knew the disease was claiming thousands of prisoners' lives, but he refused to give in to despair.

"I knew that it was not God's plan for me yet," he wrote. "I had an abiding faith that I would survive."

His faith was shored up by one mercy granted by the Butai superintendent, Captain Saegusa: a priest was allowed into the prison to hold religious services. As a devout Roman Catholic, Robert attended whenever Mass was offered, but even non–Catholics found solace and faith in the solemn rites. After regularly attending the services for several weeks, his close friend Charley Charleston decided to be baptized as a Catholic and asked Robert to stand as his godfather.

The more difficult role to fill was that of godmother, a customary though not required position in Catholic baptismal rites. Given the circumstances, however, it seemed nearly impossible someone could be found, until Father Santos, the

Filipino cleric who came to the prison to conduct the weekly masses, suggested a willing candidate:

> *[He told Charley] that a lady named Lulu Reyes agreed to be his godmother. Lulu's Christian name was Lourdes. She was a Manila society lady. As time went by we learned Lulu was active in the underground. While pretending to be a friend of the [Japanese], she was doing all she could to help the POWs and the war effort against [them].[9]*

Despite being a virtual stranger to both young men, Lulu stood by proxy with Robert to serve as Charley's godparents.

. . . .

After her brother Willie was found and eventually released from Camp O'Donnell, Lulu could have stopped there and focused on her own family's well-being and survival during the Japanese occupation. But it went against the very core of her being and every value she cherished to turn away from the multitudes of imprisoned soldiers and civilians who still badly needed help.

When the Japanese opened prisons and internment camps throughout the Philippines, Filipino internees found valuable support from their families, friends and locals who flocked to the sites in search of relatives and to offer what help they could to their captive kababayans, or countrymen. Some POWs came from wealthy families who immediately and directly negotiated their release; others from more modest

9 Dow, 34

backgrounds were at least able to receive letters and care packages shortly after they were incarcerated. Despite the much higher death rate among Filipino POWs compared to Americans, the proximity of relatives and the local community "created for them a stronger sense of hope for survival." [10] But for American POWs who were thousands of miles from home, there were no loved ones nearby to help them as Lulu had been able to help her brother.

"I could not look away. I had to keep coming back to the prison camps, to help other prisoners who looked so sick and who were suffering like Willie," she explained years later.

Lulu worked tirelessly to deliver vital supplies to prison camps, but sometimes the help she gave to internees—most of whom she had never met or would ever meet—went beyond food and medicine. As Robert later wrote, "Father Santos told us Lulu said to let us know she was willing to help us in any way she could."

Even so, a willingness to help could only go so far. It was no easy task getting relief goods into the camps as Japanese checkpoint guards and commanding officers harbored suspicions of the aid workers' intent and activities. Nevertheless, they seemed inclined to be more lenient with women like Lulu and her friend Helena Benitez, founder of the Volunteer Social Aid Committee—the Girls in Blue as they were better known.

The tolerance displayed by Japanese authorities for the women may have been due to their social standing in Philippine society as much as to their gender. Japanese culture

10 Joven

places considerable importance on hierarchy, and a person's rank, whether in a social, military, business or other sphere, often determines how others behave toward them.

As Helena later explained:

[W]e came to know some highly educated officers from the Office of the Commanding General, as we requested their permission for our group to bring supplies to the prisoners. They acknowledged us as "fujin-kai": ladies of high stature. So we were recognized officially. [11]

While such recognition was tremendously important in getting relief goods to the camps, there were times when an extra push was needed, and Lulu was just the person to get it done. She had a persuasive nature sweetened with an irresistible charm, and her innate capacity for kindness was matched by an uncanny ability to convince others to do the right thing. She knew how to appeal to the basic human spirit in anyone—even the enemy.

Father John F. Hurley, SJ, the Jesuit superior in the Philippines during the war and de facto leader of a smuggling network based in the Ateneo de Manila campus, came to know her as one of the brave volunteers who secretly loaded trucks at the school with relief goods destined for Camp O'Donnell. He witnessed firsthand the gentle force of her personality in the face of intimidating obstacles:

Often on [these] trips to camp Miss Lulu Reyes would ride shotgun. I recall warning her to be careful and to take it easy, both for reasons of her health and the fear that the Japanese might

11 Benitez, n.p.

retaliate because of her friendliness with Americans. But she was invaluable; when the truck was stopped by Japanese patrols or blocked by Japanese officials, she would last them, not with buckshot, but with her charming and disarming ways. The truck would get through.[12]

Even Robert gave testament to her talent for going above and beyond:

One day a very good friend, [Roscoe] "Piggy" Word, who also attended Mass, told me he played the violin. He said he wished he had one so he could play while I sang. Piggy knew nothing about Lulu, so his comment was just wishful thinking.

At any rate, I passed it on to Father Santos and the next week we had a violin. Naturally, Lulu had to get permission from the [Japanese] to do this. Since she had contact with some very high officers and since they really thought she was their friend, the request was granted.[13]

Some of Lulu's other actions, however, were more heart-pounding than heart-warming and posed a significantly greater personal risk. In addition to whatever food and medical supplies were sanctioned by the camp commandant, she also brazenly smuggled in contraband medicines, money and notes from the families of prisoners. When his malaria worsened, Robert appealed to Father Santos to ask Lulu for help in getting medication, which was being strictly rationed or even withheld altogether by the Japanese guards. She covertly

12 Hurley, 203
13 Dow, 34

provided atabrine and quinine to the priest, who then distributed the pills during Mass by hiding them in the palm of his hand and slipping them to Robert and others in need while they received Communion.

On one occasion, she was present at the Assumption Convent a few blocks from the Reyes family home when a Maryknoll priest and US Army chaplain named William T. Cummings arrived to meet with Sister Trinita, the Superior of the Maryknoll Sisters. Though he was a prisoner at Bilibid, Father Cummings was periodically allowed outside under armed guard to procure supplies for Mass. Seeing an opportunity, Lulu deftly distracted the Japanese officer escorting him with a rousing game of ping pong while in another room. The now uncensored priest gave the nuns news and information from inside the prison and they in turn stealthily handed him prohibited letters and money for the American POWs.

Friends worried for Lulu's safety and warned her about the risks of capture and punishment as she continued her humanitarian work and underground activities. They feared her gender and social status would not be enough to protect her if she were caught. Indeed, her good friend Josefa Llanes Escoda, a prominent suffragette and founder of the Girl Scouts of the Philippines with whom she carried out many aid missions to Camp O'Donnell, was arrested in August 1944 and held at Fort Santiago in Intramuros, where the feared Kempei-tai were headquartered and where her husband, Antonio, had been incarcerated two months earlier.

Josefa was isolated from members of her family, who were permitted to send her food and other necessities just once in the nearly five months of her captivity, and her children were hidden to prevent their capture by the Japanese to be used as leverage in their mother's interrogation. She was reportedly brutally beaten and was last seen alive being loaded onto a military truck on January 6, 1945, as the Americans launched their offensive to retake Manila and the Philippines. Her exact fate is unknown, but it is likely she was executed and buried in an unmarked grave.

Her own subversive actions almost did not end well for Lulu. The prisoner grapevine knew about her activities, and Japanese authorities may have started to suspect something, but she managed to escape detention. Others were not so fortunate: Father Hurley was interrogated several times by the Kempei-tai, who had already detained several Jesuit priests for suspicion of supporting guerrillas and the underground resistance. When he was liberated by American forces after almost a year of imprisonment in starving conditions at the University of Santo Tomas internment camp, he weighed nearly half of the strapping 208 pounds he carried before the war.

Father Santos, meanwhile, was accused of being the intermediary for an imprisoned American officer who had secretly paid a civilian on the outside to smuggle prohibited medicines into the Yamamoto Butai. The priest was sent to Fort Santiago (dubbed the "Chamber of Horrors" by POWs, according to Robert), where inmates were crowded into filthy, dank confines and starved, beaten and horrendously tortured. The bodies of about 600 captives who died from suffocation, heat exhaustion or hunger would later be discovered piled up in the Fort's subterranean cells after the Imperial Japanese Army was driven from Manila at the end of the war.

Despite the torture he most certainly endured, Father Santos never gave up Lulu or other members of the underground resistance. She would later write to Robert after the war, describing the priest's ordeal: "Father Santos[14] is back with us again. He was one of the few who survived that terrible place. When he came out, we could hardly recognize him. We are so grateful to him that he didn't squeal on us girls. If he did, I would not be writing to you."

....

Over the span of three and half years after his capture at Bataan, Robert Dow was incarcerated in several different prison camps from the Philippines to Japan: Camp O'Donnell in Tarlac; Cabanatuan in Nueva Ecija; Bilibid and the Yamamoto Butai in Manila; and finally, the transport ship Nissyo Maru docked at Moji on the island of Kyushu, Japan.

The Nissyo Maru was one of the notorious Japanese "hell ships" into which an estimated 50,000 Allied POWs were crammed into inhumanely small spaces. One survivor's account recalled 700 men were forced into a hold large enough for only 100 people. Nearly 21,000 of the men who boarded the ships died in horrific conditions.

14 Although neither Bob Dow nor my mother mentioned Father Santos' first name, there is a strong possibility that he is Father Rufino Jiao Santos, a young priest serving as secretary to the Archbishop of Manila Michael J. O'Doherty. Father Rufino was reportedly arrested after deflecting blame to himself when Archbishop O'Doherty was accused of funding the illicit smuggling of food and other items into the University of Santo Tomas camp. He was liberated in 1945 after a year of imprisonment and dreadful torture, became Archbishop of Manila in 1953 and was created the first Filipino cardinal by Pope John XXIII in 1960.

Thankfully, Robert (or Bob, as he later invited me to call him) survived all these trials. He received the Bronze Star, Purple Heart and numerous other honors and citations for his brave service, and eventually returned to America, married and raised a family. Like thousands of veterans, however, he was scarred by his experiences. He eventually wrote a book about his wartime ordeals as a form of catharsis, and he sent me a copy of the unpublished memoir with a letter explaining why he decided to write it:

I never have been able to talk a lot about what life as a Japanese prisoner of war was like. The doctors at the [Veteran's Administration] have been telling me for years to do this because I have been troubled with nightmares and intrusive thoughts all these years. I still have this problem but not to the degree I was bothered before. I was also told I owed this to my family, because they knew very little about what went on.

After his first phone call to me that late night in 1999, Bob and I regularly stayed in touch for several years. He told me how he had written to so many Philippine government agencies, politicians, diplomats and newspapers asking if anyone knew the whereabouts of Lulu Reyes. Only after the Internet became mainstream and made international communication easier was he able to find and reach out to Johnny Litton, a well-known society columnist for the Philippine Star, who led him to my godmother Nini Quezon Avanceña and eventually to me in New Jersey.

Learning more about Mom's actions during the war and Bob's firsthand accounts of the horrors experienced by American and Filipino soldiers helped me better appreciate the bravery, courage and strength of will they demonstrated in the face of grave danger and inhumanity.

I was amazed by how Bob managed to survive and how simple things, such as thoughts of his family and his girlfriend Bonnie (who later became his wife), his yearnings for his sister's chocolate cake, and the blessed power of prayer and faith, kept him alive. And in his own words written to me, he credited my mother as a critical part of his survival:

I'm sure you know a lot about the things your mother did for the POWs, but unless you were there, it is hard to realize how much she put her life on the line for strangers. For the most part… the Japanese were very cruel and would not have thought twice about putting her through torture and then killing her. Oh yes, she was a true heroine.

I am so incredibly proud of Mom's courageous actions, but I still shudder at the thought of what might have happened if she had been caught. Why did she continue to take such risks? I know very well what the answer is: her compassion for others always prevailed no matter her own situation.

"Every time I saw an American soldier in [those] prisons, I thought, 'That is someone's son, someone's brother, husband or best friend.' I cannot not do anything for them," she once told me. "I have brothers, so I know what it feels like when they go missing. I wanted to do that for other people."

A young and single Lulu Reyes bravely penetrated the most dangerous WWII prison camps in the Philippines, numerous times, to smuggle in malaria medicine, and to bring food and aid. She saved so many American POWs, including Robert Dow.

From her example, I've learned that activating the power of our hearts to love and to be kind, to see the goodness in every human, takes practice and consistent intention. But we need to keep tapping into ourselves, into the core of our souls to bring out that energy. Everyone needs to be loved and liked. Someone else always needs to be helped. Empowering ourselves to do that little act of kindness, no matter how difficult, is what makes the world better. And yes, it is hard to do, especially when there are insurmountable odds, but we are all capable of it.

. . . .

During one of our last conversations before he died in April 2006, I asked Bob why he persisted in searching for my mother for over fifty years despite so many dead-ends.

"I wanted to thank Lulu in person for saving my life," he explained. "I was able to return to the United States, marry my high school sweetheart and have a good life.

"Because of her bravery, she gave me a life."

Chapter 8

The Orphans

Whenever the news about COVID-19—runaway infection rates, rising death toll, and bitter arguments about mask mandates and vaccinations—began to feel unrelenting and demoralizing, I would turn off the television, log off my laptop and put aside my phone. Instead, I would sift through some tattered folders containing my mother's personal documents. Although it often made me teary-eyed, reading these yellowed sheets of paper brought back happy memories.

I found, for instance, a handwritten recipe for monggo con hielo, a delightfully frosty concoction of mung beans, cold milk, a bit of sugar and a lot of crushed ice. Embedded in Mom's elegant script are recollections of her preparing this treat for merienda, or afternoon snack, during the hot summer days of my childhood. I can easily picture her holding a tall parfait glass, beads of condensation sliding down its sides, and can almost hear the clinking of the long spoon against the glass as she stirred a sweet mash of mung beans into the milk and ice mixture.

Some reminiscences, however, are much more bittersweet. One letter written to her best friends Baby and Nini Quezon in the midst of the final, terrible months of World War II in the Philippines was terse yet emotional, though the words, hastily written in Spanish, gave little detail about the horrors she had witnessed during one of the most harrowing periods of the conflict:

My dearest Baby and Nini,

What can I say? How do I begin? I am so devastated, I can't even write. I don't know how to describe it. Rev. Fr. Ortiz has given me a few minutes to write you this note. We are at the Nazareth Convent with the Jesuit priests, all of us, the family. Fr. Ortiz will tell you everything.

Please come soon.

I love you both very, very much,

Lulu

. . . .

February 9, 1945

The house shuddered from yet another explosion that sounded much closer than the last. As the sounds of destruction came inexorably closer to their home, the Reyes family realized they were in greater danger the longer they stayed.

The Battle of Manila had begun six days before, when American forces reached the outskirts of the city and launched an all-out assault against the occupying Imperial Japanese Army. For nearly a week, relentless artillery fire from the would-be liberators had been targeting enemy positions in the districts, but the shelling from tanks and howitzers did not distinguish between military opponents and innocent civilians. Meanwhile, Japanese soldiers—surrounded, desperate and vengeful—were embarking on a campaign of atrocities against the trapped and helpless populace.

Every day, the blasts and street battles came closer and closer to Malate and to the house on Indiana Street until, finally, the family decided as one that it was time to leave.

Carrying not much more than the clothes they wore, Mama Nena, Lulu, Bobby, Willie and his wife, Helen, and Poncy fled north to Herran Street in the hopes of finding shelter at St. Paul College of Manila, Lulu's old school.

Acrid smoke from burning buildings shrouded the air and made it difficult to navigate the chaotic streets and sidewalks. They turned east instead, away from St. Paul and toward Taft Avenue where De La Salle College was located several blocks south. Perhaps they would be safer at that campus, where some families had already sought refuge. Lulu was acquainted with the De La Salle Brothers[15] through her charity work with the Chaplains Aid Association and was certain they would not be turned away. But detonating shells and the sharp, rapid cracks of gunfire mingling with the terrified cries of fleeing residents drove them a block past Taft to Pennsylvania Street. It was difficult to see much beyond a few feet ahead. Their eyes stung from the smoke but tears could not blur the sight of bloodied bodies of men, women and children strewn everywhere.

Lulu gasped as she nearly tripped over corpses and recognized the lifeless faces of neighbors. She whispered a broken prayer as she kept a protective arm around Mama Nena, while Bobby, Willie and Poncy flanked the women, their strides long and fast, urging them to move more quickly.

"Tulungan niyo po ako!" *Please help me!*

Sobbing, screaming and plaintive pleading rang in their ears and disoriented them even more. Lulu wanted to stop

15 The congregation is formally known as the Institute of the Brothers of the Christian Schools, founded by Saint Jean-Baptiste de La Salle in the 18th century..

Febrero 20, 1945

Queridísimas Baby y Nini,

Que voy a decir, donde voy a empezar? Estoy tan atolondrada que no puedo ni escribir, Rev. Fr. Ortiz me da algunos minutos para mandaros una nota, estamos toda la familia aqui en el convento de Nazareth con los Padres Jesuitas, ya os contará el Padre Ortiz todo!

Venid pronto, Os quiero mucho, mucho

Lulú

and help, but they simply could not risk an encounter with Japanese soldiers on the hunt, who would not hesitate to kill them.

"We need to keep running," Bobby told her.

When they reached Pennsylvania Street, they stopped at the sight before them. The road should have been as familiar to Lulu as her own street. How often had she attended luncheons, merienda cenas, bienvenidas and despedidas with the many friends who lived there? Now, she didn't recognize the once-idyllic neighborhood where blooms of bougainvillea painted in every shade of pink used to cascade from the wrought iron fences fronting elegant houses. The colorful palette she remembered was replaced by the desolate black and grey of smoldering, pulverized heaps that were once homes, churches, schools and businesses.

"Did anyone survive? Do we know anyone who may be hurt?" Lulu asked despairingly, but her brothers and mother hushed her.

Suddenly, a young man and a teenaged girl emerged from a swirl of smoke and ran towards them. Lulu immediately recognized Tomas and Victoria Quirino, the children of Senator Elpidio Quirino and his wife, Alicia Syquia, who was a close friend of Mama Nena and the eldest sister of Hector Syquia, Willie's best friend. The families knew each other well from attending many of the same dinner parties, galas and life celebrations of their social circle—all happy times that were now impossible to fathom in the midst of the city's destruction.

Lulu embraced the siblings in worried relief.

"Mama no esta mas," Vicky cried softly against her shoulder. *Mama is gone.*

It would be several months later before they learned the details of what had happened to the Quirino family — how artillery shells ignited a fire on the roof of their house in nearby Ermita, prompting the senator to send eldest son Tomas, 21, to lead his mother and three younger sisters Norma, Vicky and Fe Angela to their grandmother Concepcion Syquia's home a few blocks away, while he and second son Armando, 20, would follow after salvaging what belongings they could. How Doña Alicia and Norma, 17, died instantly when they were strafed by Japanese machine guns as they ran across a street, and how the soldiers then bayoneted two-year-old Fe Angela when they found her still alive in her mother's embrace. And how Armando, separated from their father after leaving the burning house, was also shot dead after attempting to reach his slain mother and sisters lying in the street. Only Tomas, who was wounded in the leg, and fourteen-year-old Vicky escaped because they had been running just ahead of their family.

Senator Quirino and his surviving children would eventually be reunited, and three years later he would become the sixth President of the Philippines with Vicky serving as the country's youngest First Lady at the age of sixteen. But on that horrifying day, she was just an anguished girl who had witnessed the slaughter of her loved ones.

Lulu hugged her grieving young friend tightly as tears streamed down her own cheeks. There was no time to mourn for long. Blast waves from ongoing artillery fire rippled through the air and sent dirt, wood, concrete and unimaginable pieces flying around them. Even worse, Japanese soldiers lay in wait seemingly around every corner to cut down any unfortunate Filipinos who crossed their paths. Her brothers urged them to keep moving. It pained Lulu to leave the Quirino siblings, but Vicky and Tomas needed to find their father, and so they parted in different directions.

The Reyes family sought temporary shelter in the rubble of a nearby house. They huddled together, unsure of what to do or where to go. Lulu wanted to cry out in fear and desperation, but she held herself together. She did not want to upset Mama, her brothers or Helen by letting them see her break down. As the city was being destroyed around them, the only thing she could do was to pray. She reached into her pocket for the rosary she always carried and wrapped the smooth beads around her fingers. With her other hand, she stroked the small rose gold pendant with the image of the Blessed Virgin Mary that hung from a chain around her neck. It had been a gift to her as an infant, and the soft metal still bore the tell-tale imprint of baby teeth where she had used it as a teething ring.

In a moment of quiet communion, Lulu prayed with all her heart. She prayed for the souls of Doña Alicia, Armando, Norma and little Fe Angela, and for strength and faith for Vicky, Tomas and their papa Elpidio in the face of their devastating loss. She beseeched the Lord to shield the innocent who were fleeing for their lives and for the violence surrounding them to be over soon. She implored Him to protect her family beside her and, above all, she thanked Him for keeping them together and alive.

Their respite in the ruins did not last long. They needed to keep moving, to find a safer refuge. Once again, they were running in the streets, not knowing their destination but hoping for some divine guidance. Then Lulu spotted three small children, the oldest not more than ten years old, bawling as they stood barefoot by several bodies. Their clothes were dirty and torn, and they had scratches on their faces and arms.

Despite Bobby's entreaties not to stop, Lulu pulled the children to her and asked them why they were alone. They were too scared and could barely speak, so the only information Lulu could get were their names—Albert, Eugenio, and Carmelita—and that their parents were dead. The little ones were completely alone.

Lulu decided without hesitation that the three orphans would go with them to wherever they could all find sanctuary.

"I can't leave these children behind with no one else to take care of them," she insisted over her brothers' objections. She had prayed for innocents such as these children to be protected, and she realized she could do something about it herself.

. . . .

Mom rarely spoke about those days when she and the family desperately plunged into a maelstrom in search of safety. I gleaned bits and pieces of the story over the years, patching it together with what historians and authors have written about the Battle of Manila, decades removed from the events. I know that sometime after my mother enfolded the three orphans into her care, they eventually found refuge —first, with the Jesuits at Nazareth, a former women's retreat near the campus of the University of Santo Tomas, about ten miles north of Malate and one of the first areas liberated by the Americans, and then later at the Ateneo de Manila on Padre Faura Street in Ermita, where they lived in the former chemistry building, the only structure on campus left relatively intact.

Most of all, I am so grateful for the miracle of their survival after learning how frightfully close they came to sharing the fate of hundreds of other Filipino families.

On the same day they fled the house intending to go to St. Paul College just a few blocks away, Japanese soldiers lured hundreds of men, women, and children into the school's dining hall with promises of safety, food and drink, and then detonated bombs in their midst. Those who initially survived the blasts but could not escape further were shot or bayoneted. More than 360 people were massacred at my mother's alma mater.

On February 12, three days after gunfire and explosions prevented Mom and her family from heading down Taft Avenue to De La Salle College, a group of twenty-one Japanese soldiers butchered Catholic laymen and entire families as they fled down the halls and cowered in the rooms of the school's chapel. Some say the amount of blood shed that day was so great, and the inhumanity so profound, the bloodstains could not be entirely washed from the floors and walls.

The family lived in shelters for nearly a year after the liberation of Manila. The houses and apartments that Lola Nena and Lolo Ponciano had built, and everything in them, had been shelled and burned to ashes, so they did the only thing they and their fellow survivors could do—begin rebuilding their shattered city, one house at a time. Reconstruction of all the destroyed residences in the Malate compound was completed by 1947 and an expanded Reyes family, now including three orphans of war, moved back to Indiana Street.

....

My earliest memory of Albert, Eugenio and Carmelita goes back to when I was about four or five years old. They were young adults by then and still living at the house on Indiana Street. Lola Nena had passed away in 1955 and only Tito Willie and Tita Helen lived there. Mom had developed a strong bond and affection for the three orphans and made sure they went to school, attended church, were taught family values and manners, and knew they had a home and people who cared about them. But she couldn't heal their hidden wounds. The siblings had not only witnessed their parents' deaths but had also absorbed the sights, sounds, smell and feel of war that no child should ever experience. It was just a matter of time before the trauma began to manifest in each of them, one by one.

Albert, the eldest, was the first to exhibit troubling behavior. I remember him only from photos and snatches of conversation between family members, and I asked Mom a few times what had happened to him. She tried to explain how he gradually become more violent toward other people, but she could never offer more than scant details before she became too upset over the memory to continue. All I know is that at some point, when I was still a very young child, Albert had a mental breakdown.

We recognize it today as post-traumatic stress disorder, and there are now effective outpatient treatments for PTSD. But in the 1950s and '60s, mental illness was not yet fully understood and the best therapies the era had to offer were mostly rendered in psychiatric hospitals. With few options available to help care for Albert at home, Mom decided with a heavy heart to send him to the Mandaluyong Mental Hospital[16] for treatment.

Not long after, Eugenio also began to show signs of psychological trauma. This time, I didn't have to ask my mother to recall events. I remember them myself.

One episode occurred when I was about six years old and we were visiting my aunt in Malate. Eugenio, by then in his early twenties, was watering the plants with a garden hose while I played in the yard with my friends from the compound. Perhaps our shrieks of laughter were too loud and shrill because without warning, he suddenly turned the hose on us and began yelling angrily as he chased us around the yard. We didn't understand what was happening but we knew he wasn't playing, and we were scared.

Mom dashed out of the house as soon as she heard our panicked cries. Back then, I had a child's concern only for my own need to be soothed. I now realize that I wasn't the only one who was frightened by Eugenio's actions that day. My mother worried as much for him as she did for me and my

16 Now the National Center for Mental Health

friends. She recognized the emerging behavior as the same kind that afflicted his brother but feared she could do little to stop it from overtaking him. The trauma that was seared deep in his mind could not be salved as easily as she could calm my momentary fright with a hug and murmurs of comfort. Mom faced an undeniable truth: no matter how much care and affection she offered him, Eugenio, like his brother Albert, needed and deserved more help than she could provide.

When my parents brought Eugenio to Mandaluyong themselves, Mom cried the whole way to the hospital. As far as I know, the brothers remained in institutional care for the rest of their lives. My mother rarely talked about them, and if she visited them, she never brought me or my sister or mentioned it to us.

....

After Eugenio was taken into psychiatric care, Carmelita was the only one of the orphaned siblings left. Lita, as my mom and grandmother called her, was probably around four or five years old when she and her brothers were found by Mom wandering the ruined streets of Manila.

She was a quiet girl and kept mostly to herself. No one really knew what she had witnessed during the war and how it may have affected her, but she didn't seem to display any outward signs of internalized trauma as her siblings had. She also never let on how she felt when Albert and Eugenio were institutionalized.

Mom and Lola Nena had done their best to be maternal figures to Lita, teaching her what her own mother might have. She showed an aptitude for cooking from an early age, so Lola Nena taught her all the family recipes that her own mother Lola Juana had passed along to her.

Lita was barely out of her teens when Mom brought her from Malate to live with us in Tarlac province. Our new house had just been completed and my mother needed someone she could trust to help with the household. I remember she didn't talk much and smiled even less, although her mood always lightened when she accompanied us on our weekend trips back to Manila so that she could visit her brothers, too. The house on Indiana Street was really the only home she knew, or at least could remember, so it must have been difficult for her to leave behind its familiarity and security.

The only other thing that brightened Lita's usually somber demeanor was cooking. Her obvious enjoyment of the task showed in the care and attention she put into preparing even the simplest of dishes. I have a distinct memory of her sopa de fideo, a hearty comfort soup she would make for afternoon merienda or as a starter for dinner. She knew how to perfectly balance sweet and savory flavors in the tomato-based broth and how to cook the thin, silky vermicelli noodles to just the right level of doneness.

Lita seemed at her most content in the kitchen, and I sometimes wonder now if cooking was her way to express her feelings and to voice the thoughts she otherwise kept inside. I like to think the little things she did, such as boiling a piece of chicken and shredding it finely to add specially to my bowl of sopa de fideo, showed her affection for me in place of cuddles and kisses.

It turned out, however, that some of Lita's reticence was due to keeping a secret. Mom had entrusted her with the market shopping, and sometime during one such errand, she met a man. They would meet clandestinely whenever Lita was sent to the market, which could be several times in a week. But secrets never remain secret in the marketplace, where the degrees of separation narrow and gossip is the social currency.

When Mom found out…! In my entire life up to that point, I had never seen my mother so angry. As independent-minded as she was, Mom was still a woman of her era and society, and as a surrogate mother to Lita, she reacted as she would have if her own daughters were having furtive trysts. She was hurt that the young woman would keep such secrets from her and she worried this boyfriend—a stocky older man named Avelino—was taking advantage of Lita's youth and innocence. She vehemently disapproved of the relationship, but her stern admonishments couldn't stop it. Lita and Avelino eloped soon after, leaving Mom as heartbroken as though she had lost a daughter.

The couple eventually returned to Tarlac a few months later, both of them jobless and Lita pregnant with her first child. Despite what had happened, Mom welcomed them back into our household. She was not one to hold onto past grievances, and her love for the younger woman was not readily abandoned.

Lita gave birth to a daughter soon after and named her Carmelita, too. She was close in age to my sister Isabel, and the two eventually became playmates. Meanwhile, my parents hired Avelino as a general handyman around the house and farm, but it was a poor fit. Lita's husband apparently didn't like the work, and his lax attitude toward labor annoyed my father, who never asked his employees and farmhands to do more than he would do himself. I once overheard him complain to Mom about catching Avelino asleep on the job more than once. Dad was calm, easygoing and not the type to make quick judgments about others, so for him to voice criticism of a person was out of character and pointed to a growing friction in the household.

By the time little Carmelita turned five, Lita had two more babies—a boy, Avelino Jr., and another girl named Corazon. It was clear to everyone that her children were her joy. I would sometimes catch her smiling at all of us as we sat in the living room watching afternoon kids' shows on TV and Corazon would gleefully dance along with the music. And I'm certain it delighted my mother to see the girl cruelly orphaned by war become a loving mother herself.

Mom arranged for Carmelita to attend the same Catholic school with me and Isabel, paying for her uniforms, shoes and whatever else she needed. There was never any hesitation or question on her part to provide for Lita's children; the love and care she had for their mother extended to them as well. Yet some unknown, unspoken discontent must have been festering in Lita and Avelino, and it finally reached a breaking point.

One morning just before Christmas 1966 and about halfway through Carmelita's first year of school, we woke up to find Lita, Avelino and the children gone. Their room was emptied of their belongings, the closets bare. Once again, Lita had left without explanation or goodbyes, and once again, Mom was devastated. She cried the whole day and pleaded with Dad to call the local police to search for the family, but as Lita was an adult who had left with her husband and children, the authorities could do nothing. My father did his best to reassure Mom that the family would be fine, but she was inconsolable. With Lita's departure, the three little orphans she had taken in were now all gone.

My mother loved unconditionally but perhaps this time too idealistically. On a February day in 1945, she had fled her home in fear, running through streets filled with death as the life and city she knew were being destroyed. But in the middle of the devastation, she found three innocents, and in rescuing them, she channeled her grief into purpose.

I believe that for all the good she did during the war for Tito Willie, Bob Dow and the countless POWs whose lives she helped save, my mother saw in Albert, Eugenio and Lita all of the people she couldn't help—Doña Alicia and her children, the clergymen and women with whom she had worked and prayed side by side, and the neighbors and strangers who, by cruel randomness, had lost their lives while she and her family had survived whole.

She could give the orphans love, attention and a safe home, but she couldn't erase their experience during the war and the damage it had caused to their vulnerable spirits. While Albert and Eugenio eventually acted out their trauma with anger and physical aggression, Lita was different. She was so young at the time; she may not have even remembered what her parents were like and what their deaths meant. Instead, she may have felt an inexplicable void that my mother simply couldn't fill. Despite being a part of our family for most of her life, Lita may have felt deep in her core that she didn't belong, especially after her brothers were gone. With Avelino and her children, she finally had a family that was truly, completely her own.

I would like to believe that in her heart, Lita loved my mother like a daughter would. Sadly, we never heard from her or the children again—no letters, no calls, no bits of news on the grapevine. Despite the hurt she felt, Mom couldn't help but be forgiving and hopeful. Even when it became clear that Lita and her family would not be returning, she kept the door open.

"If Lita comes back, let her in," she told Dad. "I will always love her."

Chapter 9

A Woman Called Joey

"If you can sauté garlic and onions, then you can cook anything."

My mother would often reassure me with these words while I was learning how to cook. In fact, many of her savory recipes would predictably begin with the instruction, "Igisa mo lang lahat." Sauté everything together.

Sautéing garlic and onions is the first fundamental step of many Filipino recipes. As far as I'm concerned, nothing whets the appetite quite like the satisfying hiss made by minced garlic and sliced onions hitting a super-heated skillet and the heady aroma released as they sizzle in shimmering hot oil. From there, other ingredients are added to build layers of flavor.

A perfect example of this building block approach is the classic Filipino noodle dish called pansit. Actually, pansit refers to a broad category of noodle dishes with specific types named after the kind of noodle used, such as pansit bihon (rice vermicelli) or pansit sotanghon (glass noodles), or from a place of origin, like seafood-rich pansit Malabon.

The versatility and variety of ingredients guarantees there is a recipe to suit every palate and preference, but what really helps make pansit so ubiquitous on every Filipino celebratory table is how easy it can be scaled up, from feeding a family for dinner to serving dozens of guests at a feast. There are no exact measurements for how much noodles, chopped vegetables or sliced meat should be used. The ingredients are really a cook's choice depending on preference and availability—or sometimes lack of availability.

During the COVID-19 lockdowns in New Jersey, there

were times when certain items that many of us take for granted, such as flour, butter and even chickens, became scarce or totally missing from grocery shelves. Living in a land of plenty like America, you become habitually accustomed to picking up whatever food and ingredients you need whenever you need it from a variety of sources—farmers' markets, supermarkets, convenience stores, gourmet shops and online grocers.

When I first heard about possible food shortages due to pandemic-related restrictions affecting supply lines, I panicked. I immediately went online and started looking for food stores in other counties to see if they carried what I needed. But then Elpi reminded me there was a lockdown, so we couldn't even leave our home.

The reality check calmed me down, and instead of giving in to even more panicking or indulging in self-pity, I tried to put the situation in perspective by thinking about what it must have been like for my mother, grandmother and uncles in wartime Manila.

During the occupation of the city in WWII, the Imperial Japanese Army strictly controlled the supply of food, sometimes even shooting farmers who attempted to smuggle sacks into the city, while fuel shortages and the risk of encountering Japanese ships discouraged fishermen from going out to sea. Toward the end of the war, poorly supplied enemy soldiers were given free rein to provision themselves – that is, to steal what little food could be found in the city.

Residents survived on kangkong (water spinach), camote (sweet potato) and coconut meat, but it was often not enough.

Pushcarts became a regular sight as they patrolled the districts daily to remove the dozens who died of starvation right on the streets. Mom recalled how her family gratefully subsisted on not much more than pan de sal and matamis na bao (coconut jam) during the year they spent living at refugee shelters after the war.

After the liberation of Manila and the end of the war, Filipinos once again had access, albeit via strict ration coupons, to food that must have seemed like luxuries after several years of deprivation: canned corned beef, pork and beans, powdered eggs and milk, baked bread, and chocolate and candies. And every day that my mother's family was alive and still together must have felt like a small victory worth celebrating with a meal. But even as Filipinos began rebuilding the city and country, access to food remained limited or very expensive. Food was and is such a paramount expression of celebration, and I wondered how they marked life milestones like birthdays or holidays in a time when it was still so difficult to find simple ingredients.

Several years ago, I discovered among Mom's files a photograph of a large gathering posed in front of what I immediately recognized as the house on Indiana Street. The women and men were a mix of Filipino and American, young and old, civilian, military and clergy. It was undated and had nothing written to describe the occasion or the persons depicted, but the smiling, relaxed faces in the image provided plenty of clues.

Of course, the first ones I recognized were my mother beaming radiantly, a ribboned medal pinned to her white dress, and my grandmother gazing down shyly yet happily.

Lulu Reyes (seated middle), wearing her US Medal of Freedom, with friends and family. September 1947, Malate, Manila.

I also spotted my future godmother, Nini Quezon (later Avanceña), who had returned to Manila in 1945 with her mother and siblings after her father, President Manuel Quezon, died during their wartime exile in the United States. Sitting on the ground in the front were Albert, Eugenio and Carmelita, the little orphans my mother had rescued during the Battle of Manila, and just behind Albert, with Mom's hand on her shoulder, was her dear friend Virginia "Bengie" Joseph. From the presence of these familiar faces, I knew the photo must have been taken after Lola Nena's house was rebuilt in 1947. But when exactly, and why?

Part of the answer came in a clipping from the *Philippines Free Press* and dated October 4, 1947, announcing that "Miss Lulu Reyes, prominent Manila social worker…had been awarded the Medal of Freedom by the U.S. government for her outstanding courage and resourcefulness to alleviate sufferings of American Prisoners of War during the Japanese occupation."

The accompanying photo showed Mom standing proudly between the Archbishop of Manila Michael J. O'Doherty and Major General George Moore, and wearing the same ribboned medal pinned to her dress.

According to another clip from the society pages, she and Lola Nena hosted an outdoor party at their home for a triple celebration of her distinguished award, a blessing ceremony for the newly rebuilt house on Indiana Street and Mom's 34th birthday later that month.

I am certain this merry group photo portrays that wonderful day.

I can imagine what it was like: cheerful guests arriving at the house and making their way to the back garden, where buffet tables were set up on the verandah. The society page clipping didn't mention what was served, but I have no doubt that Lola Nena would have made sure there was a large porcelain platter of pansit on the table.

Meat such as pork or chicken would have still been scarce at the time and therefore very expensive, so perhaps she made a seafood pansit like palabok, full of fresh shrimp and smoked fish, which were plentiful again in Manila Bay after several years of no commercial fishing. Or maybe she made a vegetable pansit, such as pansit sencillo, with produce grown in her own "victory garden" from some of the 50,000 kilograms of cabbage, soybean, eggplant and other vegetable seeds distributed for free to rural farmers and urban gardeners to help revive the country's post-war food supply.

Although I'll never know what was on the buffet tables on that lovely October day, I do know that my mother, a consummate hostess since she was a teenager in Manila high society, and my grandmother, from whom she learned the art of cookery and hospitality, would have made sure their guests were well and blissfully fed.

....

I didn't recognize many other faces in the group portrait from Mom's celebration, although the newspaper mentioned the guest list included US Army officers, Philippine government officials, society matrons and members of the various organizations to which she belonged. But whenever I looked at the photo, my eyes were always drawn to one young woman seated on a rattan chair between Lola Nena and an American officer perched on the armrest. Wearing a gaily striped dressed and peep-toe pumps, her smile was broad and carefree, her chin tilted up toward the glow of the late afternoon sun. I felt a sense of familiarity and connection to her that I couldn't explain, but I resigned myself to never learning her name and what relationship she shared with my mother. The universe, however, had other ideas.

In 2015, I received an email from *Tampa Bay Times* writer Ben Montgomery, who was working on a biography of the unsung WWII Filipino spy Josefina Guerrero. During his research, he came across references to my mother in the book *Under the Red Sun*, written by Mom's close friend and mentor

Father Forbes J. Monaghan, SJ, and he wondered if I could shed further light on her possible friendship with his subject. Unfortunately, I had never heard my mother talk about Miss Guerrero or even mention her name, but I was happy to share whatever information I could about that period in Mom's life.

When Montgomery's book *The Leper Spy: The Story of an Unlikely Hero of World War II* was published the following year, I immediately bought a copy. There, on the cover, was a familiar smile. It was the woman in the striped dress in Mom's celebration photo, and now I knew her name. As I began reading the book, I became engrossed in the poignant story of the woman called Joey.

Born Josefina Veluya and orphaned at a young age, Joey was raised by her modestly affluent grandparents on a coconut plantation and educated in an elite convent school in Manila where she counted future First Daughter Baby Quezon among her friends. She was married at sixteen to a young medical student named Renato Guerrero and became a mother at age eighteen with the birth of their daughter, Cynthia.

Shortly before the Japanese invasion of the Philippines in 1941, Joey began experiencing persistent headaches and fatigue. The diagnosis was devastating: she had contracted Hansen's disease, more commonly known as leprosy. She was just twenty-four years old.

Suddenly, the young woman faced a future with an incurable, progressively debilitating and socially stigmatized disease, all in the midst of a world war. Although Renato stayed by her side, Joey made the heart-crushing decision to send Cynthia away to live with his family to protect her from infection.

Her condition was soon exacerbated when the medicine she desperately needed to keep her leprosy under control became increasingly difficult to find in Japanese-occupied Manila. Rather than meekly submit to a bleak fate, however, Joey drew inspiration from St. Joan of Arc, whom she had idolized since childhood, according to Montgomery. She joined the Filipino underground resistance, gathering information on Imperial Army troop movements and garrison fortifications, smuggling medicine, food and messages to American prisoners of war, and ferrying messages between the Manila resistance and guerrilla groups in the mountains and countryside with the illicit messages hidden in her hair, clothes and even hollowed-out fruit.

To be caught meant execution, and the only thing protecting Joey was her illness. Without access to the medicine that kept her leprosy in check, she had developed its tell-tale skin lesions and swollen nodes, which she used to her advantage. These visible signs of disease were enough for Japanese soldiers to nervously wave her through checkpoints without question or interference.

Her most daring, dangerous and valuable exploits came as American forces began the campaign to retake the Philippines in late 1944. Joey drew maps by hand of Japanese fortifications and gun batteries along Manila Bay, which allowed US bombers to destroy the defenses ahead of the American advance on Manila. And when Filipino guerrillas learned the Imperial Army had mined a vast area north of the city and on the path of the planned American assault, she taped a map of the minefield to her back and walked more than fifty miles through enemy-occupied territory to deliver it into the hands of the commanding officer of the US 37th Infantry Division.

Her extraordinary action that day undoubtedly saved the lives of hundreds of American soldiers, and it was among her many courageous deeds for which she was presented a Medal of Freedom in 1948 by Major General Moore—the same American officer who, almost a year earlier, presented my mother her own Medal of Freedom that she proudly wore in the group portrait I found.

In the years immediately after the war ended and before Joey received official recognition for her heroic actions, she faced more hardship because of her illness. She had already been separated from her beloved daughter and had lost her home to bombs during the Battle of Manila, but just a few months later, she was ordered into a state-run leprosarium by the American military health authorities and their uncompromising policy of isolating patients suffering from Hansen's disease.

According to Montgomery, her mentor, Father Monaghan, immediately turned to my mother for help in hiding Joey until they could find another refuge for her. Although Lola Nena's house had been heavily damaged by shelling and the family was living in a shelter themselves, Mom did not hesitate to take in her friend.

Unfortunately, Joey could not evade the health authorities for long, and she was officially institutionalized in the infamously derelict leprosarium at Tala, Novaliches, sometime in the second half of 1945. Disappointed but not defeated, she entered the facility with dignity and with the support of her dearest friends, including my mother. As Montgomery described in *The Leper Spy:*

The next afternoon, [Father Monaghan] drove Joey to Novaliches. Lulu and her other friends came along. They joked and laughed the entire way . . .

They ate supper with the director, then packed up to leave. Lulu and the girls kissed Joey. Father Monaghan shook her hand . . . No one spoke on the drive back to Manila. They thought about how much she had given and how little she had received in return. A hero. An outcast.[17]

The fact that Joey was in the group portrait taken in Lola Nena's backyard is a testament to her friendship with Mom: by that time, she had been confined at the Tala Leprosarium for two years and would have had to receive special permission to leave the premises. Seeing her radiantly smiling face turned toward the sun, I can only imagine how she felt having a day of freedom and celebration surrounded by so many friends.

Joey would spend another year at the Tala Leprosarium, fighting tirelessly and almost singlehandedly to help improve the terrible living conditions for herself and her fellow patients. On May 29, 1948, she received her Medal of Freedom from Major General Moore, and less than three weeks later, she was given permission to travel to the United States to receive treatment at the National Leprosarium in Carville, Louisiana.

17 Montgomery, 179

After a decade of treatment in the US, she was finally free of Hansen's disease but at a deeply personal cost. Her marriage to Renato had ended; she was effectively estranged from Cynthia, who grew up barely knowing her mother; and the Philippines, her homeland, no longer felt like home. She lived out the rest of her life in obscurity in the US, just as she wanted. After so many years of fighting a disease and a war, and after so much heartache and loss, she had simply wanted to forget it all.

....

Reading *The Leper Spy* revealed a new episode in my mother's past that she inexplicably never shared with me. She and Joey very likely met through their mutual friend Baby Quezon, and they were involved in many of the same perilous activities during WWII, such as smuggling supplies into POW camps and supporting the Philippine underground resistance. As I read the book, I could see in Joey what I saw in my mother—the same resolute, unquestioning sense of duty to help others despite their personal circumstances. I have no doubt they became friends because they also recognized in each other the will and willingness to fight the hard battles.

Neither of them ever trumpeted their actions or achievements. During the last decades of her life, Joey deliberately avoided telling anyone about her exploits and preferred to live as anonymously as possible, while Mom recounted snippets of her activities during the war, leaving me to piece together the details from conversations with family and friends and through historical research.

One thing is very clear to me: my mother and her friend Joey were ordinary women who displayed extraordinary bravery and courage during one of the worst periods of modern history, and as Ben Montgomery and I realized, their stories are too compelling and inspirational to let them be forgotten.

The group photo I found captured a lighthearted moment in time, but there were dark clouds on the horizon for some of those gathered that day: Tita Nini would lose her first husband Philip Buencamino III, her mother, the former First Lady Aurora Aragon Quezon, and her only sister, "Baby," in a bloody, politically motivated assassination[18] less than two years later; and the three little orphans would struggle with lingering psychological trauma from their experiences during the war. As for Mom, she would later find herself caught in family strife and dealing with the loss of her mother and brothers to a relentless hereditary illness.

But on one October day in Lola Nena's backyard, the sun was shining and dear friends came together in celebration to talk, to laugh and to fill their plates with my grandmother's pansit. The faces that looked into the camera were bright with joy and optimism. The war was over, homes and lives were being rebuilt, and the future was hopeful.

18 Aurora Quezon, her daughter and son-in-law, accompanied by local dignitaries and an armed military escort, were on their way to open the Quezon Memorial Hospital in Baler on the central-east coast of Luzon when they were ambushed on a mountain road by an estimated 100 to 200 armed men, reportedly members of the Hukbalahap, a Communist guerrilla group. The province of Aurora, with Baler as its capital, was later named in honor of Mrs. Quezon.

Chapter 10

The Farmer and the Socialite

My mother was a beautiful woman, but she didn't think of herself as such. She would often tell me that her brothers Bobby, Willie and Poncy got the fine mestizo features of Lola Nena, who inherited them from her Spanish mother, Juana Seraller. Instead, Mom found flaws in her own looks. At five foot three, she was average height for a Filipino woman, and she occasionally wished aloud that she were more slender, had a tinier waist and longer eyelashes like her brothers.

Despite her self-criticisms, no one who knew my mother or has ever seen photographs of her could say she wasn't a striking woman. She maintained a smooth and fair complexion without the need for heavy beauty regimen, just a nightly routine of applying Pond's cold cream. She passed this ritual to me when I became a teenager, and there were many mother-and-daughter evenings when we would sit together at her three-mirror dressing table and smooth Pond's onto our faces.

Mom wore little makeup other than her favorite Revlon liquid foundation and a lipstick in a shade of pink called Mocha Polka. Her one beauty indulgence was a regular perm for her chin-length bob, which she had done at a local beauty parlor in Tarlac.

She preferred simple jewelry for everyday wear, particularly a pair of luminous pearl stud earrings and her white-gold wedding band. She didn't need diamonds to sparkle because when she spoke, she did so with an animation that made her dark brown eyes glitter like bright gemstones. Her charming grin revealed a hint of dimples just below her cheekbones and lit up the room like warm rays of sunshine.

Judging by the dozens of mentions of her in the society pages before the war, Mom enjoyed an active social life full of friends, parties and dances from the moment she emerged in Manila social circles as a lovely teenager. However, she didn't just flit from gala to gala. Many of the articles also showed she was actively devoted to civic and charitable activities, from organizing fundraisers to volunteering at Red Cross canteens.

While her friends eventually announced engagements, marriages and births, she continued her work with the Red Cross, various church groups and even the early foundation of the Girl Scouts of the Philippines. She seemed to have little time left for romance, much to the disappointment of her suitors. One young man even expressed his unrequited affection for her by publishing in the local newspaper several crestfallen poems, written in Spanish, with titles like "My Old Lament" and "The Poppy's Scorn,"which were unmistakably addressed "to Lulu Reyes."

The outbreak of World War II made the chances of a romantic relationship even less likely as Mom threw herself first into the desperate search for Tito Willie after he was captured during the Fall of Bataan and forced into the infamous Death March, and then into the hard and sometimes dangerous work of delivering food, medicine and messages to maltreated prisoners in Japanese POW camps. When the war ended, Mom was grateful she and her whole family survived when so many had not, and she re-dedicated herself to helping others.

At one point, she thought perhaps her ultimate vocation was to be a nun. She considered it seriously, albeit only briefly—she didn't want to leave Lola Nena alone. She mentioned once that one of Tito Willie's law partners and another family friend courted her with gifts, but neither of them gave her *the spark*. "When you're in love, it charges you, makes you tingle," she used to say.

If she pined for a partner and children of her own, she never outwardly let on. Instead, as a woman of deep faith, she prayed to God: "If Your will is for me to be married, then please give me the man who will be right for me."

....

December 1952

The last time Lulu was in Tarlac, the Philippines was in the grip of a brutal Japanese occupation. The province did not hold pleasant memories: her brother Willie endured the barbarous Bataan Death March to the town of Capas where he and over 60,000 Filipino and American prisoners of war were incarcerated in subhuman conditions at Camp O'Donnell. It had taken several desperate months of anguish before she finally found him and was able to get him released.

But now, seven years had passed since the war ended, and Lulu was in the town of Tarlac on a happier, more optimistic purpose as president of the Young Ladies Association of Charity (YLAC), a philanthropic organization she had co-founded with her good friend Baby Quezon in 1946 and whose mission included building rural schools and clinics. She came to organize a new chapter in the province at the urging of Luisa Lorenzo, the president of the Catholic Women's League Philippines. The CWLP's membership at the time was composed primarily of matrons whereas YLAC attracted a younger group of civic-minded ladies, and Mrs. Lorenzo felt there were plenty of young women in the community who could move forward the organization's mission and projects in the province.

Lulu received an invitation to stay for the weekend with Esperanza "Paching" Besa, head of CWL's Tarlac chapter, and her husband, Tomas Besa, a prominent local attorney. Their impressive two-story home, which townsfolk referred to simply as "the white house," was located on Panganiban Street near the town proper and across from the Besa family ancestral house occupied by Tomas's sister, Luz, and her husband, Arturo Ilagan. Their brothers, Gaudencio and Gualberto, the only unmarried sibling, also lived nearby.

Tall, slim and tanned from hours spent outdoors tending to his farm and orchards, Gualberto was not conventionally handsome, but he had a quiet, confident presence that was appealing. He spoke the way he dressed: plainly and sensibly, befitting the farmer that he was. His natural reserve might have been mistaken as stern or standoffish by someone who didn't see how relaxed and affectionate he was with his family, particularly his many nieces and nephews.

Lulu hadn't come to Tarlac to meet eligible men yet she was drawn to her host's bachelor brother, though she tried not to show any overt interest. She liked that he was down to earth and unpretentious—what you see is what you get, she thought.

Unlike some of the men who courted her in Manila, he didn't preen or strut to impress her. In fact, he didn't give any indication that he was interested in her at all. He hardly spoke to her the entire weekend, merely smiling at her during the nightly family dinners at Tomas's home. Nevertheless, Lulu felt a little spark.

From where he sat at the long dinner table, Gualberto liked what he saw in his brother's pretty and charming guest from Manila. He had heard a lot about her philanthropic work from his sister-in-law and through newspaper articles, and he thought she was unassuming and modest about her accomplishments. He was drawn to the innate quality of compassion he sensed in her. Despite the minimal conversation between them, he was instantly smitten with the lovely Miss Reyes, who was unlike any other woman he had ever met.

The weekend passed quickly for Lulu. She was kept busy meeting with the young ladies of Tarlac eager to join YLAC's nascent chapter, and soon it was time to go home. Just as she was saying her goodbyes to Tomas, Paching and their children before the three-hour drive back to Manila, she spotted Gualberto striding up the driveway toward her.

He was dressed in khaki pants, a white cotton t-shirt and a straw hat—his everyday clothes for work on the farm—and was accompanied by a farmhand shouldering a large burlap sack full of rice. Lulu was so surprised, she stopped in the middle of getting into her car. The quiet bachelor whom she secretly liked but who had barely spoke two sentences to her the entire weekend was now approaching her with a smile.

"I have a gift for you," he said rather shyly. "It's a cavan of Milagrosa. It's my first harvest of the season. I hope you and your mother enjoy it."

Over the years, Lulu had received from various suitors

enough flowers to fill a cathedral and more chocolate than was humanly healthy, but this was the first time anyone had ever given her over a hundred pounds of rice. And it wasn't just any rice: the Milagrosa variety was considered the purest, the most fragrant and of the finest quality. It was highly prized, especially since the country's farms and fields were still recovering from the war and rice remained a somewhat scarce commodity.

Deep down, Lulu knew that Gualberto's gift was more than a friendly token or pasalubong of her visit to Tarlac. He didn't say anything more, but she sensed his offering was a way of asking if she was also interested in him. He had given her a gift of something very important to him, and nothing else could have convinced her better that it was an offering from the heart. As the small spark inside her flashed brighter, she accepted the gift without hesitation.

Back in Manila, Lulu quickly returned to her routine of working as a public relations officer with the FEATI Institute of Technology[19] and devoting time to organizing YLAC chapters and projects. She had been uncharacteristically vague when Mama Nena asked about the enormous sack of rice she brought back from Tarlac.

"Oh, it's a gift from a friend," she simply said.

What if she were wrong about the meaning behind the rice? What if it really was just a generous token of friendship?

One late morning, while she helped Mama Nena cook sopa de fideo for lunch, Lulu's reveries drifted to Gualberto.

19 Founded as an engineering and technology school by Salvador Araneta and Victoria Lopez who named it after their former airline Far Eastern Air Transport Incorporated, one of the first civil airlines in the Philippines. It was granted university status in 1959

She stirred a pot of tomato-rich broth and tried to ignore her disappointment. It had been weeks since her weekend stay with the Besas and there was still no word from him. She drifted deep into thought.

If he is meant to be the one, Lulu silently prayed, *he will reach out soon.*

For his part, Gualberto wanted nothing more than to see Lulu again, but he couldn't simply show up in Manila and ask her out. He also wasn't keen on calling her on the telephone, which still relied on phone operators to connect calls from party to party. In a small town like Tarlac, the switchboard was often a source for local gossip, and any suggestion that the bachelor farmer was courting a Manila socialite would have made for juicy news. That left the mail as the only mode of communication available to him.

Gualberto wrote a short letter to Lulu asking if he could come visit her on a weekend she was free, and he gave it to Tomas for the latter's secretary to post. His brother happily tucked the letter in his shirt pocket and then promptly forgot about it. At the end of his busy day, Tomas went home, changed out of his business clothes and tossed them into the laundry basket.

Several days passed before Paching turned over the full basket to the labandera. As the laundrywoman began soaking the clothes one by one in a large wash basin called a batya, she felt the stiff crinkle of paper in one of the shirts. It was Gualberto's precious first letter to Lulu still tucked in Tomas's shirt pocket.

Imagine what might have happened if the labandera had

been less thorough with checking the dirty laundry!

Duly rescued and mailed by Paching, the nearly ill-fated missive finally made it to the house on Indiana Street, where a delighted and relieved Lulu, heart beating with excitement, quickly replied yes, she would very much like a visit from Gualberto.

. . . .

Dad later told me that for his first date with Mom, he went to the local tailor and ordered a new suit. She was used to impeccably dressed men in her social set, and he didn't know what his chances were. Despite his "take me as I am" demeanor, he realized he needed to make an extra special effort. There was still the possibility that once she spent some time with him, she could reject him.

He drove his battered old farm truck to Malate, where he planned to stay for the weekend at the Vermont Street home[20] of his brother Dr. Augusto Besa (Tio Titong to me), an orthopedic surgeon, and sister-in-law Dr. Solita Camara Besa, a physiologist and biochemist. Tita Lilit was shocked by the state of Dad's vehicle.

"You are *not* going to pick up Lulu Reyes in a truck that smells like cow manure!" she declared, insisting he take their car and driver instead. My parents later joked that the real reason my uncle and aunt lent their car was so the driver could report back to them on how the date went and what the couple talked about.

20 The street was renamed Julio Nakpil, and the house is now the restaurant Purple Yam Malate, owned by Amy Besa, daughter of the Drs. Besa, who also runs Purple Yam in Brooklyn, NY.

Mom and Dad were 39 and 44 years old, respectively, when they began dating. They were a new old couple: when they finally found each other, they were independent, accomplished adults who had lived through a devastating war with their faith in humanity intact and were fully confident in themselves as individuals. Neither had expected to find their match during a December weekend in Tarlac, but from the moment they met, my parents had the sense and wisdom to recognize immediately that they were meant to be together.

Just as he had bought a new suit for their first date, Dad continued to make an extra effort for Mom during their courtship by fitting in with her circle of city friends. He may have preferred quiet evenings of dinner and conversation at Lola Nena's home during his weekend trips to Malate, but he happily escorted Mom on group dinner dates to many of Manila's iconic night spots, such as the Brown Derby Café and the Sky Room in the gorgeous Art Deco–style Jai Alai Building.

They were headed out for one such night of clubbing with friends when Dad decided to propose. He had been wooing Mom for a little more than three months and he didn't want to wait any longer. Just as they were about to leave, he led her back into the living room for a quiet moment between them. And there, in the house on Indiana Street, where my mother grew up in idyll and which my grandmother rebuilt from the ruins of war, the bachelor farmer from Tarlac asked the Manila socialite to be his wife.

He sealed his ultimate declaration of love with a ring of white gold crafted in an intricate rose pattern that cradled a

Newlyweds Mr. and Mrs. Gualberto S. Besa. Tarlac, Tarlac 1953.

sparkling diamond solitaire. Dad remembered with amusement how Mom wouldn't leave without first telling Lola Nena and showing off her ring, and how my grandmother was so thrilled about their engagement, she followed them to the car while peppering them with questions about their wedding plans.

Their friends were equally excited and happy when they announced the news later that evening at the Sky Room. While the rowdy and jubilant group celebrated at their table, Mom's dear friend Bengie Joseph Kosloff discreetly approached the band leader and whispered a request. Everyone hushed as the band struck the opening notes of a song and the vocalist began singing in Spanish: "Besame, besame mucho…Como si fuera esta noche, la ultima vez…"

Kiss me, kiss me so much, like this evening would be our last one…

No one stepped onto the dance floor, Mom recalled. Instead, the band leader gestured to her and Dad, who was blushing deeply from being the center of attention. Encouraged by their table of friends, she held his hand and together they walked to the middle of the dance floor. The cheers and applause of their companions and the other patrons of the club faded away as the beautiful couple, so very much in love, swayed gently to their song.

Chapter 11

The House on the Highway

June 1953

The loud crowing of a rooster woke Lulu. She slowly opened her eyes and turned her head to look out the window. The room was still dark and the sky outside showed no signs of sunshine yet.

She and Bert had returned to Tarlac from their honeymoon in Baguio only the day before, and today would be her first day in her new home as Mrs. Gualberto Besa. Turning away from the window, she saw her husband sitting on the edge of the bed, already dressed in khaki pants and a short-sleeved cotton shirt, putting on his socks.

"Bert, why are you awake? What time is it?" she asked sleepily.

"It's five o'clock. This is the time I wake up to go to the farm," came the amused answer.

Lulu felt the mattress shift as he stood up to look for his well-worn rubber shoes. His next words jolted her wide awake. "What are we having for breakfast?"

In all the time they had known each other, even during their engagement, it had not occurred to Lulu to ask Bert what time he usually woke up. Still basking in the afterglow of an idyllic honeymoon, she frankly hadn't anticipated her groom asking for breakfast before the sun had even risen. She wasn't a morning person, but now that she was the wife of a farmer, that would have to change.

Lulu jumped out of bed and hurriedly put on her bathrobe and slippers before following her husband down the stairs to the kitchen where she immediately got to cooking breakfast. Bert was a punctual man, and with a farm to run, he liked to get an early start, leaving the house at precisely 6:30 every morning. A farmer's work day was governed by sunlight, so every moment counted.

A gust of cold air whipped at Lulu's cheeks as she opened the refrigerator door and leaned in to take out a couple of eggs and some slices of baked ham that Mama Nena had made for them before they left for their honeymoon. Next, she pulled a cast-iron skillet from the kitchen cabinet and poured a generous glug of cooking oil, tilting the pan in a circular motion to spread it evenly. She set the skillet on a stove burner and turned the knob to ignite a bright blue flame.

"Do you want some coffee?" she asked through the kitchen doorway. Bert had gone out to retrieve the newspaper left outside by the front gate and was now settled at the dining table to read. Even before he answered, Lulu was reaching for a bottle of Nescafé instant coffee and a ceramic jar of sugar. She quickly filled a kettle with fresh water and set it on a second burner, cranking up the flame so that the water would come to a boil right away.

Turning her attention back to the skillet, she cracked the eggs into the pan as the hot oil spit and sputtered, and sprinkled some salt on the bright yolks. As the eggs fried, she swiftly set the table around Bert, first putting down heavy linen placemats, followed by plates, cups, drinking glasses and cutlery. Her hands were deft as she folded cloth napkins that matched the placemats and tucked them under each fork. It was only the two of them, but she wasn't about to let go of the social niceties—the table had to be set properly, even for breakfast.

All of a sudden, Lulu remembered there was no bread. She felt a tiny prick of panic. Was it too late to run out to the panaderia for some pan de sal? Or was it too early? She wasn't familiar with the food shops in Tarlac, and she silently promised to acquaint herself with the local stores as soon as possible.

"Where do we buy bread?" she asked sheepishly. Bert took a moment before replying, "We can get the panadero to deliver pan de sal every morning," he explained, careful to keep the twinge of hungry impatience from his tone. "You can call them up and give the order…the day before."

In the end, Lulu made sinangag, or fried garlic rice, usually made from the previous day's leftover rice. Given her late start that morning and the longer cooking time for making the rice, the first breakfast of their marriage was delayed—something that was never again repeated for the rest of their years together.

On that early morning, Lulu Reyes Besa—Manila socialite, philanthropist and war heroine—realized she still had a lot to learn about her new husband, her new town, and her new life.

....

My parents spent the first eight years of their marriage in San Vicente, Tarlac, where life moved at a much slower pace than in Manila. Their home was located a distance from the center of town, or the población, as we call it in the Philippines. They rented a small two-story house from the Ignacios, an old Tarlac family who lived just across the street. By coincidence, it resembled my grandmother's house on Indiana Street, where Mom grew up.

The San Vicente house was a mid-century modern structure of wood and cement painted a dark forest green trimmed in white. The forest green color was such that the surrounding foliage seemed to be growing out from its walls. Potted ferns and tropical plants lined the front stoop and along the sides of the adjacent carport, while neon-bright pink and orange bougainvilleas in full bloom cascaded over a gated fence that surrounded a large front yard filled with tall coconut trees.

This was my first home after I was born in 1957. There are many baby photos of me with my parents seated on the plump cushions of rattan furniture, smiling and looking blissful, as well as pictures of them hosting lively parties with relatives and friends from around town. Even though I was very young when we lived in the San Vicente house, I clearly remember it as a place full of laughter and happiness.

I had many playmates among the neighborhood children who would come to play in our yard. One of our favorite games was called labulan—we tossed brightly colored rubber bands on the ground and then tried to make them move forward by blowing on them. The winner was whoever reached the designated "goal post" first, and the prize was to collect the losing bands. I huffed and puffed with all my childish strength to make my elastic loops move ahead of the others. How I loved collecting all those colorful rubber bands on my wrist!

On other days, my friends and I played with hula hoops,

trying to outdo each other to see who could keep their hoop revolving around their waist until it circled down to the knees, then to the ankles, and finally to the ground amid giggles and shrieks of laughter.

The only thing better than playing games was having merienda. Mom would call us to take a break for a snack as she came out of the house carrying a tray of tall glasses filled with freshly squeezed calamansi juice and slices of chilled fruit. On some days, she would make frosty buko sherbet using the young coconuts that grew in the yard. The snowy sherbet with chunks of translucent young coconut meat was a welcome sweet treat on sweltering summer days. I couldn't tell if my neighborhood playmates came for the fun games or for the merienda that Mom always offered them.

In early 1961, my sister Isabel's imminent arrival would make us a family of four, so my parents began building a larger house even farther away from the town proper, on MacArthur Highway. Its location on the road that connected metropolitan Manila to Cagayan, the northernmost province on Luzon Island, was exactly three hours' drive from the city in one direction and another three hours away from Baguio in the other.

It was, and still is, quite common for extended Filipino families to live close to each other, either as neighbors or in large shared compounds. The Besa siblings, who were always very close, were no different. My parents' new house was next to the vacant lot that belonged to Tio Titong (my uncle Augusto Besa, in whose Malate house Dad stayed during the weekends he courted Mom) and his wife, Tita Lilit. Behind us was the home of Tita Luz, and in front of her was the house belonging to Tito Tom and Tita Paching, where my parents first met nine years before.

I remember visiting the construction site with my parents. While they discussed the building progress with the foreman, I wandered around, picking up wood scraps and cement chips. To an observer, my collection of odd bits seemed random, but I had specific criteria: the pieces had to be small enough to fit in my hand and be smooth to the touch. I planned to use them as markers for playing piko, or hopscotch, with the future friends I was sure to make when we finally moved into our new neighborhood.

When it was completed, our house on the highway was painted a crisp shade of white. Decorative iron grilles covered the large screened windows that ran along the entire front façade. Inside, we had two of everything: two salas (living rooms), two dining rooms, and most importantly, two kitchens. The informal sala flowed into the everyday dining room, where we would have our three daily meals, while the formal sala and dining room were close to the kitchen. These formal areas were the domain of my mother, once and always the gracious Manila socialite and hostess, and where she loved to entertain countless family, friends and other guests for years to come.

But where she was most truly in her element was in the kitchen—or rather, kitchens. Like two halves of a whole, our two kusinas were the heart of the home. One was Mom's yellow-painted kitchen, where she baked all manner of cakes and pastries, prepared special occasion dishes, and stored all of her fine china and coveted Pyrex cookware in glass-fronted wooden cabinets.

Adjacent to this space was the "dirty" kitchen, where our daily breakfasts, lunches and dinners were cooked. Contrary to its name, a dirty kitchen is by no means unclean. The term is commonly used in many Filipino households to refer to a cooking area where the heavy-duty, daily food preparation happens. In ours, the sturdy counters were made of cement and tile, and I can still vividly recall how they withstood the impact of large Chinese cleavers coming down with shattering force on heavy wood chopping boards.

There was also an open-air cooking area just outside the kitchen back door. Here, large amounts of vegetables, meat, fish and seafood were washed and prepped in large twin sinks lined with white tile. In a space reserved for outdoor grilling, hollow concrete blocks formed a makeshift grill where uling—a type of charcoal made from dried coconut shells—was lit beneath sturdy iron grates that held all manner of ingredients to be cooked over an open flame.

I especially enjoyed watching when our kasambahay (household helpers) would barbecue marinated chunks of pork skewered on thin bamboo sticks. My mouth watered as I watched the dark, sticky marinade trickle down and drip onto the glowing embers of charcoal, which hissed and sparked and huffed indignant plumes of fragrant smoke and licks of flame until the wooden sticks were blackened and the meat was grilled to a glossy sear. Ever since then, the smoky, sweet aroma of grilled pork, charred and caramelized to perfection, never fails to fill me with hungry anticipation.

On other days, there might be a large bangus, or milk

fish, stuffed with onions and tomatoes and wrapped in banana leaves, on the grill. Inihaw na bangus was one dish my mom made regularly because it was my dad's favorite. I could tell when it was being cooked by the earthy, herbal scent of burnt banana leaves floating on the breeze from the backyard, through the screened porch and into the house.

"Luto na ba ang ulam?" I would ask as I peered at the grill with childish impatience. *Is the food cooked now?*

Mom would place the inihaw na bangus on a large bandejado and unwrap the scorched leaves at the table, sliding a large serving spoon through the slice in the belly where finely diced onions and tomatoes had been stuffed inside, and delicately open the fish so that we could serve ourselves family-style. If there were any leftovers, Dad would request that the milkfish be cooked with pinakbet, a traditional northern Philippine vegetable dish. "This fish is good when it's cooked with pinakbet," he would often say.

When Mom made pinakbet, she made it look effortless. She learned the recipe from my dad's Kapampangan cousins, who taught her first to slice and cube fresh vegetables—talong (eggplant), sitaw (yardlong beans), ampalaya (bitter melon), calabasa (squash), kamatis (tomatoes) and okra—and then layer them in a deep stock pot topped with the leftover inihaw na bangus. Then, she added bagoong (shrimp paste) and pork or chicken stock, after which the pot was covered and set on the stove to cook slowly over medium heat. Within minutes, the robust aromas of simmering vegetables, grilled fish and bagoong floated through the kitchen. Whenever Mom cooked pinakbet this way, I knew the meal was going to be marvelous.

....

When it came to what we ate at home, my mother had the final word. But my father made one important request: "Use the vegetables and fruits we have in the backyard for the food you cook."

It became our norm to eat what we grew. Dad planted just about every kind of vegetable and fruit common to Philippine cuisine, and Mom transformed them into the most delicious meals. But I didn't always appreciate their efforts. There was a time when I did not realize how privileged I was to grow up with such fresh, healthy food or with parents who loved and appreciated what nature provided for us.

I saw classmates buying food from the school cafeteria at recess and in my foolish child's mind, I somehow felt cheated that my lunchbox held a chicken salad sandwich prepared by Mom with home-baked bread and farm-raised poultry; a tumbler filled with freshly squeezed dayap juice mixed daily by Dad; and a piece or two of ripe, sweet fruit such as dalanghita (mandarin orange), guava, banana or whatever was in season from the trees in our backyard or from our fruit orchards.

Instead, I envied my classmates for buying soft drinks like Pepsi, Mirinda Orange or 7-Up, and packaged snacks, chips and chocolate candies. My parents wouldn't allow me to have any of these while I was growing up.

"My classmates buy banana-cue and fish balls from the vendor outside the gate. Can I buy some, too?" I tried wheedling Mom, hoping she would agree.

She refused, of course, warning me about the dangers of

buying food on the street cooked by strangers with dubious food safety standards. I didn't see her point. I thought my parents could not afford to give me money for a school-bought lunch, so I grudgingly accepted the merienda she made for me and Isabel after school.

It was entirely lost on me back then that almost all of the snacks Mom made from scratch used ingredients grown or raised by Dad. The sweet porridge called ginataang bilo-bilo was lush with coconut cream squeezed from coconuts from our backyard palm trees and full of plump dumplings made with flour ground from his rice crops. The mangoes for ice cream were harvested from our orchards and the squash for ukoy (vegetable fritters) grew in our garden. There was such a wealth of healthy, fresh food for my taking every day, and yet I actually felt deprived!

Now that I am an adult, I can laugh at my childish folly. I can clearly see that all the food Mom cooked and all the produce Dad planted and harvested formed the words and phrases of their language of love for me and my sister.

. . . .

My mother loved to entertain in Tarlac as much as she loved entertaining in Manila. Since our house was located halfway between Manila and Baguio, a favorite summer vacation destination of Manileños, we were never short of guests on their way to and fro. For every visit, even if it was just a stopover for an extended luncheon, Mom would prepare something special.

If visitors called ahead of time, she could plan a feast,

and if folks dropped by unannounced for lunch or merienda, she had no problem whipping together an equally fabulous meal. The freezer and refrigerator were always full, and the backyard garden provided plenty of fresh fruits and vegetables. Mom could easily put together lumpiang gulay, grill dozens of skewers of meat barbecue, and assemble fruit and buko salads for a refreshing dessert.

Her menu staples included steamed fish mayonesa, char-grilled pork and pansit palabok, a colorful dish of translucent white noodles with a flavorsome orange-hued shrimp sauce made with coconut milk from the trees in our backyard. Later, during merienda, she would serve tibok-tibok, a Kapampan-gan delicacy of carabao milk pudding laced with fried coco-nut sprinkles called latik.

A particularly special dish was kare-kare, a sumptuous Kapampangan stew of oxtails and vegetables simmered in a rich peanut sauce. If Dad did not have an ox on the farm that was headed for slaughter, then Mom used a cow's tail. How-ever, beef was only available in the Tarlac market on Tuesdays and Saturdays, when a single cow was slaughtered on each of those two days. So, if she wanted to make kare-kare for Satur-day visitors, she had to send Lita or another trusted helper to secure the cow's tail at the crack of dawn on Tuesday morn-ing. It would then take two days to soften the tail in a clay pot set over a slow kindling fire. The time, effort and expense for the main ingredient made kare-kare an extra special dish.

Of course, every recipe my mother prepared for guests was special, but sometimes her menu choices depended on how many guests would be served. Our house was often filled to the brim with large groups of family or friends, like Tita Nini, her husband Tito Bert and their brood of nine children, accompanied by their friends and other relatives, all of whom drove up our driveway in a caravan of vehicles. Invitations to lunch or dinner in a Filipino household is essentially an open house: you never know how many guests you'll be feeding until they start arriving.

Pansit palabok was a dependable crowd favorite that was easily "scaled up." Because the savory shrimp sauce used fresh coconut milk, it spoiled quickly, so Mom would instruct the house help to make the sahog, or sauce, on the morning of the visitors' arrival. On one occasion, however, an overzealous maid, eager to prove she could cook better than the others, prepared the sauce the day before. So, we ended up eating pansit palabok for dinner on Friday that was meant to be lunch on Saturday.

My mother's other favorite dish for a crowd was arroz a la Valenciana. Like pansit palabok, it could be scaled up to feed a large group by simply adding more of the key ingredients. Mom's recipe used rice from Dad's harvests, eggs from our backyard chickens, and fresh coconut milk from our ever-abundant coconut trees. The only store-bought ingredient she used was imported chorizo de Bilbao, which she bought during trips to Manila.

Arroz a la Valenciana is very similar to bringhe, a Kapampangan rice dish that also uses coconut milk and various meats and vegetables. A primary difference is the use of a more glutinous type of rice as well as banana leaves to line the bottom of the pot and to cover the rice as it cooks.

Mom learned to make bringhe because it is a specialty of the cuisine of Dad's Kapampangan ancestry, but she was more comfortable cooking arroz a la Valenciana, which reminded her of the paellas of her own Spanish heritage through Lola Nena and Lola Juana.

Bringhe and arroz a la Valenciana are so similar that some Filipinos consider them practically the same dish. But to my mother, they were distinctly different in the same way she, a Manileña born in Iloilo, was different from my Kapampangan father. In a way, arroz a la Valenciana symbolized a connection to her life in Manila.

When my parents moved to Tarlac after their wedding, Mom relied on Dad's sister and three sisters-in-law for advice about life in her new town and province, such as which businesses and sukis (favored vendors) to buy from. She also leaned on a string of Dad's older female cousins whom everyone referred to as the Atchings, meaning "big sisters" in Kapampangan. These ladies were mainstays at family parties and excelled at Kapampangan cuisine. Mom never hesitated to call on them to ask for recipes, and the Atchings were only too happy to oblige.

But despite the warm support of her in-laws, and as accomplished and brave as my mother was, she was not impervious to the feeling of being an outsider. The townsfolk were friendly enough and respectful of her husband and his family, but they were also insular and cliquish. If you weren't born in Tarlac, you might never feel like you belong, even if you married into a local family and even years after you've made the town your home.

Nevertheless, Mom's innately sociable and optimistic nature compelled her to extend frequent invitations to the ladies of Tarlac for merienda at our house on the highway. On one occasion, when I was around seven years old, she invited a dozen local matrons from church. In addition to her usual merienda fare of pansit, lumpia ubod and pitchers of chilled fresh dayap juice, she also prepared her family-famous shrimp toasts—oven-baked canapés of fluted bread cups filled with chopped and sautéed shrimp, cheese and breadcrumbs. Mom being Mom, this scrumptious midday meal was served on a table set with her finest linen tablecloths and napkins, elegant silverware and Noritake plates. I had the important task for folding the napkins and counting the shrimp toasts and lumpia on the platters to see if they needed replenishing.

Everyone who was invited attended that day, which pleased Mom. She had just rushed into the kitchen to bring out more shrimp toast, leaving open the door to the dining room and sala so she could still hear the lively chatter of her guests. Pulling a tray of canapés from the oven, she suddenly went still as the voice of one of the church ladies drifted into the kitchen: "Ali ya biyasang mag-Kapampangan!" *She doesn't know how to speak Kapampangan.*

The ladies tittered at her words. "Ayyyy, wapin!" one of them chimed in. *Yes, of course.*

Mom later told me how she felt tears well up in the corner of her eyes and a heaviness in her chest that she could not explain. All she wanted was what anyone would want: to be liked and accepted by her community.

She thought that by opening up her heart and her home, introducing her family and preparing her best dishes, the local women would fold her into their circle in the same way she was embraced by her friends back in Manila.

"No me quieren," she thought. *They don't like me.* Did they think she was a spoiled society girl who thought it beneath herself to learn the local dialect? The fact of the matter was that even to a native Tagalog speaker, Kapampangan is a difficult language to learn on one's own, especially in a time when there were no language classes or books to help.

For a few minutes, she wished deep in her heart for the comforting presence of her Mama Nena, her brothers and her dearest friends in Manila. But she was now Mrs. Besa of Tarlac, so she composed herself, picked up the tray of shrimp toast and walked back into the dining room.

She didn't give the ladies any inkling she had overheard their thoughtless comments as she continued being the gracious and charming hostess, but Mom was also human. After the incident, she discouraged Isabel and me from speaking Kapampangan at home to her and to Dad, preferring instead that we mastered Spanish like her and Lola Nena. And from that day, she would always favor making arroz a la Valenciana over bringhe.

My mother found other ways to tackle the challenge of winning friends and influencing people. To paraphrase a common adage, you can take Lulu out of Manila, but you can't take Manila out of Lulu. Reminiscent of the clubs to which she belonged as a popular young socialite in pre-war Manila, she formed Operation Birthday—a parents' social group made up of local Tarlac families and close friends of the Besa siblings. The OB group came together for various occasions, but as the name suggests, we mainly celebrated birthdays each month. Once, when I was eight years old, the entire OB group went to the beach in La Union province for a whole day of swimming and picnicking to celebrate June birthdays, including mine. For the potluck, Mom brought chicken adobo, her homemade pork tocino, a fresh tomato salad and lots of steamed rice. She always said adobo and tocino were the best picnic food because they did not spoil easily during travel and could be made in large quantity.

Although my mother shone in any party or gathering, socializing for its own sake was never her priority. Instead, she saw it as a way to do good and achieve real, beneficial results in her charitable activities. She turned the full focus of her philanthropy, organizational and persuasive skills, and vast personal network toward the town and residents of Tarlac.

Mom opened the house on the highway for fundraising dinners for such causes as establishing YLAC schools and free clinics in town. The townsfolk came in droves, eager to be part of an elegant evening for a good cause. One year, she arranged to have the Chito Feliciano dancers, from a hit TV dance show of the 1960s, perform in our house, on the outdoor cemented patio, which was elevated like a stage. The reception from the locals was ecstatic, like something reserved for huge pop stars.

Another year, she brought in the favorite models of the legendary Philippine fashion designer Pitoy Moreno for a benefit fashion show with the help of her dear friend Bengie Kosloff.

I remember that evening and being dazzled by the beautiful, impossibly tall models in our house. Some of them even lay down to rest on my bed! To my seven-year-old self, it felt like the Pope had decided to take a nap in my room.

Although fitting into a new town and adapting to a new culture was not easy for my mother, she rallied all her personal strengths and competencies, just as she had always done throughout her life, to persevere and create a beloved home for herself and for her family.

Some memories sting in their recollection—such as unkind remarks from peers who thoughtlessly judge another as an outsider, or the silly ingratitude of a child still too young to appreciate the abundance around her. But there can be a brightness and richness in such moments. We do not or cannot see when that moment is staring us in the face. We need to walk away from it first, for a while, letting time become the distance that allows us to look back and see the entire picture as a whole. And after time has passed—minutes, days or perhaps many years—we can finally recognize what those moments brought about. Like the impetus to create other meaningful ways to connect with a community. Like an appreciation for the love and care of my parents, through the home they built for me and my sister, and the food from their own hands with which they nurtured us.

The Besa family, Lulu and Gualberto (center) with daughters Maria Isabel (left) and Elizabeth Ann (right) at home in Tarlac. During the Knight of St. Sylvester Papal Awards ceremony for Gualberto. May 1977

Chapter 12

Her Christmas Spirit

The calendar reminded me it was nearly Christmas—the first Christmas of the COVID-19 pandemic—but I had only just started to plan what to serve for Noche Buena, the traditional Christmas Eve dinner. Our older son, Tim, who lived in San Francisco, told us he would not be coming home due to the rising number of cases of infection around the country. It would be the first time since he was born more than three decades ago that we would not be celebrating the holidays as a complete family. Elpi and I were heartbroken, but we understood.

Happily, our younger son, Constante, still planned to drive up from Philadelphia, and I was determined to prepare a Christmas feast as I have always done for the holidays. The centerpiece of the menu would be pinaupong manok, or "sitting chicken"– a flavorful, fragrant and fabulous-looking whole chicken roasted on a deep bed of rock salt. My family just loves it, and I love the easy recipe: I can prep the bird and then relax with a cup of tea and a good read while it roasts in the oven.

Not quite as easy to make but still a holiday mainstay is a whole category of rice cakes called kakanin. For as long as I can remember, there has been some kind of kakanin for Christmas. It's traditional in the Philippines during Pasko, when vendors set up small stalls equipped with coconut husk–fueled clay ovens and specially made tin steamers in front of churches to make and sell bibingka, puto bumbong, tupig and suman after the evening Advent services known as Simbang Gabi.

I chose to make Elpi's favorite suman cassava[21] from

21 Although it is considered a type of kakanin, suman cassava doesn't actually contain any rice.

one of Mom's old recipes, which called for three ingredients—grated cassava, grated coconut meat and inuyat, a thick Filipino molasses—combined into a dense mixture which was then wrapped and steamed in banana leaves. If using whole fresh tubers, as is common in the Philippines, it can be laborious to grate the necessary amount. Fortunately, I found that substituting frozen pre-grated cassava readily available here in New Jersey and using brown sugar instead of inuyat worked very well to produce suman cassava like the ones I remember from my childhood.

As I wrapped the suman mixture in banana leaves, I tried to work through my disappointment over Tim's absence as well as my continued anxiety about the pandemic, which we were being told could worsen as people gathered together to celebrate. I thought about one of the rare stories my uncle shared from his experiences as a POW during WWII. He described how some of the civilians gathered around the perimeter of Camp O'Donnell in search of their loved ones would furtively pass suman cassava through the fence to the starving prisoners, though it meant severe punishment if they were caught doing so. From there, my thoughts drifted to my mother, who took on such risks unflinchingly in her own efforts to help POWs during the war in the Philippines.

Over the past twenty years or so, I have compiled published anecdotes of my mother's humanitarian efforts during WWII and noticed that by some quirk of coincidence, many of them took place around the holidays. Perhaps the stark contrast between the violence and inhumanity of war and the messages of Christmas—peace, love, selflessness—imprinted these fleeting moments deeply enough that the writers felt compelled to include them in their accounts. For me, they underscored the fact that nothing could dim Mom's Christmas spirit.

The earliest account came from President Manuel Quezon on Christmas Eve 1941. He wrote of the inspiring sight he came across as he and his family prepared to evacuate from Malacañang Palace in Manila to Corregidor Island as the Imperial Japanese Army bore down on the city:

We found in the Social Hall here about fifty young girls… wrapping up the Christmas gifts for the soldiers, gifts which had been collected by publish subscription upon the initiative of my eldest daughter Maria [Baby], with the help of her sister, Zeneida [Nini], their cousins Mary Angara and Rosario Carrasco, and their friends Helen[a] Benitez, Lulu Reyes, and the Fabella girls…

In that historic palace… were those young girls completely unperturbed by the air raid and the bursting bombs, and attending to their self-assigned tasks. I thanked God that I was permitted to witness the patriotism, the courage, and the self-possession of the Filipino women…

This breathtaking scene steeled my heart for the grim struggle ahead. [22]

The Christmas endeavor with the Quezon sisters marked the beginning of Mom's wartime efforts. She worked tirelessly with the Chaplains Aid Association as well as the Red Cross

22 Quezon, 197

and the Girls in Blue to raise money and organize collection drives from whatever friends and strangers alike could spare. She personally knew most of the elite citizens in the city, and if there were any whom she didn't know, then she was guaranteed to have friends who did. As American writer George Hagar recalled in a post-war article for the Catholic magazine *Extension* observed, "From that time on, no one in Manila with money or worldly goods was safe from Miss Reyes."

She solicited donations with charming if steely determination from prominent citizens like Sergio Osmeña Jr., a future Philippine senator whose father Sergio Sr. was then vice president, to buy scarce supplies such as rice, beans and sugar. The collected goods were then packed in assorted containers, including laundry baskets, and loaded onto trucks that crisscrossed the city and surrounding provinces delivering the precious aid to POW and civilian internment camps.

During the first Christmas under Japanese rule, Mom procured a large amount of noodles with help from POW Father William Cummings, whom she first met at the Assumption Convent earlier that summer, when she lured his Japanese guard away with a game of ping pong. Author E. Bartlett Kerr, the son of an American prisoner of war who died in the Philippines, recounted the episode in his book *Surrender and Survival: the Experience of American POWs in the Pacific, 1941–1945* and noted that the noodles "made a welcome addition to Christmas supper" for American soldiers spending their first holidays as POWS in Bilibid Prison.

In his memoir *Under the Red Sun: A Letter from Manila,* Father Forbes Monaghan described how she boldly handled

a seemingly hopeless relief mission to the Los Baños internment camp where he and fellow clerics were incarcerated:

*As the last Christmas under the Red Sun drew close, [Lulu] deter-
mined to get a great shipment of food to the priests and nuns interned at
Los Baños. Everyone told her that this was impossible; the Japanese had
already forbidden it in the case of Santo Tomas. She went ahead, nevertheless . . . When [the camp commandant and his staff] came, she had glasses
of brandy and cordials ready for them. After they had drunk and drunk
again, she brought out Christmas presents for each of them. The commandant was delighted: "I am not worthy of this," he stuttered.* [23]

Having rendered the camp authority pliant and full of
holiday spirit, she seized the moment of goodwill to ask for
permission to distribute Christmas presents to the priests and
nuns inside. Not only did the commandant agree, he even
allowed her and the Jesuits who accompanied her to enter
the camp themselves, against all official regulations forbidding
civilians from doing so.

But another of Father Monaghan's recollections told of
an episode even more brazen, it would be almost unbelievable
if he hadn't recorded it in print:

*An American officer in Bilibid expressed a desire to see Dewey
Boulevard and to have a nice Christmas dinner outside. On Christmas morning [Lulu] borrowed the car of the Marquis of Tokugawa,* [24]

---

23 Monaghan, 249

24 The Marquis Yorisada Tokugawa (1892–1954) was a member of the Kazoku, Japan's hereditary peerage, which was abolished under the 1947 Constitution of Japan.
During WWII, the Marquis was chairman of the Philippines Society of Japan and
advisor to the Imperial Japanese Army.

a relative of the Emperor, put the officer in it, smuggled him out for a drive on the boulevard where every second person was a Japanese, and then brought him to her house for dinner. [25]

"What her tact enabled her to do with high Japanese officials and with sentries almost passes belief," he marvelled.

For Father Monaghan and his fellow prisoners, my mother's actions were vital: "Those Christmas shipments of food and the secret notes passed on to us saved our lives and our souls."

. . . .

Though my mother has been gone for over forty years, she is still a constant presence in my life, especially during Christmas. Despite how special she made the holidays for others even under the worst of circumstances, she once admitted to me that it was actually the saddest time of the year for her, and understandably so. Her first lesson in tragedy was the death of her father Ponciano Reyes Sr. in a shipwreck during the early morning hours of December 25, 1918. Then, there were all those Yuletides lost to war, when food like suman cassava meant the difference between survival and starvation instead of celebration. It was also the season when Lita, one of the orphans Mom took in after the Battle of Manila, left our home in Tarlac for the very last time. Finally, the heartrending death of her favorite brother, Willie, came less than two weeks before Christmas Day in 1961.

Knowing this and looking back on my childhood, I

25 Monaghan, 248–9

wonder how Mom was able to make Christmas such a happy time for Dad, my sister, Isabel, and me. She would decorate our tree, which evolved over the years from a silvery aluminum conifer to an artificially realistic evergreen, with the brightest, most colorful ornaments and set out holiday décor throughout the house. Since there is no Santa Claus in traditional Filipino culture, we went to bed soon after the Christmas Eve midnight mass called Misa de Aguinaldo and then woke up early to open the presents under the tree.

Mom made sure everyone received something special for Christmas. Her gift list encompassed a vast circle of family, friends and employees: aside from her husband and children, and her brothers and their wives, there were also Dad's siblings and his older female cousins, known in the family as the Atchings, who were indispensable in helping Mom learn all about Kapampangan cuisine as a new bride. Next came Dad's farmhands and our household staff, including folks she hired temporarily during the year, such as the seamstress, carpenter, plumber, electrician and especially the little old woman who came to cook the summer mango jam every harvest season.

She had numerous godchildren of varying ages from serving as baptismal godmother to infants and as wedding sponsor to newlyweds, and she never forgot the local clergy, from the priests, seminarians and the nuns at our local Catholic schools to the Monsignor of the diocese and the clerics at the Tarlac Cathedral. Finally, for good measure, she always made sure to have on hand emergency gifts of toys, clothes and whatnot for unexpected drop-ins. It became her mission to ensure every single person who came to our home in Tarlac at Christmas did not leave empty-handed.

To achieve this, Mom started her holiday shopping in September and reserved a guest room to store all the gifts, wrappers, boxes and ribbons, as well as a square folding table that served as the wrapping station. As if gift wrapping alone didn't keep her busy, she also immersed herself in planning and cooking the menus for Noche Buena, Christmas Day and the days leading up to the New Year and the Feast of the Three Kings, which marked the end of the festive season. Until then, she went all out with meal planning for the constant stream of Manila friends who dropped by our house on the highway on their way to Baguio for their own holidays. They came during all hours of the day—breakfast, lunch, merienda or dinner—and she relished entertaining them all.

I remember my godmother, Tita Nini, her husband, Tito Bert, and their brood of nine children plus friends arriving by the busload, which spurred Mom to prepare a lavish spread of pansit, arroz valenciana, chicken and pork barbecue, and flan and tibok-tibok for dessert. When Tita Nini's brother, Manuel Quezon Jr., whom we called Tito Nonong, made an early morning stopover during one Christmas, she nonchalantly whipped together a hearty breakfast of homemade pork tocino, eggs and sinangag for him and his friends.

Other family groups of guests included the Panlilios, the Palous, the Bowlers, the Guidotes, the Dayrits, the Riveras and the Tancos. They would arrive on successive days just before Christmas up to the New Year. Mom was never more in her element than entertaining the friends she loved.

But what really amazed me as a child was how Mom

always seemed to know exactly the perfect presents for me and Isabel year after year. For my sister, there were new dolls, a bicycle and a miniature porcelain tea set. I once received the largest set of colored pencils made from fragrant cedarwood and in every vivid hue and shade I had ever seen. Another year, she gave me a hardbound set of classic books, the smooth paper feeling wondrous beneath my fingertips as I paged through them.

As I got older, Mom's gifts became no less perceptive. One year, she gave me a pair of gold hoop earrings with a matching necklace and pendant, and in college I received a complete make-up set including my very first tube of eyelash mascara—quite the grown-up gift for a sheltered Catholic girl.

One of my mother's last Christmas gifts to me was a pair of luminescent South Sea pearl earrings set in gold. The elegant, perfectly round pearls—my birthstone—fit snugly on my earlobes, and I have worn them for every special occasion to this day. "Your face lights up when you wear pearls," she told me lovingly. "You should wear them always."

....

During the pandemic Christmas of 2020, Tim mailed us his holiday presents. The large package arrived on Christmas Eve, and Elpi and I opened it right away. It was a Portal, a smart video-calling device made by Facebook. Once it was set up, we were able to have video calls with Tim or anyone else. The nifty tablet-like device has a camera that can pan and zoom to keep us in frame, even if we were moving around. I

Lulu Reyes, humanitarian aid worker, as president of the Young Ladies Association of Charity.

set it up in the kitchen so he could watch me slice, dice, chop, mix and stir while I gave him recipe tips for his own holiday menu preparations.

Although the Portal could never replace having him at home with us, Tim had found a thoughtful way to bring us together for Christmas. As we enjoyed chatting virtually with him and my adorable grand-dog, Cinnabon, far away in California, I remembered the warmth of my mother's arms around me when I would run to hug her in thanks for the perfect, special gifts she gave me every Christmas, and I lingered on the memory.

Even when our loved ones cannot be with us physically, we can always be together in Christmas spirit.

Chapter 13

When Life Hands You Oranges

"You bought too many oranges and they're going to spoil."

Tita Helen eyed the huge bag of citrus I had just hauled back home from our local wholesale club. She had arrived from California for a weeklong visit with us in New Jersey, and knowing how health-conscious she was, I thought we could easily use up the fruit as snacks or turn them into orange juice.

"Ang dami," she tsk-tsked in Tagalog. So many.

But her gentle scolding quickly gave way as her eyes lit up with an idea. "Let's make orange marmalade!"

If anyone embodied the proverb of making lemonade out of life's lemons—or marmalade out of oranges, as it were—it was my Tita Helen. Her infectious zest for life matched that of Tito Willie, her late husband and the second of my mother's three brothers, and beneath her genteel demeanor was an ironclad resilience forged by war and loss.

....

Helen Moreno was born in Manila to an American father and a Spanish mestiza mother, Pilar Acuna Moreno, from whom she inherited her sun-kissed Mediterranean features and glossy dark brown hair. Pilar had roots in Iloilo and was a close friend of Nena Jugo Reyes; their two families often vacationed in Baguio at the same time during the summers. With such a close friendship, it was no surprise that Helen, though a few years younger, was part of the same social circles as Lulu Reyes and came into the orbit of Lulu's middle brother Willie. Even before they became sisters-in-law, Lulu loved her friend like the sister she never had, and the younger woman returned the affection equally.

Helen and Willie were married in September 1941, and the young newlyweds moved in with the groom's family as was the custom among many Filipino families. But their honeymoon period was cut short only a few months later when the Japanese invaded the Philippines in December 1941.

Willie didn't hesitate to volunteer with the Philippine Scouts, a special unit of the US Army. He was determined to fight for his country alongside the Americans, with whom he now shared a bond through his half-American bride. In April 1942, he was captured by the enemy during the Fall of Bataan and endured the infamous Bataan Death March to Camp O'Donnell in Capas, Tarlac.

He was imprisoned at the camp for several arduous months until Lulu secured his release under a Japanese POW parole program due to his grave illness with malaria. He returned to Malate to recuperate from his ordeal but was not yet ready to give up the fight. Once he regained his strength, he left again to join the large guerrilla movement in the mountains of Zambales province.

With Willie first imprisoned at Camp O'Donnell, then later joining guerrilla forces, and while the Imperial Japanese Army controlled Manila, Mama Nena and Lulu kept Helen concealed in a secret space—possibly an underground tunnel—inside the house on Indiana Street. They feared she would be picked up by the brutal military police force known as the Kempei-tai and sent to the internment camps at the University of Santo Tomas, where thousands of Americans and other foreign civilians were being confined.

They didn't dare think of an even worse possibility: Japanese authorities allowed the establishment of military brothels throughout their occupied territories in Asia. The euphemistically named "comfort stations" were filled with young women and girls, some as young as twelve, whom Japanese soldiers abducted or forcibly coerced from local communities.

This state-sanctioned sexual slavery was perversely justified, among other reasons, as a way to prevent the kind of wholesale sexual violence that occurred during the Rape of Nanking in 1937 when Japanese soldiers systematically raped, brutalized and murdered tens of thousands of Chinese women of all ages. In the Philippines, "comfort women" were victimized in army garrisons or in private homes and public buildings commandeered by the occupying army. In Manila alone, there were at least a dozen comfort stations established to serve Japanese soldiers.

But even the threat of random rape was omnipresent and hung heavy over every woman in the city and countryside. For several fearful months, the Reyes women would do their best to alter their appearance if they had to leave the house for any reason.

"Mama, Helen and I rubbed charcoal on our faces and arms, hoping the soot would disguise us and make us look ugly. We pulled back our hair in the most unflattering way, to make us look hideous," Mom remembered.

Although she was surrounded by loved ones, Helen lived a furtive life dictated by a constant dread of capture for nearly three years. When Willie finally left the guerrillas and returned home in early 1945, it was on the eve of the American forces' push to liberate the Philippines. He came back just in time to be with his wife, mother and siblings as they fled the bombardments during the Battle of Manila that would destroy the house on Indiana Street and turn the family into war refugees.

....

After the war, Tito Willie and Tita Helen harbored a short-lived dream of emigrating to the United States since her citizenship would have allowed him to accompany her to America. But as he wrote in a letter to Nini Quezon just a short time after the Battle of Manila, he felt it was his duty to stay in the Philippines to help his family rebuild their home and their lives. If they regretted the decision to stay, they never let on and instead made a happy, comfortable life for themselves in Manila.

Tito Willie followed in Lolo Ponciano's footsteps and became one of the first Filipino partners at a prestigious, American-led law firm in Manila, while Tita Helen got a job at the US Embassy. They became the primary residents of the house on Indiana Street after Lola Nena passed away in 1955. By then, Mom had married and moved to Tarlac, Tito Bobby was living in Madrid, Spain, and Tito Poncy traveled often for work with Pan Am.

When he wasn't dealing with cases, Tito Willie was the fun uncle that every child wishes for. He would shower me with gifts and would often take me to the embassy commissary to buy ice cream, toys, books and most anything I pointed to. The first time he brought me there, he treated me to a giant scoop of chocolate ice cream in a cone and a big red balloon to bring home.

For her part, Tita Helen loved to dress me up. I would accompany her and Mom to the modista from whom she would order custom-made dresses for me, and she would take me to Gregg Shoes on Mabini Street when I needed new footwear.

"You're spoiling her!" Mom scolded Tito Willie and Tita Helen whenever she heard about our trips to the commissary and shops. Her brother and sister-in-law had no children of their own, so they found delight in spoiling me. Mom understood, but she would still warn them, albeit half-heartedly, "I don't want her to get too used to it."

A world war had taken from my uncle and aunt those first few years of their young marriage, a precious time filled with bright optimism and fresh hopes for the future. Instead, Tito Willie came so close to meeting a terrible end several times—first, during the fall of Bataan and the subsequent Death March to Tarlac, followed by months in a Japanese POW camp and a severe illness induced by the harsh imprisonment, and later as a guerrilla fighter. Tita Helen meanwhile lived with the fear of being detained by enemy soldiers and the horrors they could inflict on a vulnerable young woman. But after the war, they never betrayed any sense of resentment, bitterness or anger at what had been lost or the mental and emotional burdens they had endured. Instead, they focused on their blessings and on making the most of the years they had together.

....

December 1961

It was noon on a Saturday and Dad, Mom, Tita Helen and I were having lunch at the house in Malate. It was an unusually warm day, and the faint melodies of Christmas carols playing on the radio drifted in the air and mingled with the oscillating hum of an electric fan as it cooled the dining room.

The table was crowded with tempting dishes like callos Madrileños full of chickpeas, chorizos and slices of tender tripe in an unctuous tomato sauce, and a large bandejado of steamed cabbage, sayote and green beans drenched in melted butter. Wisps of fragrant steam swirled from a mound of Milagrosa rice as Mom passed around the platters. I waited excitedly for my turn to fill a plate.

Dad sat at the cabesera, or head of the table, with Mom to his left and Tita Helen on his right. I sat next to my aunt, in the chair usually occupied by Tito Willie. He had been in and out of the hospital for months, troubled by a debilitating kidney disease. I didn't know it then but my uncle, who was only forty-four years old, was terminally ill. Yet my parents and aunt remained hopeful that he could be discharged from the hospital in time for Christmas just nine days away.

The thought of seeing my favorite uncle again cheered me. Tito Willie was fun and made me laugh, even when he tried to look serious. He always had a humorous quip or a magic trick ready for me. My favorite was when he pretended to find a coin behind my ears or on the tip of my nose, and he would dramatically declare it was exactly the amount he needed to buy me ice cream at the commissary. It never failed to make me burst into a fit of delighted giggles.

His oval face and slightly receding hairline accentuated his long sharp nose that made me think of Pinocchio, but I never told him that or else he would find a way to tease me back. Years later, Mom would often say he reminded her of Bob Hope, the American comedian, in looks and demeanor. Like the legendary entertainer, Tito Willie had a quick wit, and his rapid delivery of jokes left friends and family in tears of laughter. "Willie was always the life of the party," she would say.

I was excited that he would be coming home soon—surely it meant he wasn't sick anymore. Mom was also chatty and lively, as she always was when she was particularly happy. It seemed a long time since she was so animated. For most of the year, she had been occupied with the construction of our new home in Tarlac, as well as with Isabel's birth and my start in kindergarten, the first day of which had ended in tearful sobs and Mom waiting in the corridor to wipe away my tears and hug me tight in consolation. She never missed a beat between preparing for a big household move and taking care of Dad, a new baby and me, but it was nonetheless a busy time.

It became more stressful, however, as Tito Willie's illness progressed and Mom began traveling more often between Tarlac and Manila. Now, his expected return home had really lifted her spirits. She would admit to me when I was older that he was her favorite brother. "When I got married, Bobby gave me away because he's the elder brother, but I wanted Willie to give me away," she confided.

I remember Mom was wearing her favorite light yellow cotton housedress and her hair was in curlers—a sign we were going somewhere special later in the day. Tita Helen was as usual impeccably coiffed and dressed in a floral printed silk blouse and beige slacks.

"We will skip siesta today and go straight to La Femme after lunch," Mom said to me from across the table. I felt a thrill at the mention of the beauty parlor. It was a luxurious, elegant salon where the attendants would put me on a booster seat balanced on one of the cushioned chairs. I felt pampered and grown up on those special occasions when my mother took me there.

"What time is the wedding?" Tita Helen asked.

Mom beamed at me as she answered, "Well, we should arrive early for the Mass. This flower girl cannot be late."

A cousin, Marilyn Besa, was getting married that day, and for the first time in my four and a half years of life I was going to be a flower girl. Hanging behind the door of my bedroom was my gown, a creamy white confection of taffeta and lace trimmed with bright yellow chiffon (never mind that it was also crinkly and itchy). A matching short veil made of tulle and pinned to a spray of sunny flowers would be attached to my hair once it was styled into a trendy beehive updo at the salon. Just thinking about it made me feel so grown up.

Lunch, the beauty parlor, no siesta, a pretty gown, and a party—it was going to be a wonderful day. Reading the enraptured look on my face, Tita Helen said indulgently, "Yes, you will be a very pretty flower girl."

The shrill ringing of the telephone on the nearby credenza pierced the moment. Dad stood up from the lunch table to answer, his voice stern at the interruption. Within moments, a look of deep concern came over his face as he quickly glanced toward Mom and then to Tita Helen as he held the receiver to his ear.

Mom knew every one of my father's expressions, and she asked with a growing dread in her own expression, "Que pasa?" *What's going on?*

Her chair screeched against the wood floor as she suddenly pushed away from the table and grabbed the phone from Dad's hand.

"Hello? What? It can't be! No!" she gasped in shock before dropping the phone without ending the call. Tita Helen calmly got up from the table and replaced the receiver. She knew it was about Tito Willie, even before asking Mom what had happened.

I now sat alone at the table. I couldn't make out the solemn whispers between my parents and aunt, and I watched in confusion as they rushed out of the dining room, leaving their meals to grow cold on the table. When I saw them again just moments later, Mom had wrapped a floral scarf over the curlers that still covered her head, too distressed to even change out of her housedress. Tita Helen simply grabbed a handbag from her bedroom as they dashed out the front door to the car. I remember seeing her face strained with worry and Mom starting to sob as they left.

As a child, I rarely saw my mother cry, so I couldn't comprehend how she became so upset when just moments before, we were all laughing heartily during lunch and looking forward to the day's activities. I watched from the dining room window as the car sped down the driveway with my dad at the wheel. I wasn't sure what had just happened. But whatever it was, an awful gloom had replaced the warm, happy glow of the day.

I sat back down at the dining table, unsure of what to do. Did they forget about me? My four-year-old self fretted. Wasn't I supposed to be at the beauty salon with Mom by two o'clock? I glanced at the analog clock on the credenza. I hadn't yet learned how to read time, but I knew the hands on display were past the number 1.

As the housemaids came in to clear our forgotten lunch from the table, my yaya gently asked me in Tagalog, "Are you done?"

I was still eating, trying to finish the food on my plate, just as I'd been taught to do. I bit into a whole black peppercorn embedded in a piece of pork, and the harsh, pungent flavor seared my tongue. I frowned and nodded my head. I suddenly missed Tita Helen, who had helped me fill my lunch plate just a short while before. The last time I had bitten into a peppercorn by mistake, she had soothed me and explained what it was.

Yaya held my hand and walked me to the bedroom I shared with my newborn sister, Isabel, who was asleep in her crib. I anxiously checked to see if my flower girl gown was still hanging behind the door before Yaya bundled me to the bathroom to take a shower. It was unusual for me to take a bath at this time of day, but then again, nothing had been as usual since the phone call during lunch.

Later, as Yaya struggled to run a comb through the knots and tangles of my wet hair, the tears came. "Don't cry," she said soothingly.

But everything seemed wrong. I didn't know why I felt sad, and there was no one to explain it to me. I wished for Mom to be home; I wanted her to be the one to comb my hair, her gentle touch working out the tangles.

When I was dressed, I made my way to the living room and sat quietly on the sofa, as Yaya told me to. I didn't know what I was waiting for.

After what seemed like forever, I heard the doorbell ring. Not caring if Yaya scolded me, I ran to the window to see who was at the door, hoping that my parents or Tita Helen had come back. I felt a pang of disappointment. It was Tita Bengie, one of my mom's closest friends and the one who had whispered to the bandleader to play their song on the night my parents got engaged. She lived nearby in Pasay City, and she had come to take me to the salon.

Even in her distress, Mom had not forgotten and had called her friend to take care of me for the day. Without hesitation, Tita Bengie came over and took charge. She made sure my hair was styled and the pretty tulle veil pinned at the salon, fastened my gown that made me feel so grown up, and made sure I was at my cousin's wedding on time.

The bride, Marilyn, my cousin, was beautiful; the groom Danilo Gamboa, was handsome; and there were so many people inside the church. But I felt alone and nervous when I walked up the aisle. I missed Mom and Dad, and I missed

Tita Helen. They weren't there to see me be a flower girl for the first time.

When Tita Bengie brought me back home to Malate after the wedding, the house seemed dark and cold as we walked in the door. Yaya led me back to my room so I could change. There was still no sign of my parents or aunt. I felt a lurch inside my tummy.

I fell asleep and didn't hear the adults come home that night, but they were there at breakfast the next morning. The house was gaily decorated for Christmas but a sadness permeated the air, and there were no signs of holiday cheer on any faces.

Tita Helen sat beside an empty seat. Tito Willie was gone.

He had died of complications from polycystic kidney disease, a genetic disorder which plagued the Jugo side—Lola Nena's side—of the family. Not quite five years old, I didn't understand what a kidney ailment meant, much less the concept of death. All I knew was that it made everyone in house very sad.

Mom sat on the sofa, sobbing inconsolably. Even though it was a miracle he had survived his harrowing wartime experiences and lived sixteen happy years with his wife and family around him, it wasn't enough. She wanted more time with her favorite brother.

I hugged Mom, wanting to ease her grief. It was the only way I knew to help make things better.

"Mommy, te quiero mucho," I whispered to her. *Mommy, I love you very much.*

Tita Helen stood up from the table, her breakfast plate untouched. Wordlessly, she went into her bedroom and shut the door. I don't remember ever seeing her cry in front of us.

She was always so poised and calm, but this time, she looked bereft.

In the weeks that followed, as Tita Helen mourned stoically, I overheard my mother say how much she admired her strength. In the immediate days afterward, she would take Tito Willie's blue Cadillac and drive for hours around Malate and on Dewey Boulevard along Manila Bay. I watched from the second floor window as she maneuvered the big car in reverse and down the driveway. Few women in Manila had a driver's license in the '60s, and Mom worried when Tita Helen took off on one of these long, aimless drives. Dad reassured her, "It's her way of coping and mourning. She needs time by herself. The drive around the boulevard calms her down."

Several months after Tito Willie's passing and after we had returned to our own home in Tarlac, Mom sent me back to Manila to stay with Tita Helen for a few weeks. There was no question she would continue living at the family compound in Malate; it was as much her family home as it was her in-laws'. My mother knew how fond my aunt was of me, and she thought I could keep her company and help ease her loneliness in the house.

Tita Helen had returned to her job at the US Embassy on Roxas Boulevard and would drive herself to work every day. While I stayed with her that summer, my yaya would wake me from afternoon siesta to get dressed, and together we would take a taxi to the embassy a little before five o'clock in the afternoon to meet my aunt and accompany her home from work. Her colleagues would fuss and coo and shower me with the kind of attention any five-year-old would hapipily soak up, although I recall acting as if I just tolerated their notice as I waited for my aunt to finish work so we could be on our way. Before we left for home, Tita Helen would stop at the commissary to buy groceries, and it reminded me of all the times Tito Willie brought me there for ice cream and toys.

About three years after Tito Willie died, Tita Helen suddenly announced her decision to leave the Philippines and move to the US, just as she and my uncle had once dreamed of doing. It was shortly after my first Holy Communion in March 1965. My aunt marked the special event by giving me a beautiful silver rosary, which she had specially ordered. It bore my name engraved on the back of the crucifix and was nestled in a beautiful velvet-lined silver case. I cherished that rosary and used it throughout my school years for weekly prayers; while other girls had plain rosaries, I had my silver gift. Mom worried that I would lose it, but I was very careful. It was one of the last gifts I received from Tita Helen before she left the Philippines for the final time.

Mom was heartbroken by her decision to leave. Tita Helen was more like a blood sister than just one related by marriage, but she knew that with Tito Willie gone and being alone in the Malate house save for the household staff, it was time to let her go.

Tita Helen chose to live in San Mateo, California, where her sisters lived and where she eventually bought her own home. We stayed in close touch as I grew up. She wrote constantly, sending cards, letters and gifts that would often take weeks to arrive but were always a joy to receive. She never missed a birthday, graduation, holiday and even my wedding.

When my husband, Elpi, and I, along with our two young sons, emigrated to New Jersey in the early 1990s, Tita Helen was beyond delighted. We were once again in the same country, even if we were on different coasts separated by 3000 miles.

We talked every week by phone. Mom was gone by then, having passed away shortly before Elpi and I married. Those telephone chats felt like I had my mother back again. We talked about recipes and what I was cooking for dinner. She was always ready with helpful kitchen tips and meal ideas, mostly family heirloom recipes learned from Lola Nena so many years ago. She still referred to her late mother-in-law as "Mamà"—a sign of their close mother-daughter relationship. For me, I appreciated every single recipe and piece of advice she passed on. Hearing her talk about cooking felt like an extension of my mother's and grandmother's voices in the kitchen.

The only subjects we never talked about were the war and Tito Willie. My mother cautioned me when I was a teenager not to ask Tita Helen about either one, and when I asked why, all she would say was that perhaps the memories were too painful. Mom admitted she was hurt when Tita Helen wouldn't confide in her, given that they shared many of the same traumatic events, but she was particularly pained that Tito Willie was never discussed. She loved her brothers dearly and spoke about them all the time.

I can only guess that my aunt had internalized her wartime experiences and the early loss of her husband as a way to cope with her grief. There was one time, however, when one of our phone conversations about another person touched on my late uncle. Out of the blue, she said simply, "Your Tito Willie loved you so much."

In 1997, Tita Helen visited us in New Jersey for my younger son, Constante's, First Holy Communion. She stayed for a week, during which she immersed herself in our everyday routines. She accompanied us to the boys' soccer games, to church, to the grocery and to the park. She met our neighbors and chatted with them between the houses.

When she wanted to go to daily Mass, I drove her to our parish church after we saw the boys off to school. As she approached the front of the church, the elderly gentlemen who also attended Mass every day would rush (or what could pass as rushing for senior citizens) to open the door for her. She made an impression at the boys' soccer games, too, looking improbably elegant in her teal track suit with matching jacket and pants. I had been taking the boys to the park for years, and no heads ever turned to look at me the same way!

I do not exaggerate when I say Tita Helen was always impeccably dressed. As far back as I can remember, I never, ever saw her in rumpled clothes or looking unkempt. She would have her clothes made by a modista, taking the bus or a taxi for dress fittings and to pick up her orders. I remember watching in fascination during the weekends when she would give herself home facials, manicures and pedicures. Occasionally, she went to La Femme to have her chin-length bob trimmed or to get a perm.

Every day of her visit in New Jersey, Tita Helen and I cooked together, and she dressed just as well in the kitchen as she would at a fancy restaurant. She always wore hoop earrings encrusted with diamonds, and I never once saw her wearing a pambahay, as the colorful yet shapeless housedress is known in the Philippines. Having her in the kitchen, teaching me everything she knew about cooking, was like recapturing all the similar moments I spent with Mom.

Tita Helen taught me specialty recipes like callos Madrileños just as Lola Nena had taught her. I learned how to achieve the perfect balance of sweet and savory in the thick tomato sauce base, and the different ways to soften tripe, one of which was to cook it in a pressure cooker. I was scared of the contraption, so she patiently guided me through the steps. She revealed her secret of adding pieces from a whole pata (pork leg) and made sure I purchased the correct kind of Spanish chorizos with enough mantecon, or lard, to add an even deeper, unctuous flavor to the dish.

On the day I brought home the enormous bag of oranges, Tita Helen taught me how to make orange marmalade. The recipe itself is quite simple—mainly oranges, sugar, and water—but it is time intensive. We sliced the oranges into thin rounds, added the sugar, some lemon slices and a bit of citrus juice, and let it all soak in fresh water in a pot on the first day. Over the next three days, we returned the pot on the stove to boil the mixture and give it a good stirring before leaving it to sit for another day. After each day of simmering, the orange slices became more and more fragrant, perfuming the kitchen with the refreshing aroma of sweetened citrus, like the scent of a sunlit orchard, until the marmalade was thick and glossy and was ready to be bottled.

It took four days to make the marmalade, the better part of the week that Tita Helen stayed with us that year, and I cherished every moment of waiting for those citrus fruit, bought on a whim, to turn into a golden confiture. It was one of the last things we did together. After she returned to San Mateo, Elpi and I planned to visit California with the boys, but everyday life got in the way, and we never did make it out to the West Coast.

Tita Helen passed away at age 95 in September 2014 from complications due to Alzheimer's, which sadly also afflicted her two older sisters, Betty and Susanna. After she had been diagnosed and as the disease began to strip her of memories and cognizance, I asked her niece and primary caregiver Gigi if she could still remember me. "Oh, you have no idea," she reassured me. "She loves you very much. Of course, she remembers you."

When I learned of Tita Helen's passing, it was as if a light was turned off in the room. I felt like I had lost a mother all over again.

. . . .

During the COVID lockdowns, I would often busy myself in the kitchen. I found solace in cooking and baking because it made me feel closer to the women who had taught me everything they knew about food. When I made a large batch of Tita Helen's orange marmalade, I decided to use it for a crown roast of pork that Mom often cooked for special occasions. It was a small way of bringing together my love for both of them.

The crown roast was a stunning centerpiece of many of Mom's party tables, the ribs standing magnificently enrobed in a golden orange glaze made from Tita Helen's marmalade. It's a showcase dish, something fit for a celebration, which is exactly what Elpi and I needed after weeks of sheltering at home and dire nightly reports of infections, hospitalizations and deaths. When every day rolled into the next, each one the same as before, we craved a special day.

I thought of Tita Helen and Tito Willie, who were cruelly deprived of the precious first years of their marriage but lived every moment of the years they were gifted with joy and gratitude. They tried to make every day a sunlit day.

The resilience and grace they showed in the face of war, illness and death stayed with me through the years. So, with their example in mind, Elpi and I created our own reason to enjoy a special meal on one random day in the middle of a pandemic: we were both healthy and we were together.

What better reason to celebrate?

Helen Moreno Reyes, wife of Willie, was Matron of Honor at the
Besa-Reyes wedding. Malate, Manila, June 1953.

Chapter 14

Bobby and the Mystery Lady

The timer buzzed loudly to let me know the paksiw na bangus was done cooking.

When I unlocked the lid of the pressure cooker, a sharp tang of ginger, garlic and vinegar stung my nostrils, but I savored the tart aroma that billowed from the broth swirling gently around meaty steaks of milkfish. The soft portions of bangus were close to falling apart, so I carefully spooned them out of the deep pot while resisting the temptation to sneak a small taste from the deliciously fatty belly part. I glanced at the rice cooker on the other side of the kitchen counter, checking for the tell-tale wisps of steam that signaled the jasmine rice was also done.

During the COVID-19 restrictions that kept us at home, I often craved simple suppers like this—uncomplicated, flavorful and filled with feelings of comfort. Paksiw na isda is essentially fish simmered in vinegar, water, salt and black pepper, traditionally in a clay pot called palayok. The cooking method is not only quick and easy but is also a great preservative, which is why my mother often prepared it in the early morning hours at our house in Tarlac to take on the long drive to the family home in Manila for our weekend visits.

Such childhood recollections are mostly happy, but perhaps because we were in the middle of a pandemic, the memories that came to mind as I made paksiw na bangus were of the times Mom prepared it for her brother Bobby when he became terminally ill.

. . . .

Roberto J. Reyes, or Bobby to the family, was two years

younger than Mom and was the oldest of her three brothers. He had followed in Lolo Ponciano's footsteps as a lawyer, though his fledgling career was put on hold during World War II. After the liberation of Manila and the rebuilding of Lola Nena's properties in Malate, he revived his practice as a corporate attorney, and in 1951 he moved to Madrid, Spain for his work with the Pepsi Cola Company.

Over the next decade, he traveled extensively for both work and pleasure in Europe and America, returning to the Philippines for short visits as often as he could. One such homecoming was for a very important occasion: to walk his only sister Lulu down the aisle at her wedding to Gualberto Besa in 1953.

Tito Bobby was mostly an unfamiliar figure to me until he came home to Manila for good in early 1962, when I was nearly five years old. At the time, Mom was still in deep mourning for their younger brother, Willie, who died at age forty-four just days before Christmas a few months earlier. After the risks my mother took during the war to find him after the Bataan Death March and to bring him safely home from the brutal confines of a notorious Japanese POW camp, Tito Willie's death came far too soon and was almost too heavy a blow to bear. Mom considered her second brother as her favorite, and her grief over his passing was profound.

Tito Bobby's return from Spain provided some needed happiness. Stories about his bachelor life in Madrid filled our conversations during family meals at the Malate house. He talked about his work, of weekends spent exploring the city, and of parties and dinners spent with friends, though he never mentioned any romantic relationships.

He regaled us with stories of his travels to places such as France and Hawaii, the sights he saw and the food he ate. It was clear from his storytelling that he enjoyed indulging in rich cuisines during his many travels, but he was particularly fond of the food in Spain. Lola Nena often made traditional Spanish recipes taught to her by my great-grandmother Juana such as paella and bacalao, but it was a treat to listen to my uncle as he described the differences in the same dishes prepared in their place of origin half a world away. Even at my young age, I could hear the excitement in Mom's voice as they talked at the dinner table, and I could tell that his presence lifted her spirits.

What I didn't know then, however, was that doctors in Spain had diagnosed my uncle with polycystic kidney disease—the same inherited condition that had also claimed Tito Willie a few months earlier and Lola Nena in 1955. Now, Tito Bobby was also gravely ill and had come home to be with his family for what remaining time he had.

Although he kept an apartment nearby on Dewey Boulevard, he moved back to the house on Indiana Street where recently widowed Tita Helen still lived and where the household staff could help care for him. Even so, my mother began a regular commute between Tarlac and Manila to oversee his care. I sometimes accompanied her during school holidays; at other times, after our regular weekend visits to Malate, Dad would return to Tarlac with one-year-old Isabel while Mom and I stayed behind. It placed a heavy burden on her to divide her time and attention between an ailing brother and two young children, though she never uttered a complaint.

Tito Bobby was placed on a restrictive low-salt, low-fat diet as part of his treatment. Mom knew how dispiriting this must have been for her brother, who had delighted in tasting a variety of food during his time abroad. So she prepared dishes like paksiw na bangus, a simple and nutritious milkfish stew profuse with the aromas and flavors of peppery ginger and tart vinegar, served with equally fragrant steamed jasmine rice. Tito Bobby was no longer allowed to indulge in sumptuous dishes like callos Madrileños, full of beef tripe, chorizo, morcilla sausage and garbanzo beans simmered in a tomato sauce, but she was determined his meals would be as delectable as any he remembered from his travels.

My uncle eventually became bedridden as his condition gradually worsened, and Mom had to hire round-the-clock nursing care for him. Even so, she drove down from Tarlac more often and stayed longer each time as his dialysis treatments increased and he got weaker. It was probably the most time she had spent with him since before the war. Of all her brothers, he was always considered the quiet one—reserved, as she preferred to describe him—and despite the many stories he shared with us, it still seemed there was a lot she didn't know about him and his life in Madrid.

A few months after Tito Bobby returned to the Philippines, he and Mom agreed it was time to close his Manila apartment. No amount of optimism about his illness could deny the reality that he was unlikely to reside there again. I had accompanied her from Tarlac during that particular visit, so she took me along to be her little assistant. I was excited to be allowed to help with the important task of packing Tito

Bobby's belongings and even more thrilled to go to his place for the first time.

My uncle maintained a one-bedroom unit in the Admiral Apartments on Dewey Boulevard, less than a mile from the house on Indiana Street. The eight-story, neoclassical building was completed in 1939 and boasted unobstructed views of Manila Bay as well as elegantly themed private dining rooms that made it a favorite pre-war gathering place for the city's well-heeled. By some miracle, it survived the widespread destruction of the Battle of Manila and even served as a temporary home for General Douglas MacArthur after the city's liberation.[26]

Of course, these details were of no interest to almost-six-year-old me. When Mom and I stepped out of the car in front of the white stone edifice, the late morning sun was already blazing. A gentle breeze from the bay helped temper the heat, and a canopy of acacia trees lining the driveway cast a cooling shade on the wide cement walkway as I hopped from square to square in a spontaneous round of hopscotch. Piko, as it's called in Tagalog, was my favorite game. Anytime I saw a large, flat surface like a driveway, my first thought was to draw the familiar grid with a piece of chalk. I had no chalk with me this time, but the square pavers and my imagination did the trick.

I hopped and skipped behind Mom as we entered the building. Inside Tito Bobby's apartment, high ceilings made the space seem bigger. The living room took up most of the area with a small dining nook and kitchenette just off to the side. On the walls hung various original artwork, mostly cityscapes

26 Unfortunately, it did not survive modern-day developers: the building was demolished in 2014 to make way for a luxury high-rise hotel and condominium complex.

rendered in charcoal sketches and watercolor paintings. But it was the towering bookshelves against one side that mesmerized me. I didn't know anyone could own so many books! Tito Bobby was clearly a voracious reader. During his decade in Spain, he had accumulated boxes and boxes of books, which he periodically shipped back to the Philippines. And here they all were—fiction and nonfiction; in English, Spanish and French; and in a variety of genres that left no doubt he found great joy in reading.

I traced one chubby finger along the colorful spines of leather-bound books, leaving an uneven trail where I displaced the dust that had gathered in a fine layer. I couldn't read most of the titles and the ones I could didn't sound very interesting, but I was enthralled by the gold lettering that shimmered in the sunny apartment.

Our family driver had brought up large empty boxes, and Mom began to fill them with books, papers and photo albums which lay on tables and shelves. I was supposed to help but Tito Bobby's apartment was like an Aladdin's cave I needed to explore. On one low shelf, I found a pair of what looked like wooden shells joined by a length of bright red string. Holding one half-shell in each hand, I clapped them together. The very loud, sharp clack startled me and Mom.

"What are these?" I asked gleefully as I held up my discovery.

"They're castanets," she explained with a smile. "Flamenco dancers use them as musical instruments. You clap both parts together but with only one hand."

I stared at the castanets covetously. "Can I have them?"

She smiled patiently and told me to ask Tito Bobby later at home. Before she returned to packing, she thwarted any more exploration by giving me the task of gathering the photo albums on the dining table. I did as I was told, but I couldn't help leafing through some of the photographs, curious about the people and places in the images. As I turned a page of one album, a picture fell out.

I recognized my uncle in the black and white photo but not the lovely lady with curly light hair cut in a short bob standing beside him beneath a stone arch. They were both wearing overcoats and the sparse leaves clinging to a nearby tree suggested late autumn. They stood close to each other, their arms linked affectionately as they gazed directly at the camera. Their look of happiness was unmistakable.

"Mommy, who is this?"

Taking the photo from my outstretched hand, she considered it for a moment before replying with a curious tone in her voice. "This must be in Spain. But I don't know who this woman is."

Mom turned the picture and found "Madrid, Spain" neatly handwritten on the back, confirming her guess.

"Maybe his girlfriend?" she wondered aloud. I watched her as she studied the couple in the image, their bodies turned toward each other in a pose that suggested a personal closeness. Now I wanted to know who the lady was, too. My five-year-old logic whirred into action: if she was Tito Bobby's girlfriend, did that mean there would be a wedding? I had already been a flower girl in the weddings of two different cousins and I loved the dress-up part. Was this lady going to be my auntie soon?

Mom gave the photo one last look before tucking it into her purse. "I'll ask him when we go back home," she assured me, then turned back to boxing up the rest of his things.

She never got a chance to ask about the lady in the picture. When we returned to the house later that afternoon, Tito Bobby's nurse greeted us at the door. She was usually cheery, so the frown on her face was alarming.

"What happened?" Mom asked, but she didn't wait for an answer as she quickly walked to Tito Bobby's bedroom. I tried to follow her in but was gently yet firmly ushered out by one of the kasambahay.

I sat quietly on the sofa in the living room. I couldn't see what was happening but I could hear a flurry of activity and felt a sense of panic in the air as the nurse dashed to the kitchen and back again. She then came into the sala, where I sat unnoticed, and grabbed the phone.

"I need an ambulance…"

I heard her give the address to the house but the rest of her conversation was medical jargon that I couldn't understand. I also couldn't quite grasp the fearful feeling starting in the pit of my stomach.

Mom came into the room and sat beside me. I could see tears in her eyes although she tried to look calm and reassuring.

"I'm going to bring your Tito Bobby to the hospital. He isn't feeling well," she said to me. "Stay here with Yaya. Eat your supper, then go to bed."

She held my hand, hugged me tightly and kissed the top

of my head. "Te quiero mucho," she whispered. *I love you very much.*

I did as I was told, even though I felt like crying to see her so sad. I wanted to show her that I was brave, too, just like her.

. . . .

Tito Bobby would be in and out of the hospital several times as his disease progressed, and in his weakened state, he couldn't do much more than sit up for a bit before fatigue overtook him. It wasn't the ideal situation for an uncle to bond with his young niece, but it was enough. When it became clear he needed full-time care at home, Mom transformed the largest bedroom in the Malate house into a quasi-hospital room. I liked visiting Tito Bobby there, partly because it was the only one with air-conditioning but mostly because I was entranced by the nurse in her crisp white uniform and starched cap pinned neatly on her head—like a tiara, I thought.

"I want to be a nurse when I grow up," I later declared to Mom, as she puttered around the room while Tito Bobby napped. "I want a uniform just like hers."

A few days later, she handed me a huge rectangular box, like the kind that held her new gowns delivered from the seamstress. Inside was a nurse's uniform, complete with a cap, perfectly sized for a little girl. "Your Tito Bobby knows your dream is to be a nurse, so he asked the modista to sew this for you," she announced with a warm smile.

My uncle, who was supposedly asleep, had actually been quite awake and listening to his outspoken little niece. It wasn't my birthday or Christmas; he had simply given me a gift for no occasion at all.

That special day and gift formed an indelible image in my memory of Tito Bobby as a person who indulged a child's daydream of a future while his own precious days were dwindling. He never voiced any resentment about his plight or uttered a complaint or regret as his health deteriorated.

In hindsight, I believe Tito Bobby held off returning home to Malate until he was in the last phase of his illness because he didn't want to burden his sister, who had just lost another brother only a few months earlier. Mom commented years later that he was always the brother who did his best to cause her the least grief. But sometimes, grief can't be held at bay.

Tito Bobby died in early November 1962, about seven months after he came home to the house on Indiana Street and only a few weeks before the first anniversary of his younger brother Willie's passing. Mom's heartbreak was compounded, and she was nearly inconsolable for a period of time. She had essentially been an assistant parent for her younger brothers since she was five years old, and she mourned the loss of two of them not only as a sister but as a second mother.

Her sorrow over Tito Bobby, however, seemed different than her anguish over Tito Willie, though it was no less devastating. It was as if she were grieving not just for the Bobby she knew but also the Bobby she didn't know. His natural reserve and the fact that he lived so far away for so long meant that the last decade of his life was full of people and experiences that his sister and family would never know about—like the lady in the picture.

Mom never had a chance to ask Tito Bobby about her the day we found the photo. His illness was the primary concern and any curiosity about the unknown woman was set aside. But she was not forgotten.

Shortly after Tito Bobby's death, Mom hung up a framed photograph of him in our house. It wasn't the picture of him dressed up as a matador in front of a painted backdrop of a bullfight, a playful smile lighting his face as he held up a bullfighter's red cape. She also didn't pick the one of him sitting at an office desk, surrounded by papers and with shirtsleeves rolled up, or another of him striding nonchalantly down a city street, one hand casually tucked in the pocket of his stylish suit, looking every inch the debonair, cosmopolitan businessman. She chose, instead, that photo of Tito Bobby and his mystery companion. For years, it elicited questions from visitors to which my mother would reply, "That's the woman I never got to ask my brother about."

Mom also found another photograph of a woman at a beach, gazing out over the water as surfers rode the waves and a distant sailboat perched on the horizon. Her back was toward the photographer (was it my uncle?) but there was no mistaking the cropped, curly light hair. It was clear to Mom that this woman had been an important person to her brother.

She contacted Tito Bobby's friends and colleagues in Madrid to let them know about his passing and also to ask if any of them knew who the woman was. But no one did. It seemed that in some matters, he was just as reserved with his friends as he was with his family. To this day, we do not know who she was or what her relationship with Tito Bobby might have been.

Why did Mom choose that photo over any other to hang on the wall as a daily memorial of her brother? I like to think that the photograph represented everything she could have ever hoped and prayed for Tito Bobby and all her brothers to find in life: success, happiness, love. They had been through so much, beginning with the tragically early death of their father and through the horrors of war literally at their doorstep, and they had endured as a family.

Knowing there was so much about his life that she did not and would never know was surely a painful regret, but I hope it brought her comfort to look at the photo and see a perfect moment captured of her quiet brother radiating health and contentment and gazing confidently into the camera as if he were looking toward the future.

．．．．．．．．．．．．．．．．．．．．．．．

During the pandemic, I came to understand the feeling of regret that Mom must have felt about Tito Bobby over missed moments with loved ones and lost opportunities to make long-lasting memories together. My sons, for instance, moved away from home several years ago, but fortunately our paths converge frequently, even if it is only briefly during holidays and on vacations. But social distancing, quarantines and lockdowns changed that.

After all the cautions to maintain six feet from each other, to abstain from even shaking hands, and to wear masks that hid our smiles and our frowns from one another, it has been hard to switch back and regain the kind of personal interaction that came so easily to us before the pandemic. I used to go to lunch with a good friend once a month to catch up on our lives, but now, I admit feeling uneasy over the thought of being in a restaurant with other people, despite being vaccinated. Instead of mulling over a menu, I'm calculating how long it would be safe to remain unmasked in a roomful of people talking, eating and breathing.

Elpi and I were able to stay in touch with our sons, Tim and Constante, over video calls and messaging, but it was difficult having to miss Christmas and other special events that we once thought nothing of hopping on a plane to attend. Although we kept up to date, not being able to hug or just be in the same room with our sons left me feeling as if I had lost two years of emotional connection.

When I feel myself dwelling on this sense of loss, however, I think about Mom and Tito Bobby. They didn't have the Internet or instant messaging apps, just expensive long-distance telephone calls and handwritten letters that took weeks to travel across continents and oceans. Whatever I feel I've lost or missed out on in the lives of friends and family during the pandemic must be magnified by multiples to come close to what it must have been like for my mother and my uncle.

Then, I contemplate what I've learned from their story: there will be a time when we can come together and connect again. My uncle knew the only place he wanted to be as he faced the end of his life was with his family, and he found his

Roberto J. "Bobby" Reyes with his mystery lady. Madrid, Spain.

way home after so many years away. And my mother could mourn the lost moments between her and her brother but still cherish the knowledge that when it mattered the most, they were together in the end.

A Jar of Golden Summer

One of my father's breakfast rituals when I was growing up was to tear off a chunk of pan de sal and dip the crusty edge into a cup of instant coffee till it was a morsel of mocha-soaked sogginess. He'd then take that dunked piece of bread and give it to my little sister, Isabel, sitting next to him at the table.

My mother, on the other hand, would take her own piece of pan de sal and wipe around her plate, sopping up what was left of the soft yolks of her sunny-fried eggs. She would pop the eggy bit into her mouth and smile at us with satisfaction.

How could I forget those mornings that began with butter melting over warm, subtly sweet bread rolls baked by a local panadero before the sun had even begun to peek over the horizon? I can still picture the brown paper bag delivered to our house every morning by the baker's son on his clattering bike, hear the crinkle as Mom opened the sack and released the unforgettable scent of pan de sal baked in a wood-fired oven. Each oval of bread was delicately crusty on the outside and pillowy on the inside—perfect for a melting pat of butter or a generous slather of Mom's homemade mango jam.

My dearest memory of childhood summers is making mango jam with my mother. As she would so often say, it is a labor of love. Aside from fully ripened fruit, the most important ingredient is patience. The process is slow and lengthy but worth it in the end. Nothing else in the world is as ambrosial as homemade mango jam on warm bread.

. . . .

Summer 1967

As Dad headed out to the farm one morning, he put on his well-worn buri hat to protect his head from the scorching sun and said to me, "Put your shoes on. You're coming with me."

I scrambled to get into my sneakers and ran after him as he strode out the door.

To get to the farm, Dad drove his jeep from our house on the highway and down the long, unpaved roads of the barrio. The ride was bumpy and rough, and I had to grip the bar that ran across the dashboard just above the glove compartment. The vehicle didn't have any doors, so the warm breeze fluffed and ruffled my short hair as I tried not to get bounced out of my seat.

When we arrived at the farm, Dad parked the jeep and jumped out to come around to my side. He held my hand as I hopped out—I was ten years old and no longer a little girl, but it still seemed a long way to the ground.

We walked down the dusty pathway leading to the orchard where the thick, lush branches of the mango trees welcomed us like open arms. Mango is the Philippines' national fruit, and my sister and I grew up with an abundance of these honeyed produce from the orchard. Dad carefully nurtured the rows and rows of mango trees, which can take several years to bear fruit when first planted as seedlings and can live for more than two centuries afterward.

That morning, the farm workers were already busy collecting the ripened fruit—sun-kissed, smooth-skinned and honey-scented—in bushel baskets arranged in rows under the trees. Dad pointed out to me the unripe mangoes hanging like pendulums from the long branches and still nearly as green as the glossy leaves that shaded them. He told me the sweetest fruits were those that were tree-ripened.

We stood back to watch the harvesting. Some of the workers clambered up ladders and cut the stems with sharp knives or large clippers, but for the fruit higher up and out of reach, they worked from the ground wielding long bamboo poles tipped with hooked blades called sungkit.

Bushel baskets of woven wicker were set beneath each tree to hold the mangoes, which were carefully inspected for blemishes. Dad explained that mangoes ripened during the hot months of the dry season, from March to June, but when it occasionally rained, water could seep through the skins and create pinpoint dots inside the flesh, which he called pal-tik-paltik, or "sprinkled little spots." This blemished fruit was quickly rejected from bushels intended for the market.

My father harvested an immense number of mangoes between April and May. He brought home so much of the fruit, there were baskets and baskets around the house, inside and outside. The heady fragrance of mangoes in varying degrees of ripeness permeated our home, drifting into the hallways, rooms and every little nook.

Those summer days were far from lazy days. The huge amount of mangoes ripened faster than we could eat them, so the whole household was involved in turning fruit into jam. Even as a young child, I participated as much as my small hands and yet-to-be-developed kitchens skills could manage. It was a precious time because I got to work alongside my mother doing what she did best—cooking.

During jam-making season, I woke up at six o'clock in the morning, and as soon as breakfast was over I ran to the back of the kitchen. Baskets of ripe mangoes in shades from pale yellow to peachy gold were everywhere on the floor, filling the hot humid air with scents that flowed from sublime nectar to cloying sweetness, depending on their ripeness.

Mom had taught me one of my first tasks: how to peel a mango properly and efficiently.

"Peel it from the pointed end. Pull a strip of the skin with your fingers and keep pulling it," she instructed, demonstrating with her slim, manicured fingers how to pare the skin in a long ribbon that spiraled around the fruit and revealed lush, fibrous flesh beneath.

Mom was an expert mango peeler, but she had learned it from the true master. Dad was serious about every aspect of the mango, even after it was harvested from the tree. How the fruit was sliced at the dinner table for dessert was practically a matter of honor to him. He insisted the pit should be absolutely slim, meaning the cheeks of edible fruit-flesh on each side of the stone were to be sliced as cleanly and as closely to the seed as humanly possible. It may sound overly fussy but it illustrated just how much my father valued the sweetness and beauty of the mango. The more precise and thin the slice, the more of the fruit could be enjoyed instead of wasted.

I kept this in mind as I helped to skin mangoes all morning. I could feel every degree of the rising heat as we worked. Beads of perspiration trickled down the back of my cotton dress and my hands were sticky and smelled of ripe mangoes, but finally all of the fruit—over a hundred mangoes—was done, the curly strips of discarded peel gathered in a tangled pile inside a drum container.

Next, we crushed the fruit against a giant sieve. I pressed hard, rotating the treacly fruit around the rough surface to extract the juice and pulp, which flowed into a giant basin underneath. When we finished, I stood back as my mother and the house staff assessed the amount of golden pulp that had been collected so they could determine how much white sugar would be needed.

My favorite part of the jam-making process began when The Old Woman arrived, dressed in a long plaid-patterned traditional skirt called a saya and a cotton kimona top, and her white hair coiled into a tight bun. I never knew her name and she never spoke a word to me, but I couldn't wait for her to come to the house.

The Old Woman began by transferring the mashed mango into an enormous and deep copper pan the size of a batya[27] set on a pile of kindled wood. She fanned the flames with a pamaypay, an anahaw-leaf fan shaped like an upside-down heart with a woven handle, which she used to control the heat of the flames as she cooked.

She stirred the mango pulp for hours, slowly and gently, with a long wooden spatula, pausing to add cup after cup of glittering white sugar that melted languidly into the molten mixture as she resumed her stirring. Pretty soon the jam turned deep gold in color and thickened in consistency until it became more difficult to move the wooden spatula around the pan.

27 A wok-shaped basin used for washing clothes

At this point, Mom used a spoon to scoop a small sample to taste, and then let me try it, too. She held the spoon as I leaned in and inhaled the honeyed scent.

"Aaaah, it's hot!" I yelped. The tip of my tongue was scorched by the super-heated jam, but it didn't stop me from wanting another taste. Mom promised I could have more for dessert after supper.

Once she and The Old Woman agreed that the mango jam was finally done, the copper pan was taken from the fire and the sweetened cooked fruit was left to cool before bottling.

My mother spent the year between mango seasons collecting a variety of jars in anticipation of the annual jam production. Any and every glass bottle was saved—pickle jars, peanut butter jars, mayonnaise jars, and more. She hoarded the ones we used at home and solicited neighbors and friends for their empties.

"Do you still need this?" she would ask politely during visits, picking up a used glass container while Dad shook his head in exasperation behind her.

On rare occasions, she bought new Mason jars, but most of the time she relied on a motley assortment of recycled bottles. They would be carefully sterilized in boiling water and set out to dry on pristine kitchen towels laid on a tray. I remember Mom even used the stove-top sterilizer meant for my sister's baby bottles.

Cooling the mango jam required perfect timing; if left too long, it would thicken into a sticky clump that made a mess when it was time to bottle. Mom knew just the right moment to start spooning the glossy and still pliant jam into her jars. She preferred to do this part herself as she was very particular about cleanliness during the canning process. She placed the lids on top of the jars but did not close them tightly right away; instead, she covered them with a cloth and waited until the jam cooled to room temperature. Then, she let me help twist the caps to fully seal them.

As promised, my first taste of the season's mango jam was for dessert after dinner. Mom simply spooned the confection onto a small dish, like a pudding, and I let every little bit melt on my tongue before I took another taste.

....

The flavor and fragrance of Dad's mangoes were deeply imprinted in my memory, and I can honestly say that after many years of our homemade version, I could tell if a mango jam was made from fruit grown by my father or by someone else.

Several jars were kept for our household and the rest were given as gifts to family, friends and neighbors. Dad's siblings were always the first recipients. Mom would send them in a basket along with fresh produce in season from the farm.

While I would have been perfectly content turning every mango into jam, Mom showed more creativity. Whether they were still green, crisp and sour, or mottled and on the cusp of overripeness, she found ways to turn them into an entirely new food. Together we pickled tart, unripe mangoes and made chutney from the ripest selection. In between, we prepared pastillas, pies, cakes, ice cream or purees for juice.

During the summers of my childhood in Tarlac, there seemed to be no end to the harvest of mangoes that had to be peeled and squashed into a thick pulp. To another child, helping with the post-harvest processing was a tedious chore that took time away from games and toys. It's a wonder, then, that instead of developing a dislike for mangoes, I grew up loving them like no other fruit. Mangoes represent the very best lessons I ever learned from my mom and dad.

Unfortunately, there is a bittersweet irony to the whole experience. For some reason, I never got around to asking Mom for the mango jam recipe—the ratio of ingredients, the cooking times, the cues and hints and tips learned over time that resulted in the flavor of a summer orchard. Her mango jam was such an ingrained part of my life, I thought there would always be a jar on the shelf waiting for me.

Years later, as a food writer in America, I wrote an essay about my regret over never asking my mother for her recipe. I realized my painful mistake when I attempted to recreate the mango jam of my childhood for the first time in my kitchen in New Jersey.

I couldn't do it. I didn't know how. And Mom was gone.

No matter how many mangoes I had, how ripe or plump or sweet they were, I could not seem to replicate the jam the way Mom used to make it. I felt awful for never having asked her for the recipe. But I persisted, drawing as deep as I could into my memory and visualizing those moments in Tarlac when I watched fruit and sugar transform into gold.

After what felt like a million attempts and failures, innumerable hours of stirring, and too many burns on my wrists from the spits of molten lava of sugar and pulp that bubbled and spluttered in the pot, I finally produced a thick, rich golden jam that tasted just like Mom's. By then, I was in my American kitchen, far from the small town where I grew up having warm pan de sal and homemade mango jam for breakfast.

Even without a written recipe, it seems some things I learned from mother stayed in my heart forever. I'm not sure what the final piece to the puzzle may have been. Was it the copper-bottomed pot? Did I finally hit the right combination of time and temperature or the magic number of stirs with my trusty old wooden spoon? Or perhaps I simply realized the mangoes I was buying in America were not my father's mangoes, and I figured out how to parboil them first so they mimicked the soft texture of the orchard fruit I remember from my childhood.

Deep down, though, I knew the secret: Mom was right there in spirit, next to me, showing me how to do it the right way. I just knew she was beside me. I could tell by the longing for her that jabbed at my heart while I stirred the jam.

During the pandemic, I baked a lot, especially pan de sal. Whenever I put on my thick oven mitts to pull out a hot tray of buns from the oven, the aroma fills the kitchen and immediately transports me back to those long ago mornings in Tarlac, where my days began with Dad dunking a piece of pan de sal in his coffee and feeding it to Isabel, Mom mopping up every last gooey bit of egg yolk, and me reaching for a jar of golden summer.

Lulu Reyes Besa with daughters Maria Isabel and Elizabeth Ann. 1964.

Chapter 16

"It's Just Me and Poncy Now"

$\mathcal{I}$ have absolutely no doubt my mother loved her brothers without limit or reservation, but her relationships with each of them were as different as the siblings were themselves.

Bobby, the eldest of the three Reyes boys, was the quiet one who made a new, exciting life in a city thousands of miles away from the house on Indiana Street—a life revealed to Mom and the rest of the family through letters, photos and lighthearted anecdotes during his visits home. Some of what we knew about his personality and preferences, such as his love of art and literature, came later, from what we gleaned from the personal effects he left behind. His introversion created a distance that was not so easily bridged by a phone call or a plane ride. When he died, there were some things about him and his life in Spain that would forever remain an enigma, to Mom's sad regret.

Willie was her confessed favorite brother and the one for whom she risked her life and safety to find in a Japanese prisoner of war camp after the Fall of Bataan. As former POW Bob Dow demonstrated with his decades-long search for my mother, whom he never even met, saving a life can create an extraordinary bond between two people. For a sister and brother, it can transcend even the bond of blood they already share. Perhaps it is the reason why the depth of Mom's grief over Tito Willie's death seemed extraordinarily profound.

Poncy was the baby of the family, and in many ways Mom was more like a mother than a sister to him. He was named after their father, Ponciano Sr., and born a little over six months after the latter's tragic death on Christmas morning in 1918, when the ferry he was on capsized en route from

Manila to Zamboanga during a typhoon.

Lola Nena became a widow at the age of twenty-one, and there were many days when her sorrow weighed so heavily, she couldn't even get out of bed. Instead, her eldest child and only daughter took on a mothering role to her younger siblings. When Poncy was an infant, it was Lulu, not yet six years old, who would run into the bedroom to check on him, lifting him out of his crib to soothe and cradle him in her child's arms before bringing him to their mama.

She continued to dote on her baby brother as they grew up; some might even say she spoiled him shamelessly. Years later, whenever she spoke about him, she often mentioned the unhappy circumstances surrounding his birth, as if trying to explain—or justify—why he was coddled and indulged even in adulthood.

I only really got to know Tito Poncy after my two other uncles, Bobby and Willie, passed away within a year of each other when I was about five years old. I remember his handsome Spanish mestizo features from Lola Nena's side of the family, and that he had a talent for photography. In fact, he took most of our family photos at the time, many of which were some of the best photos any of us had of ourselves.

A plum corporate job with Pan American World Airways allowed him and his wife, Fortunata, known as Atang, to travel abroad for work. They lived in Hawaii during one assignment, and upon their return to Manila, they brought back those souvenir dancing Hawaiian dolls, which my uncle displayed on his desk at home. I was so fascinated by the bobbly figures wearing grass skirts and colorful leis and playing little ukuleles.

Tito Poncy enjoyed entertaining my parents with stories of their distant travels and the interesting people they met, and I can still hear Mom's delighted laugh when his stories took an amusing turn. As fun-loving as he could be, however, he could also be prickly and obstinate, and he harbored a conceit about his abilities and judgment. His jet-setting for Pan Am fostered a taste for an affluent lifestyle and socializing, but he lacked a practical sense for finances. He dreamed big and foolishly. He relied on, and perhaps even expected, his big sister to help him achieve what he wanted but often refused to accept her advice or counsel. And yet my mother found it difficult to deny him whatever he asked.

My uncle's impulsive nature coupled with a lack of foresight eventually led to a decision that kicked off a domino effect of events whose impact would be felt many years later. Despite a secure and well-paying corporate job, Tito Poncy decided to turn his photography hobby into a full-time profession. Exasperated and sounding more like a parent than a sister, Mom voiced her concerns that being a studio photographer couldn't provide an adequate living. She warned him that he would be giving up any severance pay if he quit his job, but he was stubbornly determined to do as he pleased. After the deaths of Tito Willie and Tito Bobby, ownership of Lola Nena's house in Malate and the income from the rental homes in the compound were shared equally between him, Mom and their sister-in-law Helen as Willie's widow. This steady though modest source of money convinced him he had enough cushion to change careers.

So, Tito Poncy resigned from Pan Am, and he and Tita

Atang moved into the house on Indiana Street. After purchasing professional photographic equipment, he converted a large storeroom into a darkroom and designated the living room as his studio space. He also joined the Camera Club of the Philippines, which counted many of the country's most prominent photographers as members.

Unfortunately, the business failed to prosper, although I was too young to understand the reasons why. With clients scarce, Tito Poncy fell back on being the family property administrator, responsible for the rental houses and the collection of rent, which provided a good income. Sympathetic to his struggle to keep his photography studio running (even though she had urged him not to quit his job in the first place), Mom ceded her share of the rent collection to him. Still, he grumbled about the considerable chunk of money required to pay property taxes. The remainder was modest yet enough to live on—that is, if one lives equally modestly. But my uncle seemed unable or unwilling to live within those means.

One year, he decided he needed a new car, so he nagged Mom to ask my father to loan him the money. When she finally relented with the admonition not to buy a flashy vehicle that might attract the attention of thieves, he immediately purchased a flaming red Toyota Corona sedan. Predictably, it was stolen off the street not too long afterward, while Tito Poncy was at the dentist's office. Car insurance barely covered the loss of the theft, but soon after he was once again pleading with his sister and brother-in-law to lend him more money to buy another car. At least for this next purchase, he finally heeded his sister's advice and bought a white compact Toyota Corolla.

Then in 1965, Tita Helen moved to California, leaving Tito Poncy and Tita Atang as the sole family residents of the Malate house. Before leaving, she also generously gave her portion of the rental income to her brother-in-law. She might have sensed a brewing conflict in the family regarding money, and with a job and new home waiting for her in the US, she had no reason or need to take the money when Poncy needed it more.

For several years afterward, life for our family unfolded smoothly and uneventfully. My parents, sister and I continued to visit the house on Indiana Street on weekends. As she had always done since she married and moved away, Mom would prepare special dishes at home in Tarlac to bring to Manila.

One such dish, and a particular favorite of Tito Poncy, was chicken curry with mango chutney. Mom would fill a plastic container full of plump pieces of chicken and chunks of potatoes covered in a robustly fragrant yellow curry sauce, and then two large glass jars of homemade mango chutney. Everything went into a big red-and-white Coleman cooler with bags of ice placed underneath and on top of the food to keep it cool and well-preserved during the three-hour drive to Malate. In fact, Dad often refused to make any stopovers during the trip as he didn't want the food so painstakingly prepared by Mom to spoil. "We need to reach Manila quickly," he would say, when Isabel or me would ask to stop for a roadside snack.

But my mother loved road trip stopovers, especially in the neighboring province of Pampanga, where we would stop at Café Fernandino and the iconic Everybody's Café to buy assorted Pampango specialties like yema, a sweet custard candy made with egg yolks; pastillas, a soft carabao's milk candy; uraro, or arrowroot cookies; and candied sampaluk, as tamarind is called in Kapampangan. She also bought boxes of local pastries such as caramel boat tarts and coconut macaroons gaily wrapped in colorful cellophane to give as souvenir gifts known as pasalubong for Tito Poncy and Tita Atang.

"It's just Poncy and me now," Mom would say to me. The two of them were all that was left of the little family that had been forged by early tragedy and strengthened by wartime adversities. As the last of the siblings, their bond remained strong, until one weekend visit drastically changed the tone of their relationship.

On a Saturday evening as we all sat down for dinner, Tito Poncy casually brought up the idea of selling the Malate compound. The property included the family home as well as two other large houses in a lot approximately 2500 square meters. Thanks to its size and central Manila location, it had a good market value.

I was twelve years old then and old enough to instantly recognize how incendiary the topic was. Our parents had taught me and Isabel that mealtimes were sacrosanct; we always began and ended each meal with a prayer. The table was a safe place where we could leave behind our conflicts, however briefly, to enjoy our meals in harmony. Arguments, or sensitive topics that could lead to arguments, were to be settled in private.

Mom's spoon clattered onto her plate, startling everyone. She looked as if someone had slapped her in the face. Tension stiffened her posture and her demeanor was a mix of shock and anger. She did not say a word and did not take another bite as the rest of us finished our meal in awkward, uncomfortable silence. Tito Poncy had the good grace to recognize his proposal had unnerved his sister, so he backed off the topic and didn't bring it up again that night.

The next afternoon, as our weekend visit came to an end, we prepared to return to Tarlac. Isabel was still inside the house with our parents, but I had a pre-teen's impatience to get back to the comforts of our own home. I waited in the car parked on the driveway, hoping the adults would be quick with their goodbyes.

Then, the sound of an argument—loud and contentious— exploded from the house and easily reached where I was sitting inside our car. Inexplicably, Tito Poncy had chosen that moment to bring up the sale of the house and property again.

"We can't sell—this is our home!" I heard Mom shout. The sound of her raised voice was jarring and immediately upsetting to me. I didn't recognize this side of my mother. It was so unlike her to speak with such indignation. She was not escandalosa, prone to making a scene in public. Their argument was so loud, I could hear it clearly outside in the driveway.

Every word, every accusation they hurled at each other carried to where I sat in the car and echoed throughout the property. I cringed in embarrassment, wondering if the families who rented the homes in the compound could also hear the argument between sister and brother, and what they must be thinking.

"I'm paying too much in taxes now," my uncle retorted, disregarding how Mom and Tita Helen had generously given him their rightful shares of the rental income. "Malate has become expensive and I need to cash out."

Mom's fury turned to despair. "It's all I have left of Mama," she cried as she begged her brother not to even consider selling. But he was insistent, and his next words came out callously.

"Mama is gone. Bobby and Willie are gone, and Helen has moved to the States. This property is of no use to them anymore."

He salted the wound even more when he accused her—the sister who had only ever doted on him all his life—of selfishness for her refusal.

I heard in Mom's voice how hurt she was over his words. "You have no idea what you're asking me to do. I cannot give up the only home we have had together as a family," she cried, each word a labor to speak.

I never heard my father among the raised voices. If he spoke, it would have been calmly, sensibly. I couldn't see him, but I could picture him standing quietly in the living room as the unbelievable scene between his wife and his brother-in-law unfolded. Ever since Dad married into the Reyes family, he never attempted to act like some kind of patriarch over his in-laws or assert any fraternal authority over his brothers-in-law. His presence supported Mom, but I think he knew that he could not take a direct role in this dispute and that if he inserted himself on her side, then Tito Poncy might feel they were ganging up on him.

In the car, I put my hands over my ears as the sound of their heated quarrel became unbearable. It felt suffocating inside our Oldsmobile. As I sat there sweating profusely, I considered going back inside the house, but that would have meant witnessing up close my mother and uncle bickering. The thought of seeing Mom so distraught and hearing her cry pierced my heart like a sharp knife.

Tito Poncy knew how much she loved their mother's home. The house on Indiana Street had nurtured a fatherless family, sheltered them during a war and was resolutely rebuilt from the rubble of that conflict. She lived for the weekends when we would visit, and Lola Nena's clothes and furniture were still stored inside.

But my uncle was financially desperate. His inability to manage his finances despite a steady income from rentals and his struggle to build up his photography business found him almost dependent on borrowing from Mom and Dad—loans they willingly gave him without conditions and without demanding repayment. He was dead set on selling the compound.

Their argument that day was the beginning of frequent squabbles between them, and I came to dread going to Manila on our weekly visits for fear that at any moment a fresh quarrel would ignite. There were periods of calm, of course, in large part because Tito Poncy had some difficulty finding a buyer for several years. During that time, my mother and uncle would briefly regain some of the easy relationship.

On a July night in 1969, not long after that weekend, Tita Atang suddenly collapsed in the kitchen after dinner and died in the hospital from a brain aneurysm. It was Isabel's birthday, and I remember being woken up by Mom early the next morning so we could all travel to Manila.

Tito Poncy was distraught. Some people can weather the storm of such an unexpected loss, but he was not so emotionally strong. Tita Atang's death left him floundering and helpless, but Mom was there for him without being asked. For several months, she traveled frequently between Tarlac and Manila when her brother seemed to have difficulty settling into life without his wife. He got into arguments with the house staff and fired them, so Mom took charge of hiring new maids and training them, only to have Tito Poncy quickly find fault and fire them as well.

These staff turnovers persisted at regular intervals for nearly four years, much to my mother's frustration. She continued to travel to Malate frequently as she found herself essentially overseeing two households and feeling torn between caring for her husband and children and watching over her adult brother.

During one of Mom's trips in July 1972, powerful Typhoon Gloring[28] wheeled its way across the Pacific just north and east of the Philippines. Even though it didn't make landfall in the archipelago, the storm enhanced the seasonal monsoon, leading to several days of heavy rains that flooded huge swathes of Central Luzon in chest-deep waters. It was some of the worst flooding in decades as the sustained deluge broke through dams and dikes, and cut off communities throughout the provinces of Tarlac, Pampanga and Bulacan.

---

[28] International name: Typhoon Rita

Manila was also badly affected. MacArthur Highway, the primary thoroughfare connecting these provinces to the city, was closed off to all automobiles except military vehicles distributing relief goods. Mom was stranded in Malate for weeks as most of the island of Luzon was practically underwater.

I had just turned fifteen years old and started my senior year of high school. Our town was inundated after the Tarlac dam failed, so I volunteered to help distribute aid to local flood victims as the relief trucks finally reached our province. When I started feeling poorly, I thought it was simply the flu. But later that night, I woke up trembling and my teeth were chattering. I had a high fever, chills and severe congestion exacerbated by my asthma. Isabel jumped out of bed when she heard me moaning and ran to get Dad.

It turned out I had contracted both dengue and typhoid fevers, likely from the floodwaters and the mosquitoes that thrived in them. My father, usually so capable and unflappable, didn't know what to do. Due to severe flooding throughout town, the doctor couldn't make it to our house and I couldn't be taken to the clinic. Dad was finally able to reach the doctor by phone to describe my symptoms and receive a prescription for medications, only to discover I had a previously unknown allergy to the kind of antibiotic when I suddenly broke out in hives.

All the while in Manila, Mom was beside herself with worry at not being able to rush home. She could only listen as Dad kept her posted about my condition over the phone, and she dictated step-by-step instructions on how to care for me. I eventually received the appropriate antibiotics and recovered from the double infection, but as a mother myself now, I can imagine Mom's anguish and sense of helplessness at not being there to care for her sick child.

If she ever felt angry or resentful over being stuck in Manila while I was so ill because Tito Poncy had another self-inflicted staffing issue, my mother never voiced them to me or anyone else as far as I know. Just as she had always given him broad leeway due to the sad circumstances of his birth, she displayed tremendous tolerance of his neediness because he was now a widower. She continued to worry over him like a mother hen when she wasn't in Malate. She asked her brother-in-law Augusto Besa, who lived nearby, to check on Tito Poncy now and then. As the Besa siblings were close and affectionate, Tio Titong didn't hesitate to visit Mom's brother despite his busy doctor's schedule.

Then, four years after the death of his first wife, Tito Poncy married a lovely woman named Tessie, whom he met on a blind date arranged by friends. My uncle at first wanted to try a live-in relationship before marriage, but Mom would have absolutely none of it and quickly planned a proper wedding in Tarlac, officiated by the Bishop of the Diocese, Monsignor Jesus Sison. She was frankly relieved her brother had found such a compatible partner. The new Mrs. Ponciano Reyes Jr. was malambing, meaning someone who is particularly warm and affectionate—a trait my mother credited to her Visayan heritage—and she knew how to anticipate my uncle's needs. In short, she was a perfect fit for his dependent nature.

If Mom harbored any hope that his new domestic bliss

might make her brother forget his plan to sell the Malate compound, she was quickly disappointed. Tito Poncy doubled down on his determination, taking any opportunity to try and wear her down. I'll never forget how Mom recoiled at every mention and reminder. When he borrowed money, for instance, he would say nonchalantly, "Don't worry, I'll pay you back when Malate is sold."

What he really wanted, however, was to move to Baguio with his new bride. He knew Mom always worried about him, so he played on her caring by pointing out how hot and crowded it was in Manila and how he could invigorate his photography business by opening a new studio. She protested that there were equally pleasant areas in Manila for a new studio and more opportunities to find clients in the city, but he would not be deterred.

Tito Poncy finally found a buyer in 1973, when I was in my last year of high school. The prospective new owner made a very attractive offer, and my uncle excitedly (insensitively, I thought) relayed the news to Mom. It set off another huge argument between them on our next weekend visit.

The mood afterward on the drive back to Tarlac was beyond somber as Mom cried during the entire three-hour trip from Manila. For the first time in my memory, we didn't even have supper when we got home. Instead, my mother rushed to the bedroom and slammed the door behind her. Through the walls, I could hear her weeping. Tears streamed down my own cheeks as I fell asleep emotionally exhausted.

A loud knock on my bedroom door woke me up around midnight. It was Dad.

"Mommy is having chest pains. I'm bringing her to the hospital," he said calmly but with a worried frown I had never seen on his face before.

A cold feeling of dread slithered throughout my body. My mouth went dry and my legs felt as if they were tied down to the bed. I felt my own heart suddenly palpitate in rapid thumps. As I stumbled out of bed and dressed as quickly as possible, I knew deep down what had just happened. The anguish of losing her childhood home and its memories of Lola Nena, Lolo Ponciano, Bobby and Willie was too much to bear. Poncy, her adored baby brother, didn't realize what he had just done to his devoted sister.

We almost lost Mom that night. She had a heart attack, we were told at the hospital. Though she later recovered and was able to come home, something had changed. It felt as if we had started down a path toward an inevitability that I wasn't sure I would be ready for.

Poncy Reyes with second wife Tessie. Malate 1973.

Chapter 17

To Be a Friend

I look back on my childhood in Tarlac and I'm flooded with idyllic memories of loving parents and a beautiful home; afternoons playing with friends in the fresh, pure air of the countryside and summers spent making mango jam; and all the amazing, delicious food prepared by my mother. But if I'm honest with myself, I didn't always feel this way while I was growing up, especially during my school days.

I attended the private Holy Spirit Academy,[29] an all-girls Catholic school in Tarlac City and the alma mater of generations of Tarlac families, from kindergarten through high school. From my earliest days in school, I was often excluded when classmates formed cliques during recess. It hurt a lot, and I began to learn how emotionally painful it was to not belong.

My schoolmates seemed to think I was some kind of "señorita"—a spoiled little miss—because I lived in a nice house and was brought to school every day by the family driver, and they teased me mercilessly for it. We also spoke Spanish instead of Kapampangan at home because my mother was once mocked by guests in her own home for not being able to speak the local language. As a result, she forbade me and my sister Isabel from speaking Kapampangan in her presence. She didn't know that it would contribute to making me feel like an outsider among my peers.

"Nobody wants to be my friend," I sobbed to my mother one day after school.

"Be patient," she soothed. She told me how it took years for her to nurture her truest friendships, and how they could

29 Now called the College of the Holy Spirit of Tarlac

last for a lifetime.

I thought about her closest friends, all of whom I called tita, or aunt, because they were as close as sisters—like my godmother, Tita Nini, and Tita Bengie, who made sure I was at my cousin's wedding to be a flower girl for the first time on the same day my Uncle Willie passed away. There was Tita Ampi Palou, the widow of Tito Willie's best friend Hector Syquia, who remarried after the war to Bill Palou and had six more children. Tita Ampi's friendship stayed strong with Tito Willie because she asked him to be godfather to her son Arthur. I remember when we used to visit at her Forbes Park home in Makati, she would greet my mother so joyously with a shriek of "Luluuu…!" and the biggest hugs. She even gave Bambi, one of our fluffy white Japanese Spitzes, as a special gift to Mom.

They and other close friends—Chit Dalupan Sebastian, Loleng Panlilio, Gin Mata, Lourdes Alunan Fernandez, and Mary Guidote—were the first to come to the hospital without hesitation to support and comfort my frantically worried mother when three-year-old Isabel had to undergo emergency surgery for an aneurysm.

These wonderful women were some of her closest friends since before World War II and from when she co-founded the Young Ladies Association of Charity. Their unbreakable friendship was forged from common goals, shared compassion and caring for others before themselves. For the rest of their lives, they celebrated every life milestone, shared every success and disappointment, and offered solace for every sorrow together.

"How did you make friends?" I asked Mom, wishing the same for myself.

"To have a friend, you must first be a friend."

She taught me that I must be the first one to reach out and to choose friends based on love and kindness, not on money or status. "Good friends help you and others without being asked and without expecting anything in return. Help your friends, even if they don't ask, and never ask for any favors in return."

I took her words to heart and eventually found good friends who made my elementary school years brighter. Still, by the time I was in high school, the soft schoolyard barbs I continued to suffer became more pointed, sharper and meaner. By then, we were all old enough to understand the ability of words and actions to hurt another person, and yet some of my classmates continued to do so.

Their taunts stung deeply because I simply wanted to be a part of a barkada, to belong to a group of friends who spent their free time and experiences together, forming friendships that last a lifetime. I wanted to fit in with my classmates and be accepted as a peer. Unfortunately, the differences others saw (or thought they saw) about me were sometimes amplified by the people I loved most.

Once, during my senior year of high school, I forgot my baon, or packed lunch, at home. When Mom realized this, she sent our family driver Ding to deliver it to my school. Following her strict instructions to hand me my lunch in person, he made his way to my fourth-floor classroom. There, he stood squarely in the open doorway, holding my baon neatly packed picnic-style inside a wicker basket as my English liter-ature teacher Miss Castillo stared at him in surprise.

I cringed in embarrassment at my desk as Ding tried to catch my attention. "Elizabeth Ann, I think that's for you," announced Miss Castillo.

I could hear my classmates' whispers as I stood up and took the basket from Ding, urging him to leave quickly with a furtive motion of my hand. I returned to my desk and placed the basket on the floor next to me, where it stayed until class was dismissed for lunch. In the meantime, the aroma of fried food filled the rows beside and behind me. My classmates snickered and jeered, "Pengi ha!" *Give us some.*

The teasing wasn't funny to me. I loved my parents with all my heart, but my adolescent craving for approval and acceptance from my peers found such parental gestures mortifying rather than loving. Having my lunch delivered by the family driver only validated their poor judgment of me as maarte, or uppity; they didn't see it as a mother simply making sure her child had a proper meal that day. Instead of whetting my appetite, the aroma of home-cooked food was like a green light for unpleasant teasing to begin.

At lunch, I sat at a table with several friends who were having sandwiches and soft drinks purchased from the cafe-teria. I slowly unpacked the wicker basket. It was an elegantly dainty container that I recognized as one Mom often used to send gifts to friends and neighbors. My classmates watched with curious amazement as I opened Tupperwares of fried chicken, steamed rice and coleslaw; a plastic tumbler of chilled dayap juice; and even cutlery and linen. I had an amazing feast

in front of me, but all I wanted at that moment was a sandwich and soft drink just like everyone else.

I hated the attention I was getting from other students
for the lavish lunch Mom had sent. I felt so embarrassed and
even more separated from my peers that I couldn't recognize
what I had before me. I couldn't appreciate how expertly my
mother had fried the chicken in a thick batter coated with
bread crumbs so that it stayed crunchy until lunch. I couldn't
register the crispness of the coleslaw made with cabbage,
carrots and cucumbers grown in our garden. And I could
barely taste the tart sweetness of the dayap juice my father had
prepared himself as I quickly gulped it down so that I could
pack the plastic containers—and my embarrassment—back
inside the wicker basket.

Although deep down I knew everything my parents
did for me came from a place of love, I was still an immature
teenager to whom their protective bubble began to feel more
like a suffocating cocoon.

. . . .

My heart felt close to bursting with excitement in the
summer of 1973 after I graduated from high school and was
preparing to attend college in Manila. I could hardly wait to
have some measure of independence, to create my own path
in the world, even if it meant making mistakes.

Although I loved my parents dearly, I was excited to
leave home and become my own person. My mother remained anxious to keep me safe, so they had steered me toward her alma mater, St. Paul College of Manila.[30] She firmly

30 Now St. Paul University

believed that the same education she received from the nuns at St. Paul would provide the right foundation for me as well.

The college campus occupied an entire large block in the Malate district, a short distance from the palm tree–lined Roxas Boulevard that ran along the banks of Manila Bay. The grounds were larger than the academy I had attended from primary to high school, and there were so many more students than I had ever seen or been with before. I eagerly anticipated the luxury of attending classes in air-conditioned rooms inside modern multi-story buildings, and I was mesmerized by the rows of books and long mahogany study tables in the huge library located on the ground floor of the famous St. Paul's Chapel. I looked forward to spending hours and hours reading in this repository of knowledge.

Underneath my excitement, however, I felt the strong currents of anxiety. The hurt from the taunts of classmates in Tarlac still lingered, and I was worried about making new friends.

"Make as many friends as you can because you need friends in your life," Mom had often counseled. She knew firsthand what can be accomplished, especially for a greater purpose, if one can get others involved.

I was afraid of being bullied again, thinking it would follow me from high school. In the first few days at college, I walked into class uncertain and too shy to start conversations with my new classmates. I even lacked the confidence to raise my hand in class because I didn't want to draw the attention of strangers to myself.

But I soon realized the very fact my classmates were

strangers—people who didn't know anything about me or my family—made them more accepting of me. Soon, as my anxieties settled and my confidence grew stronger, I began making friends among my dorm mates.

. . . .

I was an interna, as students who lived on campus were called. The dormitory housed about fifty girls who came from all over the Philippines, from as close as metropolitan Manila to the mountainous Northern Luzon and the even more distant Visayas and Mindanao regions in the central and southern parts of the country.

Despite our different geographic origins, we all had one thing in common: for most of us, it was the first time we had lived far from home and the first time we were independent from our parents and families. As such, many of the girls were often homesick and found comfort in clustering with others who came from the same region and spoke the same provincial languages. Because I had ties to different areas—Manila and Western Visayas through my mother and the northern provinces around Tarlac through my father—I befriended girls from the different groups that formed in the dorm.

We internas bonded over shared meals in the dormitory dining room. Our campus board and lodging included a plan for three meals a day, but it was mostly during dinner time that nearly all the girls were present, as there were no other options in the evening after the off-campus restaurants and food stalls closed for the day. There were four of us assigned to each rectangular Formica table, with two girls on each side.

The tables were lined up short-end to short-end to create two very long mess tables that spanned the dining hall. Dinner started at 6:30 pm and consisted of a meat or fish entrée, a vegetable side dish, a bowl of steamed rice, and fruit for dessert.

I had never tasted a truly horrible meal until I went away for college and ate in the dormitory dining hall.

Friday dinners always seemed especially bad. One such supper consisted of a watery green porridge that was meant to be monggo guisado but bore no resemblance to the traditional stew of mung beans simmered in aromatic onions and garlic, and richly flavored with fatty slices of pork or briny flakes of smoked fish that I always enjoyed at home. Accompanying the bland slurry were two minuscule fried galunggong, the once-crisp little fish turned limp and stone-cold by the time they were slid onto our plates. And dessert was an unrecognizable mush masquerading as a fruit pudding. No matter how hungry I was, I could barely muster the willpower to take another bite of that particularly disastrous meal, and every Friday meal that followed. By Saturday, I couldn't wait to go home to Tarlac for the weekend, if only to savor Mom's cooking again.

Like clockwork, Dad and Isabel would drive to Manila to pick me up at St. Paul early on Saturday morning. We would arrive at the house on the highway around noon to the delirious sound of Bambi barking and yapping at my return. As soon as I walked through the door, I could smell the garlicky aroma of pancit Molo simmering in the kitchen. The sight of plump pork wontons bobbing amongst shreds of cabbage and carrots in the clear broth was the best welcome home.

My mother cooked the most phenomenal meals for us on my weekends home from university—Spanish cocido, paella, adobado, steamed fish mayonesa and fresh lumpia ubod, among so many other dishes. I felt like I was in seventh heaven, and the lingering aftertaste of subpar dormitory food in Manila dissipated with every bite of a home-cooked meal.

I told Mom about the miserable fare at school and how my dorm friends received care packages filled with foodstuff mailed by their parents from as far away as Iloilo, and how I would drool at the sight of one mother's siopao asado, another's homemade buttery baked buns, and the cans of corned beef and SPAM and tins of lengua de gato cookies they would generously share with me.

I didn't mean to hint—well, perhaps I did—but Mom picked up the cue and began preparing cooked food for me to bring back to school. Every weekend visit home thereafter ended with me returning to St. Paul laden with one or two delicious meals prepared by my mother.

As the months progressed, however, I began to notice something alarming during my visits home. There was something amiss about the way Mom walked and moved around the house, though I couldn't quite put my finger on it at first. She didn't jump up from the table and bounce into the kitchen with enthusiasm, as she used to do. It was as if some inner energy that once glowed and pulsated within her was slowly draining away.

She had suffered a heart attack several months before,

after her younger brother Poncy sold the family home in Malate to her great distress, but she recovered well—or so I thought. I was too scared to ask my parents if something was wrong. Whatever was ailing her was something I did not, could not, face just yet.

Even if she was not feeling one hundred percent, Mom would get up from the couch or from her bed where she was resting to make her way slowly to the kitchen and prepare the weekly baon I was to bring back to the dorm. One weekend, when she was in bed for two whole days, I finally gathered the courage to ask how she was.

"Hija, my blood pressure is too high, so the doctor told me to rest this weekend," she reassured me. She also admitted, almost apologetically, that she was suffering from angina and heart palpitations, so she could not get up to cook. I had never seen her like that before, and it worried me. I tried to be cheerful and volunteered to cook our family meals from then on, whenever I was home from school.

And so, Isabel and I eventually began to take over Mom's role in the kitchen, recreating her staple weekend dishes. I was more confident in my cooking, and I could bake cakes and pastries, too, having taught myself by reading cookbooks and watching cooking shows on TV. I was especially proud of my chocolate cakes, butter cupcakes, cookies, pies and even ensaymada.

Mom was generous with her praise for my newfound baking abilities. "Your Lola Nena would have been so proud to see you baking ensaymada," she declared with a fond smile. "Mama used to bake them, too."

One Sunday, when it was time for me to return to Manila, Mom insisted on packing some adobo she had cooked the day before, even if it took every drop of strength she had to get up from bed. She patiently transferred a huge serving of chicken and pork adobo into a large recycled Coffee Mate jar, first spooning the meat into the glass container and then pouring in the adobo gravy. As I watched, I caught a potent whiff of garlic and vinegar. Adobo can keep for many days in the refrigerator, and it's common knowledge that it tastes even better days after cooking as the garlic and vinegar flavors deepen. Mom figured there was enough for two large servings of adobo and suggested I could either have two meals or share a supper with a friend.

As soon as I returned to the dorm that Sunday evening, I immediately put the adobo in the communal refrigerator. I had sealed the lid with duct tape, and wrote my name on the jar with a black marker before stashing the bottle way in the back on the very bottom shelf of the fridge. There was an unspoken rule among those of us who shared the refrigerator: no one touched what did not belong to them. After all, who can you trust if not a dormitory full of good Catholic girls?

I was so looking forward to enjoying Mom's adobo, anticipating the taste of morsels of chicken and pork made tender and fragrant from a long, slow stew in soy sauce, vinegar, peppercorns and lots of garlic. Mom put so much garlic in her adobo that the scent of it rolled all around the dining hall and made heads turn whenever I brought some back from Tarlac and asked the manang (matron) in charge of the kitchen to heat it up for me.

I had not yet eaten after a long day of exams and all I could think of while in class was Mom's adobo waiting for me in the dorm refrigerator. When I finally went to pull out the jar, I immediately noticed it felt light—too light. I saw the duct tape had been peeled off the lid, and I desperately twisted the cap open to find the jar completely empty. My adobo was gone, except for some chicken bones picked clean of meat. The cruel thief had also left a note, written on a piece of paper torn from a notebook and stuck to the jar with a strip of discarded tape: "Ha, ha, it was delicious!"

I could barely read the words through my tears, and the lump in my throat threatened to choke me. I was hungry, tired, sleep-deprived and homesick, and all I had wanted was my mother's adobo. I knew how much it had taken out of her to cook it, and I suddenly felt angry. It was not just about the effort she had made but also the realization, made acute by seeing how her health had begun to decline, that Mom would not be around forever to lovingly cook such a meal. What else would soon be taken from me?

I felt a deep anger build up inside me. I was certain who the culprits were. Several weeks before, the barkada of girls from Bacolod, many of whom were the daughters of wealthy, sugarcane plantation–owning families, had suddenly stopped speaking to me. I was baffled by their snub as I thought we had become friends; after all, I shared a connection and common Visayan heritage through my mother. One of my roommates later whispered to me, "The Bacolod girls won't talk to you because they saw you chatting with the Ilocano girls."

The very thing that offered comfort to many of my

homesick dorm mates—gravitating toward other girls from the same province or region, or who spoke the same language—had created a kind of tribalism and rivalry along regional differences. It was trivial and petty, and I suddenly found myself in the middle of it.

Dejected and feeling friendless, I called my parents. My mother, who only saw the goodness in other people, didn't condemn the theft. Instead, she told me to pray for whoever had taken it.

"Be kind to them. It will surprise them how kind you are, no matter what they did to you," she told me. "There must be something wrong in their lives that is making them unhappy and makes them bully others.

"Be kind. Be nice. It will be worth the effort."

Despite my hurt and anger, I took my mother's advice to heart. I decided not to let this incident dictate how the rest of my time at school would proceed. I didn't rail at the girls I suspected and I didn't reciprocate their snubs. I wanted to show them that their actions would not influence or impact my own values and behavior and that their shortcomings would not become mine.

I began my college life full of doubt and insecurity about making friends and finding my own place away from home and family. I was unsure how to navigate this new life until I realized that I had a perfect example to follow: my mother, the Manila socialite turned farmer's wife.

She, too, had found herself in a completely unfamiliar setting, surrounded by strangers who weren't altogether welcoming. But instead of letting other people and circumstances determine her place in Tarlac, Mom drew upon her personal values and strengths, such as the belief in helping anyone in need and the ability to bring people together to achieve a common good, to carve out a place in the community that was uniquely hers.

She figured it out. She found a balance for herself, and I needed to do the same. I had to find the equilibrium within myself to accept the person I was in order to be happy with who I was.

Before I left for college, Mom gave me her gold Immaculate Conception pendant, the one she had held in prayer as she and her family fled their home as Manila was being bombed during WWII. It had been a talisman of her faith that she could persevere, and now it was my turn to draw strength and courage from it to face my own challenges.

By the end of my time at St. Paul, I was thriving in college. I made the Dean's List every semester, joined the Spanish Club, honed my public relations skills with the Public Relations Unit (PRU) of Miss Juco, a contemporary and former schoolmate of my mother; joined the school's drama club Paulinian Player's Guild, and created content for *The Paulinian,* our class yearbook.

I have loved writing since I was a little girl, and I used to write short stories, poetry and even storybooks which I illustrated myself. I knew by high school that I wanted to pursue a career in a writing-related field, so I chose to major in Mass Communications in the hopes of one day landing a job in broadcasting, advertising or print journalism.

At St. Paul, I wrote and produced TV shows in an actual

Good friends Vicky Quirino, Nini Quezon, Lulu Reyes, Chona Kasten.
Malacanang Palace, Manila 1949.

studio and was even part of the production team for a live radio program called *Lunchbox*. Much to my delight, I received job offers during my senior year in college and had a position waiting for me right after graduation as a copywriter at an advertising agency in Makati City in metro Manila.

Far from the little girl who went home crying because no one at school wanted to be her friend, I was elected dormitory president for two consecutive years. My dorm mates had become good friends, and they applauded and cheered me on when I won. Even the Bacolod girls became friendly, if not outright friends; after all, my elections were unanimous, which meant that even they, who had once snubbed me, had voted for me.

But the best things to happen from my time at St. Paul were the classmates who became my dearest friends for life: Veng Miranda, Tepton Quimbo, Lily Yap and Irene Obligacion. Soon after, close friendships were forged with Marissa, Pooch, Bibs, Suj, Idz, Melot, Pura, and Popi. We started by sharing common interests in our field of Mass Communications, but our camaraderie evolved into deep, lasting friendships as we shared joys and sorrows together, even after our college graduation.

We didn't just share the same class schedules; we grew together during a vital phase of our lives. We saw each other during some of our worst moments as well as our best times when the world was ours for the taking. To this day, we can pick up our friendship wherever we left off, as if we weren't continents apart. I finally found in these friends what anyone longs for: unconditional acceptance, true understanding, selflessness, and love.

It will be worth the effort, Mom had assured me. And as always, she was right.

Chapter 18

Evening Blossoms

March 1981

$\mathcal{M}$om did not want to fall asleep yet.

She was waiting for Isabel to arrive at the hospital. I warned her that it was stormy outside. A typhoon had been forecast and the increasingly fierce winds would likely delay my sister, who was taking her final exams and planned to ride the bus afterwards to the Philippine Heart Center for Asia in Quezon City where Mom had been admitted more than three weeks ago.

Maria Isabel was nineteen years old and two weeks away from graduating with honors from the College of the Holy Spirit in Manila. She had worked long and hard to earn her bachelor's degree in food and nutrition, and our parents couldn't have been more proud and excited for her. Mom was especially eager to see her graduate. She held out hope that she would be well enough to leave the hospital to attend, even if it meant having to be wheeled on a gurney into the college auditorium.

Four years younger than me, Isabel had been skinny and sickly for most of her childhood, suffering from constant ear infections that plagued her into her teen years and respiratory infections that developed into a full-blown and severe asthmatic condition. When we were children, I would sometimes find her curled up in her bed or on the couch, gasping for breath. Perhaps these attacks affected her appetite as well because she was also a fussy eater from infancy. One of the few dishes she tolerated as a toddler was Mom's misua soup. Every day, our mother made it just for her. She would ladle the soup

broth, redolent of pungent garlic and savory pork, from a large
tureen into a small bowl. Chunky meatballs, silky tendrils
of misua noodles and tender slices of patola, or luffa gourd,
followed. It never failed to tempt Isabel to eat.

From a picky eater as a child, she grew up to be an
excellent and versatile cook. Like me, Isabel learned her way
around the kitchen from Mom, but she also had a natural
knack for developing her own versions of family favorites, like
her tangy paksiw na bangus (vinegar-stewed milkfish), which
she prepared in a pressure cooker to render the fish belly ever
so tender and tasty. There was also her specialty kinilaw na
tanguigue, with cubes of fresh, raw Spanish mackerel, sliced
cucumbers, red onions and bell peppers soaked in a punchy
marinade of vinegar, ginger and fiery siling labuyo (bird's eye
chilies). As wonderful as her savory dishes were, however, her
desserts were even better.

No one could resist Isabel's sweet creations. For Christmas, she baked multitudes of traditional fruit cakes and dec-
adent date bars called Food for the Gods to be given as gifts
to friends and family. Her delicate mango crepes laden with
heavy cream were nothing short of divine. And for guests
who dropped by for dinner, there was always her light and
sweet lychee-buko gelatin dessert.

For all the times my sister struggled with her health as
a child, our mother knew how to nurse her back to healthy
wholeness with her cooking. And now, Isabel was about to
graduate with a degree in food and nutrition, and she was determined to reciprocate Mom's care of her through the years.
"I'll go home to Tarlac with Mommy and Daddy after

graduation," she told me. "I'll take care of Mommy. Dad needs all the help."

I did not mention Isabel's plans to our parents, waiting instead for my sister to share the good news herself. It would make Mom so happy to have one of us back at the house. Dad had previously brought up the idea of supporting Isabel for graduate school at the University of the Philippines to earn a master's in food technology, which elated Mom. No matter how fragile her health was at the moment, our parents stayed on course and continued to make plans for me and Isabel. Their optimism and positive outlook were like beams of sunshine keeping at bay the somber aura that was slowly seeping into our lives.

....

Mom had developed polycystic kidney disease, the same debilitating illness that had taken her mother and then two of her brothers, Willie and Bobby, within a year of each other in the early 1960s. The hereditary condition ran in Lola Nena's side of the family and spared none of her children: the youngest, Poncy, was also afflicted and hospitalized at the same time as his sister. While Mom was being treated at PHCA, Tito Poncy was about six miles away at the Medical City Hospital in Mandaluyong.

As the siblings were fighting for their lives, we, their families, decided together not to tell them about each other's condition. After the first terrible fight over Tito Poncy's decision to sell their childhood home in Malate, the ongoing disagreement strained their relationship. When my uncle finally succeeded in selling the house, Mom suffered a heart attack over the stress of the news. But it wasn't the reason we kept quiet. We knew they still cared for each other deeply, despite their partial estrangement, and that neither would receive news of the other's illness well. None of us wanted them to worry about each other when they needed their strength to fight for their own health.

Dad, Isabel and I regularly checked on Tito Poncy through phone calls with his wife, Tessie; when we could manage it, we also visited him in Mandaluyong. We never let on how badly Mom's condition was progressing.

After she was diagnosed in 1979, Mom began treatment at PHCA where some of the best nephrologists in Manila practiced. Every month for two years, we drove three hours from Tarlac for her hemodialysis sessions. It was a grueling trip, but she never complained.

One month, however, something changed. Even after the hemodialysis, Mom seemed worse off than before, and her doctors decided she should remain longer at the center for observation. Her malfunctioning kidneys were now affecting other organs in her body. Her blood count went off in all directions and her blood pressure fluctuated from extremely high to dangerously low, only to climb high again. Her liver was severely impacted: the doctors had found a tumor, which required emergency surgery between her dialysis sessions. She also developed diabetes and her underlying cardiac condition worsened. The incessant bloodwork and IV infusions had left her hands and arms mottled with black and blue patches of bruising.

Mom had lost a lot of weight due to the low-salt and no-sugar diet prescribed by her doctors, and she appeared so thin and frail. I feared her legs would crumple whenever I helped her get up from bed to walk to the bathroom. She had gotten so weak, Dad and I had to lift her so she could sit upright in bed. There was not a single organ in her body that was physically alright, and yet her determination to put up a brave front for her family was strong and steady.

As we waited for Isabel, Mom asked me to turn on the radio so she could listen to music and stay awake. I could tell she was mustering her strength to stay alert for her younger daughter's arrival. The lilting voice of Debby Boone singing "You Light Up My Life" filled the hospital room.

"I love this song," Mom murmured, smiling at me as I tucked a beige thermal blanket around her thin legs. I reached for the small yellow transistor radio I had placed on the bedside table and turned up the volume a little bit more. The table was filled with an assortment of medicine bottles surrounding an image of Our Lady of Perpetual Help with Mom's rose-red rosary draped on one side of the frame.

She shivered a little, so I adjusted the buttons of the pink flannel top she wore over her hospital gown. I smoothed tendrils of her hair that fell over her forehead. Once a glossy midnight black, her hair was now completely gray, and I fixed it daily into a neat bun atop her head.

"Do you need another blanket?" I asked.

"No, hija. Can you give me my rosary?" Mom turned her face toward the side table.

"My ahijado Ben gave me this," she said in happy remembrance, as I lifted the delicate rosary from its perch and placed it in her hands. I already knew the story, but Mom enjoyed reminiscing about how her favorite godson Ben Avanceña, the son of her best friend and my own godmother Tita Nini, had given her the rosary when he recently visited her in the hospital. She spoke of him with all the love and affection she held for his mother.

"He came from Europe and brought me this rosary as a pasalubong. How thoughtful of him," she recounted again, as her fingers lightly stroked the beads. "Remind me to write him a thank-you note."

I placed my hand over hers as she held the rosary, and I felt how chilled her fingers had become. Mom clasped my hands, appreciating their warmth.

"Tita Nini left after you fell asleep," I told her, and she smiled at the mention of her dearest friend.

Through the long weeks and months of my mother's illness and prolonged hospital stays, Tita Nini visited regularly and it was obvious how her presence brightened Mom's day. "She said she'll be back this week," I reassured her.

The thought of my godmother visiting again strengthened me. Tita Nini's name and phone number were the first entry in my address book, highlighted in yellow and underlined in red ink. She was the first call I made when we rushed Mom to the hospital a few years ago after her monumental argument with Tito Poncy over the fate of the house on Indiana Street.

"Call me if anything happens, anytime," Tita Nini later insisted, offering herself unconditionally as a lifeline in case of any emergency with Mom. It meant the world to me. Many years later, her daughter Nene Quezon Avanceña would tell me, "More than anyone else, she understood what pain and sorrow was, and what it did to a person. So she knew how to bring you comfort on the darkest days…"

Outside the room, I could hear the muted sounds of doctors being paged over the intercom. Faint whiffs of chlorine bleach and sanitizing alcohol seeped in from the hallway. I looked through the sliding glass door of the room, toward the hexagonal nurses' station where doctors and nurses were checking patients' charts as electronic monitors around them beeped and flickered. I was getting tired of the hospital. I knew Mom was, too, as well as Dad, though neither of them ever complained.

My father never lost faith throughout Mom's illness. He kept his spirits high and never grumbled during the seemingly endless weeks of her hospital stay. Day after day, he sat quietly on the sofa by her bedside, reading a book, the Bible or the newspaper. He never asked for anything more than what he needed at the moment.

"When your mom gets better, we'll get a house here in Manila, so she can be closer to the hospital," he announced one day. It was surprising news to me. Dad loved our home in Tarlac and had always been inflexible about living anywhere else. Mom could never convince him to have a second house in Manila. Though I doubted it would happen, I found comfort in hearing him make plans for a future with Mom.

Her previous stays at PHCA didn't last longer than a week, but now, three weeks had already passed. Unlike her other hospital confinements, Mom didn't seem to be getting better this time. Her nephrologist Dr. Soriano gave no sign of losing hope, but we dreaded what seemed more and more to be inevitable.

The dialysis treatments became more frequent, from once a month to three times a week. And it was no longer hemodialysis but rather peritoneal dialysis in which a tube was inserted directly into her lower abdomen. I cringed whenever they stuck the long, large needle and tube into Mom's stomach. I tried not to flinch so she wouldn't see how it pained me to think of how it must hurt her.

Always practical, Mom told me frankly, "Peritoneal dialysis is the last resort."

"How do you know?" I asked, trying not to sound despairing.

"It's what they did to Willie before he died."

My heart lurched with pain at that thought.

....

The morning passed and Mom had no appetite. She was hungry, she told me, but she didn't care for the strict and flavorless diet imposed on her. She missed the comforts of our home on the highway, the warmth of the kitchen and the delicious, home-cooked meals prepared there. She missed being healthy enough to be up and about and busy cooking for us.

Mom's lunch tray remained covered, turning cold and even more unappetizing on the moveable table at the foot of her bed. She refused to even look at it.

"Where will you and Isabel take Dad for lunch?" It was

typical of her to worry about how we were eating when she was ignoring her own hunger. I glanced at Dad, who looked up from his reading and smiled at me without saying a word.

Just then, Isabel noisily arrived, sliding open the glass door with an audible swoosh and a jubilant announcement, "I'm here!"

She was dressed in a t-shirt, blue jeans and her shoulder-length hair tied in a pony tail. A backpack was slung over one shoulder and she held a dripping-wet umbrella, which she set on the floor as she leaned over the bed to give Mom a kiss and then sat down next to Dad on the sofa. "Hello Mommy! Hi Dad!" she greeted them cheerily.

Mom's face lit up with joy at the sight of her younger daughter. I had never really paid attention to how she looked at me and Isabel whenever we walked into a room to greet her. But this time, I saw clearly her luminous expression as she weakly lifted her arms to embrace my sister. Despite her pallor, her whole being seemed to glow brightly with happiness.

"Has comida ya?" she immediately asked. *Have you eaten?*

Isabel laughed, playfully rubbing her tummy to acknowledge her hunger. "Not yet, Mommy."

It was then decided she and Dad would go to the cafeteria for lunch while I stayed with Mom. My fiancé, Elpi, was coming to the hospital, so he and I could have a late lunch together after the two of them returned. Dad quietly slid the glass door shut behind them, and I watched as they walked past the nurses' station toward the elevator. His head was bent and his shoulders drooped; he looked tired. Isabel walked beside him, talking animatedly, no doubt excited about her upcoming graduation.

I turned off the radio and switched on the television, turning the dial to find a show. I looked back at Mom on her bed to ask what she wanted to watch, but I already knew the answer.

"It's okay. You watch. Estoy cansada," she said. *I'm tired.*

I sat on the chair next to her and rested my arm on her bed. It was moments like these, when I was alone with Mom, that she often chose to tell me stories of the past or things that were weighing on her mind but didn't want Dad to hear.

"Your Daddy is having a hard time with me in the hospital."

Her voice was calm but I didn't want to look at her, knowing it would make me cry. I didn't want her to see me in tears.

"You are finding it difficult to take time off from work to be with me."

"It's okay. My boss is understanding," I quickly reassured her. "They let me bring home my writing, so I can fulfill my deadlines."

She looked directly into my eyes. "Hija mia, tell your dad to look for a hospice for me. One that has nuns who can take care of me."

I felt my insides tremble. I knew what putting her in a hospice meant. I didn't like hearing Mom talk like this, as if she knew she was at the end of her life. My heart was already breaking, though I tried to control myself.

She continued gently, "Help your dad find a place. I am not getting better. It's time to find someone else to look after me. I don't want to burden your dad or you girls anymore."

I didn't trust myself to answer. How do you respond when your mother tells you that only palliative care is the best thing for her now? How do you answer a plea to hand her over to strangers, even caring ones? A raw sense of grief clawed at my insides.

I was turning twenty-four in a few months, but I didn't feel like an adult who was ready to accept what my terminally ill mother had apparently already accepted. I wanted to be a five year old again, clutching her hand as she comforted me.

I didn't know what I would do without Mom, if I could live without her. But I was afraid to tell her these painful thoughts. So I stayed silent. Just this once, I wished a nurse would pop in like they always did to ask my mother how she was feeling or to take her pulse or any of the dozens of things they always seemed to be doing every few minutes. But no one interrupted us.

I hoped Mom would fall asleep so that we didn't have to finish this conversation.

"Hija," she said softly. *Daughter.*

I finally turned to look at her, to ask if she was in pain or uncomfortable. Her tired eyes were brimming with tears. I felt a lump in my throat as I held back my own tears to hide the fact that my heart seemed to be shattering into a million pieces.

"Take care of the house. Take care of your Daddy and your sister, always," she whispered.

"Cuidate bien. Te quiero mucho." *Take good care of yourself. I love you very much.*

She spoke so softly, I had to lean closer to hear her. I stared blankly at the television, holding her hand as she fell asleep.

....

Mom slipped into a coma later that day. We never got to talk to her again. She died a week later, on March 14, 1981—the day before Isabel's college graduation. She had fought so hard with every bit of her formidable will to be there.

At first, I questioned why God would take His most faithful daughter just one day before an event that mattered so much to her, but then I thought perhaps it was His gift to me, Dad and Isabel. Perhaps He meant to show us that our lives would continue and that we would be fine because of everything Mom had taught us by her own example. She knew we would be okay when she was gone because she had shown us how to be brave, to have faith, to retain hope and to give infinite love.

The days that followed, as we prepared our farewell to Mom and then mourned at her funeral, were clouded with grief. For the first time in my twenty-four years of life, I saw my father weep. It was a quiet, private moment when we were alone, and only Isabel and I were with him.

"It's time to say goodbye to your mother—" Dad said in a trembling voice, unable to finish his sentence. We rushed to his side, and the three of us embraced tightly, crying without restraint.

My father's courage was indomitable, especially during the last years of Mom's illness. On her most difficult days, when pain engulfed her, he would hold his wife's hand and smile at her, easing all her pain. Now, at this moment, Dad's sobs pierced through my heart like shrapnel and tore through whatever inner strength I had left.

But we still had one more difficult task to face: we had not yet told Tito Poncy that his sister had died.

Tita Tessie feared the news would be so upsetting, it might worsen his condition. So, three weeks passed before Dad suggested it was finally time. She remained reluctant, but he urged her gently, "This is when you leave it in the hands of God."

Elpi drove me and Isabel back to Manila to see our uncle. Before we entered his room, we stood outside with Tita Tessie to discuss how best to break the news. I was elected as the messenger. The thought of how upset Tito Poncy might be unsettled me, but I opened the door and walked in as bravely as I could ahead of the others.

The curtains were drawn and cold air rushed from the air-conditioner. I sat down on a chair next to his bedside. He seemed to be asleep, but as if sensing my presence, he opened his eyes and turned his head to look at me. He greeted me by name and asked after Isabel, his gaze clear and lucid. I cleared my throat and painfully started the conversation.

"Tito Poncy, I have something to tell you. A few weeks ago, Mommy got very sick. It was more serious this time. Even with frequent dialysis, she did not get better."

I was avoiding what needed to be said, and I tried hard to keep the tears from falling. Tito Poncy looked at me direct-ly. He was calm and peaceful, which gave me the strength to continue. "I'm sorry. Mommy got very sick and fell into a coma. She died."

I hurriedly tried to explain, "I'm sorry we didn't tell you sooner, but she's gone now."

Tito Poncy's expression remained serene, and his reply surprised all of us in the room. "I know. I know she died. I've known all this time.

"Lulu came to me," he revealed. "She came to say good-bye."

I stared at my uncle, unsure of how to process what he had just told us, but I didn't question him or voice any doubt or skepticism. He didn't say he dreamed of her. He was not emotional or upset in any way. By the tranquility that gentled his features, I knew he spoke with true belief and a sense of reconciliation.

Somehow, some way, in some dimension that defied logic, physics and human rationality, and for reasons only God knew, Mom had come to make peace and say goodbye to the baby brother she had doted on all her life. Her capacity for love and forgiveness, though tested by their estrangement, was infinite, boundless and too strong to let death prevent a final extraordinary reunion.

Tito Poncy was in and out of the hospital for the next two years as he continued to fight his kidney disease. He died in December 1983 and was laid to rest in the Manila North Cemetery next to his parents and brothers.

....

Day after day, time passes languidly yet inexorably, like water flowing down a stream. I remember how Mom and I would pick her favorite florals from the yard every evening at five o'clock, before she started cooking supper. As the sun set slowly over the Tarlac countryside, turning the skies a warm copper color, we gathered tiny and delicate jasmine growing on the trellis, intoxicatingly fragrant sampaguita garlanding the walkway, and pristine white camias from bushes lining the front of the house. She would string light green ylang-ylang into a lei, and after dinner, she would stand by the window to inhale the heady scent of night-blooming dama de noche. She treasured the wonderful perfume of these evening blossoms— the result of years of tending to every vine, every shrub and every flower bed so that they bloomed into their full beauty when the time came.

The end of a person's life arrives inevitably and on its own terms, and we have no control over it. But we can find solace and meaning in it. In her last conscious moments, Mom asked me to take care of my father, my sister and myself, as she always used to do for us. Would she have asked such a thing of me, handed me such a responsibility, if she didn't think I could handle it? Just as she had tended the flowers in our garden, she had taken care of me, so that when the time came, I could blossom on my own.

When I think of all my mother's accomplishments, adversities and triumphs, I always ask myself if I have even an ounce of her courage, if I am strong enough and capable enough to persevere through any hardship.

As I look back to my last conversation with Mom, when she asked me to continue caring for our family as she had always done, I realize that she had answered for me.

Yes.

Lulu Reyes Besa,
October 31, 1913 – March 14, 1981

Chapter 19

**Afterword:
Words of Gratitude**

My mother neither sought nor expected laurels for her efforts to help others, but there was no question in the minds of many people that she deserved them. She was presented with plaques, trophies and medals—too many for me to count. There were presentations in recognition for her work with the Young Ladies Association of Charity establishing branches around the country, raising funds for YLAC projects and helping to build community clinics and public schools. In 1953, she received the Ateneo de Manila University's Ozanam Award, named for French Catholic scholar and social advocate Blessed Frédéric Ozanam, and awarded annually to a person or group who has demonstrated a deep commitment to social action guided by their Christian faith. And her alma mater St. Paul University Manila bestowed on her its highest honor for distinguished alumni, the Fleur de Lis Award, in 1962 for her lifelong philanthropy and civic work.

She received international recognition as well: for her efforts in raising funds to build the National Shrine of Our Mother of Perpetual Help, known simply as Baclaran Church, Pope Pius XII and the Holy See in Rome inducted her in 1954 as a dame of the Order of the Holy Sepulchre, a nearly millennium-old Catholic order of knighthood. Before then, she was awarded two Medals of Freedom in 1947 by a grateful US government for her courageous actions in aiding American POWs during World War II.

Through the years, there must have been hundreds of visitors to our house in Tarlac, yet not once did I hear Mom mention these awards to them, much less bring them out to show off. I have no doubt she was grateful for the accolades, yet she remained humble and down to earth about them. The medals and plaques—still in their original boxes—remained tucked away in Dad's home office, where they filled the two-shelf cabinets that stood like squat sentinels behind his desk.

Dad used the office to conduct his business affairs and to meet with his farmhands and employees, so Isabel and I were allowed to enter only during the evening to have our home-work checked.

One day, I snuck into the office and gingerly opened one of the cabinets where Mom's awards were kept. I was awe-struck by the neat stacks of velvet boxes containing medals; shiny plaques nestled in silk-lined cases; crisp certificates filed in leather folders; albums filled with photographs of different ceremonies; and scrapbooks bulging with news clippings. I wondered why she didn't display them on the walls or in a glass case, like the sports trophies I saw exhibited at school.

She later told me Dad had promised to build her a vitri-na, or glass display case. It was a promise he was never able to keep—but not for lack of trying. Every time Pedro, one of the farmhands and a skilled carpenter, would come to the house to start building the case, Mom would suddenly remember that my sister or I needed a new headboard or a side table, which would then take a few weeks to build, paint and var-nish. When the project was done and he was ready to start on the vitrina, something else would be needed more urgently: a sideboard to store dishes; a stereo cabinet for Dad; or barstools for the kitchen. As far as Mom was concerned, there were always more important projects for Pedro to make than a display cabinet to showcase her awards.

But tucking away the medals and citations along with her reticence about sharing her experiences had the unfortunate effect of leaving me and my sister to grow up with little awareness of her accomplishments during the war. Perhaps she did so out of a desire to spare us, as children, the knowledge of how cruel the world and people can be; or maybe she had simply learned to live in the moment, to enjoy the present rather than dwell on the past. Whatever her reasons, Mom didn't tell me or Isabel the whole story about her wartime exploits, and as a result we may not have fully appreciated what all those awards really represented.

In 1972, a deluge of rain from Typhoon Gloring caused severe flooding throughout Central Luzon, including our province and town. Our house on the highway did not escape the deep floodwaters when the Tarlac dam failed, and Mom's awards were badly damaged. Her two Medals of Freedom rusted terribly and the ribbons could hardly be cleaned of the dirty floodwater that had soaked into them. Various plaques were also ruined as the metal parts corroded and the wood mounts warped from being waterlogged. The only items that avoided substantial damage were the Papal award and certificate, which I eventually brought with me to the US. The rest—too damaged to display now—remain in storage back home in Tarlac.

I could dwell on the loss of these material items but after spending twenty years researching my mother's story, I discovered an even more valuable, indestructible trove of tributes in the words left behind by people who knew her, witnessed her efforts and were directly impacted by her humanitarianism.

Before my mother was awarded her two Medals of Freedom, there first came nominations from former prisoners of war and civilian internees—at least thirty-seven of them, according to historian Dr. Ernesto de Pedro. These nominations were supported by poignant written evidence left behind by POWs who had scribbled her name on scraps of paper found hidden in the walls or protectively buried in the ground at Bilibid, Cabanatuan and other Japanese prison camps. Dr. de Pedro noted that even Japanese seminarians who were part of the "Catholic unit" of the Japanese Propaganda Corps' Religious Section left admiring accounts about her.

When Mom received her awards from the US government—first a standard Medal of Freedom given on August 11, 1947, followed soon after by another with the distinguished addition of a Silver Palm on September 25—the citation that accompanied them succinctly described her honorable actions and cited "her inspiring bravery and unfaltering devotion to the cause of freedom." General George F. Moore, who was himself a POW for three years, personally presented the medals and called her "more than a soldier" and "one of the outstanding heroines of World War II."

In reading personal memoirs and letters written by former prisoners like Bob Dow, and articles by historians and journalists, the testimonials to Mom warmed my heart and filled me with such pride. Commodore Ramon Alcaraz, for instance, commended her bravery and patriotism, and compared her to Joan of Arc in his diary of his time inside the Malolos POW camp.

Likewise, Father Edwin Ronan, CP, who had established the Chaplains Aid Association with Mom as its first president and who spent two years as a POW in Japan, shared his warm memories of her in a letter written to Bob shortly after the war ended:

There are not to be found better than Lulu. For years she worked with me and was always the generous, patient and reliable person . . . She is the same good soul, always willing to work for others.

And her longtime friend Father Forbes Monaghan described her in his memoir, *Under the Red Sun*, as "a girl of a quiet beauty and a sincere friendliness that evoked in every one who met her the same sincere admiration." He wrote further:

To this wonderful girl Lulu, thousands of American and Filipino prisoners owed the fact that their lives were endurable, and hundreds that their lives were saved at all. [31]

Others spoke their words of admiration for my mother directly to me. Father James B. Reuter, SJ, was a twenty-six-year-old seminarian when he was imprisoned with other Jesuits, including Father Monaghan, in the Los Baños internment camp. He credited Mom's determination to provide food and medicine as a crucial part of his survival during his three years as an internee. I met him for the first time when I

31 Monaghan, 249

was fourteen years old and he was visiting Mom at the Manila Doctors' Hospital while she recuperated from surgery.

"Your mother is a very, very brave woman," he told me then.

A few years later, Father Reuter was the chaplain of St. Paul College where I was a student. I will never forget how his deep blue eyes looked into mine as I greeted him after Mass one Sunday.

"Do you have any idea how brave your mother is? God bless her," he said simply. He didn't say much more, but his gaze was steady and piercing, as if he were trying to etch the depth of his gratitude directly into my soul.

Some of the books and articles which mentioned Mom were published during her lifetime, but if she had read or even been aware of them, she never mentioned it to Dad or me and my sister. I also don't know if she was allowed to see the nominations submitted for her Medals of Freedom, or if she knew about how her name had been furtively written on random pieces of paper by suffering prisoners of war, many of whom did not live to feel freedom again.

Just as I finished writing this book, I received a copy of an article about Mom in a 1948 issue of the Catholic magazine *Extension,* and it contained a beautiful, stirring passage from the writer George Hagar that encapsulated the significance of those bits of paper and indeed all that has been written about her:

The men who wrote these testimonials to her help and loyalty speak from their thousand scattered graves. They were willing to die, but not without the hope that someday Lulu Reyes would know that they were grateful.[32]

All of these words about Mom are proof that the substantial and lasting impact she had on people's lives were well worth the hard work and dangerous risks she willingly accepted in order to help others, and I am absolutely certain she would have cherished them more than any medal or plaque on display. What greater reward could there possibly be than to be remembered with such admiration, respect, affection and gratitude long after events and persons have passed?

Among the reasons I finally wrote this book were so that her story can serve as an inspiration for everyone who reads it as well as to give my sons an opportunity to know their grandmother and her legacy of bravery, her devotion to faith and her commitment to humanity. But writing about my mother's trials and triumphs and researching her wartime heroism have also helped me to process her absence in my life, to recall the lessons she taught me and to learn to face fears as courageously as she did.

For all of this, I am grateful too.

32 Hagar, 18

Lulu Reyes receiving an award from First Daughter Vicky Quirino, as Nini Quezon looks on. Manila 1949.

Chapter 20

Recipes

ENSAYMADAS

Makes 20 to 24 ensaymadas

Ingredients

For the first rise:

1½ Tablespoons active dry yeast

1½ teaspoons granulated sugar

1 cup lukewarm water (about 98°F)

½ cup milk, at room temperature

½ cup all-purpose flour

For the second rise:

5 large egg yolks,
   at room temperature

¼ cup granulated sugar

1 cup all-purpose flour

For kneading and the third rise:

5 large egg yolks,
   at room temperature

½ cup melted unsalted butter

½ cup granulated sugar

3½ cups all-purpose flour,
   plus more if needed

1 Tablespoon vegetable oil

Cooking spray

For shaping and filling:

All-purpose flour, for the
   work surface

1½ cups grated cheddar cheese

For the topping:

1 large egg

½ cup milk

2 cups grated cheddar cheese

1 cup melted unsalted butter

1 cup granulated sugar

Procedure

First rise (10 minutes): In a the bowl of a stand mixer, combine the yeast, sugar, water, milk and flour. Mix well with a wooden spoon. Cover the bowl with a clean, dry kitchen towel and leave it in a warm spot in the kitchen for 10 minutes.

If the mixture has formed large bubbles after 10 minutes, it's ready for the second rise. If bubbles have not formed, then start the recipe over with new yeast.

Second rise (1 hour): Add the egg yolks, sugar and flour to the yeast mixture. Fit the mixer with the paddle attachment and combine the ingredients until smooth. Cover the bowl again with the kitchen towel and let the mixture rise for 1 hour in a warm spot of the kitchen, until dough mixture has risen to almost double in size.

Kneading and third rise (1 hour + 10 minutes): Add the egg yolks, melted butter and sugar to the yeast-flour mixture in the bowl. Mix well. Gradually add the flour as you mix. As the flour is incorporated and the dough starts to take shape, turn off the mixer and switch from the paddle to a dough hook.

Add the oil to the dough, then knead the dough with the hook for 8 to 10 minutes, until it is smooth and pulls away from the sides of the bowl. The dough should be soft but solid, not liquid like pancake batter. If it is still sticky and wet, add more flour a tablespoon at a time as you continue to knead, but do not add more than ¼ to ⅓ cup, or the ingredient proportions will be off for baking, and will result in dense buns.

Grease a clean bowl with a little cooking spray. Shape the dough into one large ball and place it in the bowl. Cover the bowl with a clean, dry kitchen towel and keep it in a warm spot in the kitchen. Let the dough rise for 1 hour, until it doubles in size.

Filling and forming the ensaymadas, and fourth rise (1 hour + 10 minutes for rising): Grease 20 to 24 (4-inch) fluted tart tins with cooking spray. (Do not use melted butter because it will burn on the bottom during baking!) Arrange the tins on a rimmed baking tray and set aside.

Punch the dough down with your fist. Take it out of the bowl and place on a clean, dry floured surface. Pinch off about ½ cup of dough and shape into a ball. Sprinkle flour on a rolling pin and flatten the ball into a long, flat rectangle, about 8 x 3 inches. Sprinkle about 1 tablespoon of the grated cheese over the rectangle. Be careful not to overfill or it will be hard to coil. Roll the cheese-topped rectangle lengthwise into a long rope. Pinch the dough with your fingers to seal the edges so that the cheese doesn't spill out.

To form a bun, hold down one of end of the rope on the surface. Holding the other end loosely, wind the rope around the center into a coil. Tuck in the ends within the dough. Place the spiral bun in a prepared tart tin. Repeat the process for the remainder of the dough and cheese filling. You should have 20 to 24 medium buns.

Cover the ensaymadas loosely with plastic wrap, then cover lightly with a clean, dry kitchen towel. Set the baking tray in a warm spot and let the buns rise for 1 hour and 10 minutes. The ensaymadas should double in size and fill in the sides of the tart tins.

Topping and baking the ensaymadas (25 minutes): Preheat the oven to 325°F.

Combine the egg and milk in a small bowl to make an egg wash. Gently brush each risen ensaymada with a few drops of egg wash.

Bake for 18 minutes, until the tops are light brown.

Remove the baking tray from the oven. Sprinkle about 2 teaspoons of cheese on each bun and return them to the oven. Continue baking for 7 minutes more, until a cake tester pierced through comes clean, or buns have an internal digital temperature of 185°F.

Let the ensaymadas cool for 5 minutes for easier handling.

Use a small sharp knife to loosen each ensaymada from the sides of the tart tin. Carefully remove each bun and place on a rack to cool. While the ensaymadas are still warm, brush the tops with the melted butter and sprinkle the rest of the grated cheese and the sugar over them.

Serve the ensaymadas warm or at room temperature. Or wrap individually in parchment or wax paper and store in refrigerator for 1 week or the freezer for 1 month.

PANCIT MOLO SOUP

Servings: 4 to 6

Ingredients

For the wontons:

1 pound ground pork

¾ cup minced peeled singkamas
   (jicama) or turnips
   (see Cook's Comment)

1 carrot, peeled and minced

2 large eggs, beaten

½ cup chopped scallion stalks,
   white parts only

2 Tablespoons soy sauce

¼ cup breadcrumbs

1 teaspoon salt

1 teaspoon ground black pepper

1 large egg, for egg wash

½ cup water

30 to 35 wonton wrappers

For the soup:

2 Tablespoons vegetable oil

1 medium onion, chopped

2 garlic cloves, minced

1 teaspoon patis (fish sauce)

8 to 10 cups chicken broth

2 scallion stalks, white and green
   parts chopped

2 cups shredded cabbage

1 teaspoon salt

1 teaspoon ground black pepper

Procedure

Make the wontons: In a large mixing bowl, combine the pork, singkamas, carrots, beaten eggs, scallions, soy sauce, breadcrumbs, salt and pepper. Mix well.

Make an egg wash by beating the egg and water. Set aside.

Lay out the wonton wrappers on a flat surface. Place a tablespoon of the pork mixture in the center of each wonton wrapper. Brush egg wash on the edges of the wrapper. Wrap by bringing one side of the wrapper over the filling but not covering it completely. Continue all around so that the wonton looks like an open flower. The filling should be visible from the top of the dumpling. Continue until all the wonton wrappers are filled and shaped. Cover the wontons with a clean, dry kitchen towel.

Prepare the soup: Heat the vegetable oil in a large stockpot over medium-high heat. Add the onions and garlic and sauté until onions are soft in 1 to 2 minutes. Season with the patis. Pour in the chicken broth and add the scallions. Cover the pot and bring the soup to a boil. When it is boiling, lower the heat to a simmer.

Carefully drop the wontons one by one into the soup. Add the shredded cabbage and continue cooking covered, until the wontons are cooked through, about 15 minutes.

Season the soup with the salt and pepper. Serve warm.

Cook's Comment: If singkamas (jicama) and turnips are not available, you may use peeled fresh or canned water chestnuts.

CALLOS

....

Servings: 4

Ingredients

1 to 2 pounds pata
 (pork hock or pig's knuckle)
1 pound pork belly,
 rind trimmed off
1¼ pounds ox tuwalya (tripe)
2 Tablespoons extra virgin olive oil
2 Spanish chorizo links, sliced
6 to 8 garlic cloves, minced
1 large onion, chopped
1 jar (6.5 ounces) pimientos,
 drained and chopped, or
 1 cup sliced red bell pepper
2 large potatoes, peeled
 and cubed (about ½ inch)

1 medium carrot, peeled
 and cubed (about ½ inch)
3 cups beef broth
1½ cups tomato sauce
1 cup tomato paste
1 cup garbanzos (chickpeas),
 drained
1 cup pitted Spanish olives,
 drained
¼ teaspoon salt
¼ teaspoon ground black pepper
½ cup grated Parmesan cheese
Steamed rice, for serving

Procedure

Tenderize the meats on the stovetop (Option 1): Place the pata, pork belly and tuwalya in a large stockpot and pour in enough water to cover (3 to 4 cups). Place the stockpot over high heat and cover it. Bring to a boil, then simmer over medium heat for about 2 hours, until the meats are tender. Skim off the filmy or foamy residue that comes to the top of the liquid during cooking.

When the pata is soft, remove it from the stockpot and place on a chopping board. Cut the meat from the bone and slice into 1-inch pieces. Set aside.

Remove the rest of the meat from the stockpot. Cut the pork belly and tuwalya into ½-inch pieces and also set aside. Discard the cooking water and rinse out the stockpot.

Tenderize the meats in an Instant Pot or electric pressure cooker (Option 2): Combine the pata, pork belly and tuwalya with enough water to cover in the interior pot. Close and lock the lid, then set the release valve setting to Sealing. Click "Manual" + "High Pressure" + "Meats or Stew" + "45 minutes." (If using another brand of cooker, please check the manual for equivalent instructions.)

When the cooking is complete, do a "Natural Release." Unlock the lid and remove the meats. Cut the pata meat from the bone. Slice the pata meat, pork belly and tuwalya into uniform 1-inch pieces and set aside. Discard the cooking water.

Cook the callos: Heat the olive oil in a large stockpot. Add the sliced chorizo and stir for 2 minutes to season the oil. When the edges of the slices turn crisp, remove them from the pan and set aside to drain on paper towels.

In the same stockpot, add the garlic, onions and pimientos or bell peppers to the oil and sauté until onions and pimientos are soft in 1 to 2 minutes.

Add the potatoes, carrots, pata meat, pork belly and tuwalya and stir to combine. Pour in the beef broth, tomato sauce and tomato paste and stir to distribute the paste. Simmer for about 20 minutes over low heat, until vegetables are soft and cooked.

Add the garbanzos and olives and return the chorizo slices to the pot. Season with salt and pepper and sprinkle with Parmesan cheese. Serve warm with freshly steamed rice.

CHICKEN RELLENO

Servings: 6

Ingredients

For the marinated chicken:

¼ cup soy sauce

2 Tablespoons calamansi
  or lemon juice

½ teaspoon salt

¼ teaspoon ground black pepper

1 whole (4-pound) roasting
  chicken, deboned (ask the
  butcher to do it for you)

For the stuffing:

½ pound lean ground pork

2 Spanish chorizo links, chopped

2 large eggs, beaten

1 medium onion, chopped

1 large celery stalk, chopped

1 cup chopped peeled carrots

½ cup sweet pickle relish

1 cup raisins

¾ cup grated cheddar cheese

2 Tablespoons all-purpose flour

½ teaspoon salt

¼ teaspoon ground black pepper

2 hard-boiled large eggs, sliced
  (about 6 slices each)

2 cans (4.6 ounces each) Vienna
  sausages, drained (about 12
  pieces per can)

½ cup unsalted butter, softened

For the gravy:

Drippings from the roasted
  chicken (you should have
  about 1 cup)

2 cups chicken broth

1 teaspoon Worcestershire sauce

2 Tablespoons cornstarch

¼ cup water

Salt and ground black pepper

Procedure

Marinate the chicken: Combine the soy sauce, calamansi or lemon juice, salt and pepper in a large bowl or heavy-duty plastic bag. Add the chicken, cover or seal and set aside to marinate for about 1 hour in the refrigerator.

Position a rack in the center of the oven and preheat to 375°F.

Stuff and roast the chicken: In a large bowl, combine the ground pork, chorizo, beaten eggs, onion, celery, carrots, pickle relish, raisins, cheese, flour, salt and pepper. Mix well.

Remove the chicken from the marinade and pat dry. Discard the marinade. Fill the chicken with the stuffing mixture by spooning one-half of the stuffing into the deboned bird. Insert the slices of hard-boiled eggs and sausages, distributing them evenly. Finish by spooning in the remaining half of the stuffing. Close the cavity of the chicken by securing the loose skin together with toothpicks, so that the stuffing does not fall out.

Rub the softened butter all over the chicken skin. Wrap the entire bird in aluminum foil and place it breast side up in a foil-lined roasting pan.

Roast the chicken for 1 hour and 30 minutes, or until completely cooked, and the juices run clear when the thickest part is pierced. If using a thermometer to check doneness, the internal temperature in the thick part of the thigh should read 165°F. The temperature should also be the same for the stuffing, indicating it is cooked as well.

When the chicken is fully cooked, carefully open the foil and let the bird roast for 10 minutes more, until golden brown. Remove the pan from the oven and cool on the counter for at least 15 minutes. Pour the drippings from the roasting pan into a medium pot, skimming off excess fat, and set aside.

Place the chicken relleno on a bandejado (oval plate) or large serving platter and slice into serving pieces. The slice should have the stuffing encased by the chicken meat. Cover relleno loosely with foil to keep warm while cooking the gravy. *(continued)*

Cook the gravy: Add the broth and Worcestershire sauce to the drippings and bring to a boil over medium heat. In a small bowl, dissolve the cornstarch in the water, stirring briskly to remove any lumps. When the drippings mixture starts to boil, add the cornstarch slurry. Continue stirring until the sauce thickens, about 2 minutes. Season with salt and pepper. Serve the gravy on the side.

CANONIGO

Servings: 4 to 6

Ingredients

For the caramel syrup:

1 tablespoon unsalted butter, softened

1 cup granulated sugar

For the meringue:

8 large egg whites

½ teaspoon cream of tartar

¾ cup granulated sugar

For the custard cream sauce:

8 large egg yolks

3 Tablespoons granulated sugar

1 can (12 ounces) evaporated milk

1 teaspoon pure vanilla extract

2 Tablespoons unsalted butter

1 Tablespoon rum (optional)

Procedure

Preheat the oven to 350°F.

Prepare the pan and make the syrup: Grease the sides of a 9-inch round cake pan with the softened butter and set aside.

Add the sugar to a small, heavy saucepan set over medium heat. In 5 to 6 minutes, the sugar will melt and start to bubble and turn a light golden brown. As the sugar cooks, tilt the pan around to level off the caramel syrup. Once the sugar has transformed entirely into a thick syrup, quickly pour the syrup into the prepared cake pan. Make sure the syrup is distributed evenly by tilting the pan, then set it aside.

Make the meringue: Use an electric mixer to beat the egg whites and cream of tartar at the highest speed until fine bubbles form. Gradually add the sugar, a tablespoon at a time, until soft peaks form. Pour the meringue into the caramel-lined cake pan.

Prepare a water bath in a larger baking pan that can accommodate the 9-inch pan. Place the smaller pan inside the larger pan and pour in enough tap water to come halfway up the sides of the smaller pan. Place the pans in the oven and bake for 30 minutes, until firm, and cake tester comes clean.

Cook the custard cream sauce: While meringue is baking, combine the egg yolks, sugar and evaporated milk in the top pan of a double boiler and fill the lower pan with water. Bring the water to a boil over medium-high heat and cook, stirring continuously, until the mixture thickens, 20 to 25 minutes.

When the custard has thickened, remove the pan from the heat. Whisk in the vanilla, butter and, if desired, the rum. Set aside to cool for at least 30 minutes.

Unmold the meringue from the cake pan by loosening the sides with a knife, then inverting it on a rimmed dessert platter. The caramel will coat the top and drip down the sides of the meringue. Spoon the custard cream sauce on top and slice individual pieces to serve.

CHICKEN AND PORK ADOBO

Servings: 4

Ingredients

1 cup white vinegar

2 Tablespoons soy sauce

1 garlic head, separated and
   peeled (about 8 cloves)

1 Tablespoon black peppercorns

1½ to 2 pounds bone-in chicken
   cuts (about 6 pieces)

1 pound pork shoulder or pork
   belly, excess fat trimmed off,
   cut into 2-inch cubes

2 cups chicken or pork broth

2 bay leaves

½ teaspoon salt

½ teaspoon ground black pepper

Steamed rice, for serving

Procedure

Combine the vinegar, soy sauce, garlic and peppercorns in a large bowl or shallow baking pan. Add the chicken and pork pieces. Cover the container and refrigerate for 6 hours or overnight.

When you're ready to cook, transfer the meats and marinade to a large stockpot. Pour in the chicken or pork broth, then add the bay leaves, salt and pepper. Cook uncovered at a slow simmer for 1 hour and 30 minutes, until the sauce is reduced to a thick gravy and the meats are cooked completely, the juices run clear if thighs are pierced. Or the instant read thermometer registers 165°F.

Remove the bay leaves from the gravy. Serve the adobo warm with steamed rice.

Cook's Comment: If desired, once the adobo is cooked, remove the chicken and pork pieces from the gravy in the stockpot. Pan-fry the meats in vegetable oil in a large skillet over medium heat until crisp. Pour the gravy over the fried adobo pieces and serve while still crunchy and warm.

BEEF MORCON

Servings: 4

Ingredients

For the marinated beef:

2-pound piece lean beef
   tenderloin or skirt steak

¼ cup soy sauce

2 Tablespoons calamansi or
   lemon juice

For the sauce:

2 Tablespoons vegetable oil

2 garlic cloves, minced

1 onion, chopped

1 cup chopped tomatoes

½ cup tomato paste

1 cup tomato sauce

2 cups beef broth

½ teaspoon salt

¼ teaspoon ground black pepper

For the filling:

2 hard-boiled large eggs, sliced

10 canned Vienna sausages,
   drained

2 ham slices, deli-style,
   cut into 2-inch strips

2 whole sweet pickles, sliced

2 red or green bell peppers,
   seeded and sliced

1 medium carrot, peeled and
   julienned into 2-inch strips

Butcher's twine for tying the
   beef roll

Procedure

Tenderize and marinate the beef: Prepare the beef by pounding the whole slab with a meat mallet to tenderize. You want it to be about 12 x 10 inches and ¼ inch thick.

Combine the soy sauce and calamansi juice in a shallow baking dish. Add the beef, cover and set aside to marinate.

Start the sauce: Add the vegetable oil to a large, heavy stockpot over medium heat. Sauté the garlic and onions for about 1 to 2 minutes, until onions are soft. Add the tomatoes and cook until soft.

(continued)

Stir in the tomato paste, tomato sauce, and beef broth, and season with salt and pepper. Let the tomato mixture simmer on low heat for at least 25 minutes, until thick and tastes sweet.

Meanwhile, fill the beef: Remove the tenderized beef from the marinade and pat dry with paper towels. Place the beef on a chopping board. Following the long edge, neatly arrange in separate and alternate rows the hard-boiled eggs, sausages, ham, pickles, bell peppers and carrots. Roll the beef away from you, like rolling a burrito, to close, tightly enclosing the fillings inside. Tie both ends and the center with butcher's twine so that the ingredients will not burst out while cooking.

Place the beef roll in the simmering tomato sauce. Cook on low heat for 40 minutes, turning the roll halfway through cooking, until the beef is tender and cooked well-done, with an internal temperature of 160 F if using a digital thermometer, and the sauce has reduced to a thick gravy.

When done, transfer the beef morcon to a platter. Cut off the twine and discard. Spoon the tomato sauce over the morcon. Slice the roll into individual servings.

FRIED LUMPIA UBOD

Makes 12 to 14 lumpia

Ingredients

For the filling:

2 Tablespoons vegetable oil

4 garlic cloves, chopped

1 medium onion, chopped

2 scallion stalks, white and green
parts separated, chopped

1 pound shrimp, shelled
and chopped

1 medium carrot, peeled
and julienned

2 Tablespoons patis (fish sauce)

2 pounds fresh or canned ubod
(heart of palm), julienned,
about 3 cups

½ teaspoon salt

¼ teaspoon ground black pepper

For the lumpia:

1 large egg

½ cup water

12 to 14 lumpia (egg roll)
wrappers, at room temperature

½ cup vegetable oil, for frying

For the dipping sauce:

½ cup white vinegar

2 Tablespoons soy sauce

1 Tablespoon finely chopped
onions

2 garlic cloves, minced

Pinch of salt

¼ teaspoon ground black pepper

Procedure

Make the filling: Heat the vegetable oil in a large skillet and sauté
the garlic, onions and scallion whites. Add the shrimp, carrots and
patis. Stir well to blend. Add the ubod to the mixture. Season with
salt and pepper. Cook for 8 to 10 minutes, until ingredients are soft.
When done, set the filling aside to cool.

Wrap the lumpia: Mix the egg and water to make an egg wash.
Place 2 tablespoons of the cooled filling in the center of one lumpia
wrapper and shape it into a long line. Brush the edges of the wrapper with egg wash, then fold the left and right edges inward before

(continued)

carefully rolling the wrapper like a burrito. Lumpia should be about 4 to 5 inches long, and 1 inch wide. Seal the edge with a brush of egg wash. Set the filled lumpia aside on a large plate. Repeat for the remaining wrappers and filling. Refrigerate the uncooked lumpia, covered loosely with foil, for about an hour to firm up. Chilled uncooked lumpia tends to result in crispier logs after deep-frying.

Make the dipping sauce: Whisk together the vinegar, soy sauce, onions and garlic in a small bowl. Season with salt and pepper, then set aside until you're ready to serve the lumpia.

Fry the lumpia: Heat ½ cup of vegetable oil in a large nonstick skillet over medium-high heat. When the oil is hot enough, and heat is up to 370°F, add several pieces of lumpia, taking care not to crowd too many in the skillet. Fry the lumpia for 3 to 5 minutes, until crisp, turning them to cook evenly. When the wrapper is golden brown, remove the lumpia from the skillet and drain on paper towels. Repeat with the remaining lumpia pieces. If amount of oil decreases while cooking, pour ¼ cup more, and give it 3 to 4 minutes to heat up again.

Garnish with the reserved scallion greens. Serve warm and crisp with dipping sauce on the side.

Cook's Comment: Fresh ubod (heart of palm) are sold in Asian markets seasonally in America. It is easier to find canned ubod in Asian groceries and online sources year round.

BOBBY'S PAKSIW NA BANGUS

Servings: 2

Ingredients

1 pound whole bangus (milkfish),
   gutted, scales left on, sliced
   into 3 or 4 pieces

3 cups water

2 Tablespoons salt

1 medium onion, sliced

6 garlic cloves, minced

1-inch piece fresh ginger,
   peeled and sliced

1 large Asian eggplant
   (about 4 to 5 ounces),
   sliced diagonally

1 ampalaya (bitter melon),
   about 20 grams, seeded, white
   membrane removed, then sliced
   lengthwise about 2 inches long

1 cup white vinegar

1 cup vegetable or fish broth

1 Tablespoon vegetable oil

1 Tablespoon patis (fish sauce),
   plus ¼ cup for dipping sauce

1 teaspoon black peppercorns

½ teaspoon salt

¼ teaspoon ground black pepper

2 pieces whole siling mahaba
   (finger chiles)

Steamed rice, for serving

Procedure

Place the cleaned bangus portions in a bowl and add the water and salt. Soak the fish for 30 minutes. Drain and discard the salted water and set the fish aside.

Layer the sliced onion on the bottom of a medium stockpot. Arrange the fish portions on top of the onions. Sprinkle the garlic and ginger over the pieces. Nestle the eggplant and ampalaya slices around the fish, then pour the vinegar, broth, oil and 1 tablespoon of the patis over the fish and vegetables. Season with the pepper-

(continued)

corns, salt and ground pepper. Add the whole siling mahaba last; if added too soon, their spiciness may overpower the other flavors.

Simmer the fish uncovered and over medium heat for 25 to 30 minutes, until the fish is cooked and the vegetables are soft. Remove the stockpot from the heat and let cool to room temperature.

When the paksiw has cooled, transfer the fish, vegetables and broth to a covered container and refrigerate for one day.

The next day, reheat the paksiw na bangus and serve warm with steamed rice and a side of patis for dipping.

Cook's Comment: Salmon belly makes a good substitute if bangus is not available.

WILLIE'S BEEF POCHERO

Servings: 4

Ingredients

For the pochero:

¼ cup vegetable oil

2 large fully ripe plantains, peeled
and sliced diagonally into
2-inch pieces

2 Spanish chorizo links, sliced

3 pounds beef stew meat,
cut into 2-inch cubes

4 garlic cloves, minced

1 large white onion, chopped

1 Tablespoon patis (fish sauce)

2 medium potatoes, peeled
and quartered

1 medium carrot, peeled
and sliced in rounds

1 can (15 ounces) tomato sauce
or 2 cups Homemade Tomato
Sauce (see following recipe)

6 to 8 cups beef broth

½ teaspoon salt

¼ teaspoon ground black pepper

1 Tablespoon granulated sugar

1 cup sliced green beans
in 2-inch pieces

2 cups shredded cabbage

For serving:

Steamed rice

Eggplant Sauce
(see following recipe)

Procedure

Make the pochero: Heat the vegetable oil in a large stockpot over medium heat. When the oil is hot enough in 1 to 2 minutes, add the sliced plantains. Turn the pieces for 2 to 3 minutes to brown, then transfer them from the pot to paper towels and set aside. Do not drain or discard the oil in the pot.

In the same stockpot, stir-fry the chorizo for 2 minutes until lightly browned. Remove the chorizo from the pot and set aside to drain on paper towels. *(continued)*

Add the beef to the still-heated stockpot and brown the meat for 2 minutes. Toss in the garlic and onions and sauté for about 2 minutes, until garlic is crisp, and onions are soft. Add the patis, potatoes and carrots, followed by the tomato sauce and broth. Season with salt and pepper. Stir slightly to incorporate the flavors. Cover the stockpot and lower the heat to a simmer. Cook for about 1½ hours, until the beef is tender and the vegetables are soft.

Sprinkle the sugar over the pochero and stir, then add the green beans and cabbage. Cover the stockpot again and cook for another 8 minutes until the last vegetables added are soft. Finally, toss the reserved chorizo and plantains into the pochero.

Serve warm with steamed rice and side dishes of sliced plantains and eggplant sauce.

HOMEMADE TOMATO SAUCE
Makes 2 to 3 cups

2 Tablespoons extra virgin olive oil
1 Tablespoon minced garlic
1 medium white onion, chopped
6 to 8 large tomatoes, peeled
  and coarsely chopped

2 cups water
1 teaspoon granulated sugar
½ teaspoon salt
¼ teaspoon ground black pepper

Heat the olive oil in a medium saucepan over medium-high heat. Sauté the garlic and onions until soft. Stir in the chopped tomatoes. Add the water and cover the saucepan. Adjust the heat to low and continue cooking for 30 minutes, until the tomatoes are soft and mashed and the sauce has thickened. Season with the sugar, salt and pepper. Refrigerate any leftover tomato sauce for use in future sautéed dishes. Sauce will keep up to 1 week in refrigerator, and 1 month in the freezer.

EGGPLANT SAUCE
Makes 1½ cups

4 or 5 large Asian eggplants,
  about 4 to 5 ounces each
1 Tablespoon minced garlic

¼ cup white vinegar
½ teaspoon salt
¼ teaspoon ground black pepper

In a small stockpot over medium-high heat, boil the eggplants in enough water to cover them for 25 minutes until soft. Drain the eggplants and set them aside to cool.

When cool enough to handle, peel the eggplants and mash them. Sprinkle the mashed eggplants with the garlic and vinegar, and season with salt and pepper.

ELIZABETH'S CHOCOLATE CAKE

Servings: 6 to 8

Ingredients

For the cake:

Baking spray, for greasing
  the pans

2¼ cups cake flour

2 teaspoons baking powder

2 teaspoons baking soda

1 teaspoon salt

1 cup unsweetened cocoa
  powder.

2 cups water

1 Tablespoon pure vanilla extract

1 cup unsalted butter, softened

3 cups granulated sugar

4 large eggs

For the mocha custard filling:

1 can (12 ounces) evaporated milk

2 large egg yolks

¼ cup granulated sugar

2 teaspoons powdered
  instant coffee

2 Tablespoons unsalted butter

For the chocolate fudge icing:

1 can (12 ounces) evaporated milk

1 can (14 ounces) sweetened
  condensed milk

1 cup unsweetened cocoa powder

2 Tablespoons unsalted butter,
  softened

Procedure

Make the cake layers: Grease two 9-inch round baking pans with baking spray, and line the bottom of each with parchment paper. Set aside. Preheat the oven to 350°F.

Whisk together the cake flour, baking powder, baking soda and salt in a bowl, then set aside. In another bowl, combine the cocoa powder, water and vanilla. Set aside.

Using an electric mixer, cream the butter and sugar. Alternately add the cocoa liquid and the cake flour mixture to the creamed butter mixture, beginning and ending with the cocoa liquid. Add the eggs one at a time, beating well after each addition.

Pour the cake batter into the prepared pans and bake for 30 to 35 minutes. Test if the cake layers are done by piercing the top of each one with a cake tester, like a toothpick or the tip of a small sharp knife. If the tester comes out clean, the cake layers are ready.

Invert each cake layer onto a cooling rack. Carefully peel off and discard the parchment paper. Cool the cake layers for at least 1 hour, until at room temperature.

Make the mocha custard filling: Mix the evaporated milk, egg yolks, sugar and coffee in the top pan of a double boiler. Cook over simmering water while stirring continuously until it thickens, about 20 minutes. The mixture should coat the back of a spoon. Add the butter at the end of cooking, then set the custard filling aside to cool.

Make the chocolate fudge icing: Combine the evaporated milk, condensed milk and cocoa powder in the top pan of a double boiler. Stir to blend well. Cook, stirring, over simmering water over medium heat until it thickens, about 25 minutes. The chocolate mixture should be a creamy consistency, yet stiff enough to spread on the cake and hold its shape if curls and florets are formed. Add the butter when the icing has thickened. Cool the icing for at least 45 minutes before using.

Assemble the chocolate cake: Place one cake layer on a cake plate. Spread the mocha custard filling evenly on top with a spatula. Place the second cake layer over the filling and frost the entire cake with the chocolate fudge icing. The cake can stay on the counter for 1 day. After that, keep cake, loosely covered in foil or a plastic cake cover, refrigerated, up to 1 week. The cake can be frozen, in a plastic container for up to 1 month.

SOPA DE FIDEO

Servings: 4

Ingredients

3 large ripe tomatoes,
coarsely chopped

2 Tablespoons vegetable oil

8 ounces dried pasta (such as thin
spaghetti or elbow macaroni)

2 garlic cloves, minced

1 small white or yellow onion,
chopped

8 to 10 cups chicken broth

Pinch of salt

¼ teaspoon ground black pepper

¼ cup grated Parmesan cheese

1 Tablespoon chopped parsley,
for garnish (optional)

Procedure

Puree the tomatoes in a food processor or blender, about 2 minutes. Set aside.

Heat the vegetable oil in a large stockpot over medium heat for 1 to 2 minutes, then add the uncooked pasta. If using spaghetti or long noodles, break the pasta in half or smaller pieces. Stir the pasta in the hot oil for 3 to 5 minutes, until it is lightly browned and becomes a bit puffy.

Toss the garlic and onions in with the pasta and continue sautéing together for 2 minutes till onions are soft. Stir in the tomato puree. Pour in the chicken broth. Cover the pot and simmer until pasta is cooked, about 11 minutes. Season the soup with salt and pepper, and sprinkle with the cheese.

Serve piping hot with a garnish of parsley, if desired.

Cook's Comment: For a wholesome soup meal, add a cup of shredded cooked chicken.

LOLA NENA'S PANSIT BIHON GUISADO

Servings: 4 to 6

Ingredients

For the noodles:

1 pack (8 ounces) dried bihon
   noodles (rice vermicelli)

For the guisado:

1 pound fresh head-on shrimp

1 cup water

2 Tablespoons vegetable oil

4 garlic cloves, minced

1 medium onion, chopped

2 scallion stalks, white and green
   parts separated, chopped

1½ cups chicken or
   vegetable broth

2 Tablespoons soy sauce

1 Tablespoon calamansi
   or lemon juice

1 carrot, peeled and julienned

3 cups shredded cabbage

2 cups shredded pechay
   (bok choy)

2 cups togue (mung bean sprouts)

Pinch of salt

½ teaspoon ground black pepper

6 bacon slices, cooked
   and chopped

½ cup patis (fish sauce),
   for dipping

Slices of fresh calamansi or lemon

Procedure

Prepare the noodles: Soak the noodles in water for 10 minutes.
Drain and set aside.

Prepare the shrimp juice: Remove the heads from the shrimp.
Shell the shrimp, discarding the shells and tails. Set the shrimp aside.
Place the shrimp heads in a small saucepan and cover with the
water. Bring to a boil, then lower the heat to simmer for 10 minutes.
When the shrimp heads turn to pink, squeeze them against the side
of the pot with a fork to extract the juices and give the simmering
liquid a rich flavor. Save ½ cup of the shrimp juice and discard
the solids.
(continued)

Cook the guisado: Heat the oil in a large skillet or wok over medium heat and sauté the garlic, onion and scallion whites until onions are soft in 2 minutes. Add the shelled shrimp and continue sautéing until the shrimp turn to pink, 8 to 10 minutes. Pour in the broth, shrimp juice, soy sauce, and calamansi juice. When mixture starts to simmer, add the carrots and give it a good stir. Add the cabbage, pechay and togue, and cook for another 5 minutes, until soft. Do not overcook or the vegetables will wilt.

Add the pres-oaked bihon noodles. Combine all the ingredients well until the cooking liquid coats the noodles and is evenly distributed. Continue cooking for 5 minutes more, until the flavors blend and the noodles are soft. Season with salt and pepper, sprinkle the cooked bacon bits all over and garnish with the chopped scallion greens. Serve with the patis for dipping and calamansi slices.

FISH MAYONESA

Servings: 4

Ingredients

1 whole white fish (such as red
   snapper, pompano, striped
   bass or trout, 2 to 3 pounds),
   cleaned, scaled and gutted
2 Tablespoons calamansi or
   lemon juice
1 teaspoon salt
1 teaspoon ground black pepper
1 medium onion, sliced
2 scallion stalks, white and green
   parts separated, chopped
1 medium carrot, peeled and
   sliced crosswise

1 cup vegetable or fish broth
1 Tablespoon vegetable oil
1 cup mayonnaise
2 hard-boiled large eggs, yolks
   and whites separated
   and chopped
1 red bell pepper, seeded
   and chopped
1 green bell pepper,
   seeded and chopped
1 cup chopped peeled carrots
1 cup sweet pickle relish, drained
1 pitted black olive

Procedure

Before cooking, wash the fish in cold running water to remove any remaining traces of blood. Pat dry with paper towels. In a shallow baking dish, marinate the fish with the calamansi or lemon juice, salt and pepper for 20 minutes.

Meanwhile, preheat the oven to 375°F.

Lay the fish on a roasting pan large enough to accommodate the whole piece. Scatter the slices of onions, scallion whites and sliced carrots all over, then pour in the broth and vegetable oil. Cover the roasting pan with foil and bake for 30 to 35 minutes, until fish flakes when pierced with a fork, and internal temperature on a thermometer is 145°F.   *(continued)*

When the fish is cooked, remove the pan from the oven, uncover and let the fish cool to room temperature.

Transfer the cooled fish to an oval platter or large serving tray. Discard the vegetables and liquid from the roasting pan.

Spread the mayonnaise all over the top of the fish, from head to tail. Decorate the fish by arranging the following in diagonal strips on top of the mayonnaise: egg yolks, egg whites, red bell pepper, green bell pepper, chopped carrots and pickle relish. Repeat the lines as needed until all the garnishes are used. Place the black olive where the fish eye should be.

Sprinkle over the chopped scallion greens for garnish, then cover the fish loosely with foil or plastic wrap. Keep refrigerated until ready to serve.

Cook's Comment: If a whole fish with the head and tail is not available, cook fish fillets, then nestle the pieces together in the shape of a large fish with tail and head. Decorate as described.

MOM'S SHRIMP TOAST

Makes 12 toasts

Ingredients

2 Tablespoons vegetable oil

2 Tablespoons butter, unsalted

2 garlic cloves, chopped

½ cup chopped white or
  yellow onion

2 scallion stalks, white and green
  parts separated, chopped

½ cup chopped red bell pepper

½ pound shrimp, shelled
  and chopped

2 Tablespoons calamansi
  or lemon juice

1 Tablespoon soy sauce

¼ teaspoon salt

¼ teaspoon ground black pepper

Cooking spray

12 slices white or whole wheat
  bread, crusts trimmed

½ cup grated sharp
  cheddar cheese

Procedure

Heat the oil and butter in a saucepan set over medium heat. Sauté the garlic, onions, scallion whites and bell pepper until soft in 1 to 2 minutes. Toss in the chopped shrimp, then sprinkle with the calamansi juice and soy sauce. Mix the ingredients well. Cook until shrimps turn to pink, 8 to 10 minutes. Season the filling with salt and pepper and set aside to cool.

Preheat the oven to 350°F. Grease a muffin tin with cooking spray. Place a piece of bread over each cup. Using your fingers, gently push down the middle of the bread into the cup, until the sides look like petals of a flower and the bread forms a cup. Toast the bread cups in the oven for 3 minutes or until light brown.

Take the muffin tin out of the oven and fill each bread cup with about 2 tablespoons of the shrimp mixture. Sprinkle grated cheese on top of each shrimp toast and garnish with the scallion greens. Toast the cups for 6 to 8 minutes more, until the cheese has melted.

(continued)

Use a pair of tongs to remove each shrimp toast from the muffin tin. Serve warm.

ARROZ A LA VALENCIANA

Servings: 4

Ingredients

1½ cups uncooked white rice

2 cups coconut milk

1 cup water

2½ teaspoons salt

1 pound boneless, skin-on chicken cutlets, cut into 2-inch cubes

1 pound boneless pork belly, rind sliced off, cut into 2-inch cubes

1¼ teaspoons ground black pepper

2 Tablespoons extra virgin olive oil

2 chorizo de Bilbao (Spanish sausage) links, sliced into ¼-inch-thick rounds

4 garlic cloves, minced

1 medium white or yellow onion, chopped

2 plum tomatoes, chopped

2 large potatoes, peeled and cubed

1 large red bell pepper, seeded and sliced into strips

1 teaspoon paprika

½ cup chicken or pork broth

1 cup green peas

2 hard-boiled large eggs, sliced

Procedure

Wash the rice grains in the removable pot of a rice cooker or Instant Pot under running water, then drain the rice thoroughly. Stir in the coconut milk, 1 cup of water, and 1 teaspoon of the salt. Press the appropriate settings of the rice cooker or Instant Pot to steam the rice. When the rice is cooked, about 12 minutes, fluff the grains with a fork and set aside to cool.

Season the chicken and pork belly cuts with 1 teaspoon of the remaining salt and 1 teaspoon of the pepper. Set aside.

Heat the olive oil in a large skillet over medium heat. When the oil is hot, add the chorizo and sear the slices for 2 minutes, till the edges get crisp. Remove the slices and set aside to drain on paper towels. In the same skillet, add the chicken and pork cuts. Sauté for about 5 minutes until the meats are browned.

Add the garlic, onions and tomatoes, and continue sautéing until onions are soft in 1 to 2 minutes. Add the potatoes and bell pepper strips. Sprinkle the medley with the paprika. Pour in the broth and continue cooking at a simmer until the meats and potatoes are tender, about 10 minutes more.

Add the cooked rice, mixing all the ingredients well. Add the green peas and incorporate them into the rice mixture. Season with the remaining ½ teaspoon salt and ¼ teaspoon pepper. Garnish with the hard-boiled egg and chorizo slices and serve warm.

TIBOK-TIBOK

Makes 20 pieces

Ingredients

1 banana leaf

2 Tablespoons coconut oil

2 cups goat's milk

1 cup cornstarch

¾ cup granulated sugar

1 teaspoon grated lime zest

½ cup coconut cream

Procedure

Wash the banana leaf with soap and water, rinsing well to ensure no soapy residue remains. Pat dry with paper towels. Trim it to fit the bottom of a 9 x 11-inch or an 8 x 8-inch baking pan. Line the pan with the banana leaf, then grease the leaf with the coconut oil and set aside.

Combine the goat's milk, cornstarch, sugar and lime zest in a medium stockpot set over medium heat. Bring the mixture to a low simmer, stirring continuously until it thickens to a pudding-like consistency and separates from the sides of the pot, 15 to 18 minutes. Do not leave the mixture alone, or it could burn.

When the mixture has reached a creamy, nearly solid consistency, pour it into the leaf-lined pan. Set aside to firm up while you make the latik (coconut sprinkles).

Pour the coconut cream into a small skillet. Over medium heat, cook the cream while stirring continuously until it solidifies into small brown curds, 8 to 10 minutes.

Sprinkle the coconut latik over the now-firm tibok-tibok. Cover the pan loosely with plastic wrap or foil and refrigerate until you're ready to serve.

To serve, slice the tibok-tibok into 2-inch squares. Store any leftovers in the refrigerator, covered, for up to 2 days.

Cook's Comment: If banana leaves are not available, pour the tibok-tibok directly into a greased pan.

GINATAANG BILO-BILO

Servings: 4 to 6

Ingredients

Cooking spray

1 bottle (12 ounces) ube
(purple yam) jam, refrigerated

1 camote (sweet yam),
(about 6 ounces), peeled

1 cup Mochiko (sweet or glutinous
rice flour)

2 to 4 tablespoons + 3 cups water

2 large ripe plantains
(see Cook's Comment)

½ cup brown sugar

2 cans (13.5 to 14 ounces each)
coconut milk

¾ cup granulated sugar

1 cup canned langka (jackfruit),
drained and sliced into
2-inch strips

1 cup bottled cooked sago
(tapioca pearls), drained

Procedure

One day ahead, for easier handling, grease a teaspoon and your hands with cooking spray. Take 2 teaspoons of the ube jam and shape into a 1-inch ball; a 12-ounce bottle makes about 27 balls. Lay the ube balls on a dinner plate, taking care not to overlap or place them too close to touch. Refrigerate, covered loosely with foil, until ready to use.

Boil the camote or sweet yam in water for about 35 minutes, until soft. Drain and let cool for a few minutes, Cut into cubes about ¼ inch in size. Set aside. *(continued)*

Combine the rice flour and 2 tablespoons of water in a medium bowl. Mix well with a wooden spoon until the flour comes together in a soft, slight elastic dough. Add 1 to 2 more tablespoons of water if the dough is still crumbly. Pinch off about a tablespoon of the dough at a time and roll into ½-inch round bilo-bilo (dumplings); it should yield 12 to 14 dumplings. Place on another plate, cover, and refrigerate to firm up.

Peel and cut the plantains into ½-inch cubes. Toss in a small stockpot with the brown sugar and 1 cup of water. Bring the plantains to a boil, then lower the heat to a simmer and cook until the liquid thickens and becomes syrupy, 5 to 6 minutes. Do not overcook, or the plantains will turn mushy. Remove the plantains from the syrup and transfer to a container. Cover or seal the container and refrigerate until ready to use. The syrup can be saved for another dessert, if desired.

Combine the coconut milk, 2 cups of water, and the ¾ cup granulated sugar in a large stockpot, stirring to blend. Bring to a boil over medium–high heat, then lower the temperature to a simmer. Be mindful and stir occasionally to avoid burning or curdling the coconut milk. Add the prepared ube balls, sweet yam cubes, sweetened plantain cubes, jackfruit strips and sago to the coconut milk mixture and stir gently. Continue to simmer while stirring for about 5 minutes, until slightly thick.

Add the bilo-bilo and cook for another 5 minutes, until all the dumplings swell, are firm enough, and thoroughly cooked, and all the ingredients are coated with the coconut milk sauce.

Serve warm or cold as snack or dessert. To store, keep the ginataang bilo-bilo in a covered container and refrigerate for up to 2 days.

Cook's Comment: Make sure to use ripe plantains. To ripen plantains, keep them in a paper bag until they change color. To tell if they are ready, the peel should be dark brown, almost black, but still a little firm to the touch.

SUMAN CASSAVA

Makes 12 pieces

Ingredients

1 pound fresh cassava, peeled and grated, or 16 ounces thawed frozen grated cassava

1 cup fresh or thawed frozen grated coconut meat (do not use sweetened or desiccated coconut flakes)

¾ cup brown sugar

12 banana leaves, cut into 8-inch squares, for wrapping

Butcher's twine

Procedure

Combine the cassava, coconut meat and brown sugar in a bowl. Mix the ingredients until smooth and light brown in color.

Place 2 tablespoons of the cassava mixture in the center of a banana leaf square. Wrap by tightly tucking the left and right sides of the leaf inward, then roll the leaf like you would a burrito. The suman packet should be about 3 inches long. Tie each suman with twine on both ends to help keep the filling inside while it is being steamed. Repeat with the remaining cassava mixture and leaves.

Place the suman in a large stockpot, in overlapping layers to fit if necessary. Add enough water to cover the top of the packets. Cover the pot and simmer over medium heat for 2 hours. Check the water level occasionally and add more water if the liquid has evaporated and is less than half of the original level.

When the suman are solid, firm and done, remove the packets from the stockpot and discard the liquid. *(continued)*

Cool the suman to room temperature, then refrigerate at least 6 hours or overnight.

Unwrap to serve. Serve warm or chilled.

Cook's Comment: Cassava, also known as yuca, can be found in Asian or Latin American markets, fresh or frozen.

PINAUPONG MANOK

Servings: 4

Ingredients

1 whole chicken (4 to 5 pounds)
1 Tablespoon garlic powder
1 Tablespoon onion powder
1 teaspoon ground black pepper
5 to 6 cups + 1 teaspoon
  kosher salt
1 medium white or yellow onion,
  chopped

4 scallion stalks, white and green
  parts separated
¼ cup soy sauce
Juice of 1 lemon
Steamed rice, for serving

Procedure

Preheat oven to 375°F.

Wash the chicken thoroughly and pat dry with paper towels. In a medium bowl, make the seasoning blend: combine the garlic powder, onion powder, pepper and 1 teaspoon salt. Rub the seasoning blend all over the chicken. Stuff the chicken with the onions and scallion whites.

Pour 5 to 6 cups of salt into a 9 x 13-inch roasting pan or other pan large enough to fit the whole chicken. Level off the salt to make a flat, even bed about ½ inch thick. Place the chicken, breast side up, on top of the bed of salt. Cover the pan tightly with foil. Roast the chicken for 2 hours and 40 minutes (see Cook's Comment).

When the chicken is cooked through, remove from the oven. Transfer to a chopping board, rest the bird for 10 minutes, and then carve into serving pieces. Discard the salt bed.

Combine the soy sauce and lemon juice to make a dipping sauce. Chop the scallion greens and use to garnish the carved chicken. Serve warm with steamed rice and the dipping sauce.

Cook's Comment: To check if the chicken is cooked, pierce the thickest part of the thigh. The meat should not be red or pink and the juices should run clear if pierced. If using a thermometer to check if the chicken is cooked, the internal temperature should read at least 167°F. If the meat is still pink or has not reached 167°F, return the chicken to the oven and cover loosely with foil. Continue roasting, checking at 5-minute intervals, until the chicken is cooked.

TITA HELEN'S ORANGE MARMALADE

Makes two 12-ounce or three 8-ounce jars

Ingredients

5 or 6 unpeeled oranges, sliced
   into thin rounds, seeds reserved
1 unpeeled lemon, sliced into
   thin rounds, seeds reserved

Granulated sugar
1 Tablespoon calamansi juice

Procedure

Day 1: Place sliced oranges and lemon in a large, deep stockpot and add just enough water to cover the fruit. Cover and let stand at room temperature overnight. Place the seeds of the oranges and lemon in a small cheesecloth bag, to be used when simmering the next day. Tie the bag with a long piece of twine. Set aside.

Day 2: Simmer the fruit in the pot for 30 minutes over medium heat, with the cheesecloth bag containing the seeds tied to the handle, hanging into the pot. The bag should be immersed in the liquid. Turn off the heat and let the fruit cool before covering the pot. Let stand overnight at room temperature.

Day 3: Simmer the fruit and cheesecloth bag of seeds for 1 hour over medium heat. Turn off the heat and let the fruit cool before covering the pot. Let stand overnight at room temperature.

Day 4: By the fourth day, the orange and lemon slices should be immersed in a thick liquid. Measure the amount of fruit and liquid, then return them to the pot. Leave the cheesecloth bag of seeds in the pot, tied to the handle.

Add 1 cup of sugar for every cup of fruit-and-liquid mixture, stirring well so that the sugar dissolves. Pour in the calamansi juice and mix with a spoon. Bring mixture to a boil over medium-high heat, then cover the pot with the lid slightly askew. Lower the heat to a slow simmer and cook for 3 hours. Stir once in a while to prevent the fruit from sticking to the bottom of the pot.

By the last hour, the mixture should be glossy with a thick, jam-like consistency and dark caramel color. Turn off the heat and uncover the pot to let the marmalade cool slightly. Remove and discard the cheesecloth bag of seeds.

Spoon the marmalade into two large (12-ounce) or three medium (8-ounce) sterilized glass jars. Leave them uncovered until they have cooled to room temperature, then cap and store in the refrigerator. The marmalade will keep for up to 3 months refrigerated.

ORANGE CROWN ROAST
OF PORK RIBS

Servings: 4

Ingredients

2 garlic cloves, minced

1-inch knob fresh ginger, peeled
    and julienned

1 cup orange marmalade (use
    Tita Helen's Orange Marmalade,
    page 330, if desired)

¼ cup pineapple preserves or jam

2 teaspoons grated orange zest

½ cup soy sauce

½ cup ginger ale

Pinch of salt

½ teaspoon ground black pepper

4-pound crown roast of pork ribs
    (see Cooks' Comments)

Fresh orange slices

1 Tablespoon chopped parsley

Procedure

Whisk together in a bowl the garlic, ginger, orange marmalade, pineapple preserves, orange zest, soy sauce, ginger ale, salt and pepper. Place the pork ribs in a baking pan or heavy-duty plastic bag. Pour one-half of the marinade over the meat, distributing it evenly. Set aside ¼ cup of the marinade for serving, and the rest of the marinade for basting. Cover the pan or seal the bag and leave it to marinate in the refrigerator for at least 6 hours or overnight, turning the ribs occasionally.

Preheat the oven to 350°F.

Remove the ribs from the marinade and discard any remaining marinade. Stand the marinated ribs in a large roasting pan and cover loosely with aluminum foil. Bake in the oven for 2 hours, basting the ribs every 30 minutes with some of the reserved marinade. When the ribs are cooked (see Cook's Comments), remove the foil. Broil the crown for 5 minutes, until golden brown.

Transfer the crown to a serving platter. Pour the remaining ¼ cup of marinade over the ribs.

Garnish with the orange slices and chopped parsley, and serve warm.

Cook's Comments: Ask a butcher to shape a rack of pork ribs into a crown if you do not want to do it yourself. Some butchers refer to it as a rack of bone-on pork loin, tied together, end to end, and it creates a large round roast, with the bones standing vertical, that look like a crown. If you prefer the pork is not shaped like a crown, cooking time for ribs at 350°F: 2 hours for baby back ribs, 2½ hours for pork spare ribs; and 30 minutes per pound for bone-in country-style ribs.

PAN DE SAL

Makes 20 buns

Ingredients

1 Tablespoon active dry yeast

1½ teaspoons granulated sugar

½ cup lukewarm milk

⅔ cup lukewarm water

¼ cup unsalted butter, softened

1 teaspoon salt

2 large eggs

4 cups unbleached bread flour,
  plus more for shaping

Cooking spray

1 cup plain dried breadcrumbs

Mango Jam, for serving
  (see following recipe)

Procedure

Mix together the yeast, sugar, milk and water in a large bowl or the bowl of a stand mixer. Cover and let stand for 10 minutes. The yeast mixture should produce bubbles in this time.

Add the softened butter, salt and eggs to the yeast mixture, stirring very well with a wooden spoon so that the yeast is evenly distributed and the mixture looks like a thick liquid with large bubbles. Slowly add the bread flour, about ½ cup at a time, and mix with the wooden spoon or use the dough hook attachment on the mixer. Continue to add flour, mixing and kneading the dough until it looks smooth, about 10 minutes.

Grease a large bowl with cooking spray. Place the dough in the greased bowl and cover with plastic wrap. Let the dough rise in a warm spot in the kitchen for 1 hour, until almost doubled in size.

Place the dough on a floured surface and flatten with a rolling pin to form a large rectangle about ½ inch thick. Roll the dough into a long shape resembling a baguette, about 2 inches in diameter and 20 inches long. Slice the dough crosswise into 20 even piece. Shape each individual piece into an oblong bun. Roll each bun in breadcrumbs.

Arrange the buns 1 inch apart on an 11 x 17-inch rimmed baking tray lined with parchment paper. Cover the tray loosely with a clean, dry kitchen towel. Let the buns rise for 1 hour in a warm place, until doubled in size.

Preheat the oven to 350°F.

Bake the buns for 18 to 20 minutes, until they are light brown outside. Serve warm with mango jam. Store Pan de Sal buns in an airtight container for up to 3 days at room temperature. After that, refrigerate for up to 5 days.

Cook's Comment: When baking bread, follow the exact times for rising. Do not go over the time required, or the bread may taste yeasty after baking.

MANGO JAM

Makes two 8-ounce jars

10 ripe Ataulfo mangoes
(also called Manila mangoes,
or carabao mangoes in the
Philippines)

½ cup granulated sugar
2 Tablespoons calamansi juice

Peel the mangoes. In a large stockpot, over medium heat, parboil the mangoes in water to cover for 5 minutes to soften. Do not leave unattended or they might burn.

Remove the mangoes from the stockpot. Slice the mangoes from the center where the pit is, slicing off two cheeks. Peel and slice off any flesh from the sides of the pits. Discard the pits.

Using a food processor or blender, puree the mango flesh for 1 to 2 minutes, until thick. Place the puree in a heavy, medium stockpot. Add the sugar and calamansi juice. Blend well by stirring.

Over medium heat, stir the jam continuously using a long wooden spoon. When the pulp boils in about 8 minutes, lower heat to a slow simmer. Continue stirring every so often, and cooking over low heat for about 55 minutes. The jam will start to thicken and change to a darker orange hue after about 30 minutes, and should turn thick and coat the spoon. Do not get distracted or leave the jam; it can burn.

When jam has cooked and coats a spoon, remove the pot from the stovetop and let cool on the counter for 20 minutes, until it is at room temperature. Spoon the jam into sterilized glass jars. When cooled to room temperature, cap and store in the refrigerator for up to 3 weeks.

CHICKEN CURRY WITH MOM'S MANGO CHUTNEY

Servings: 4

Ingredients

2 Tablespoons vegetable oil

1 large onion, sliced

1 Tablespoon minced garlic

2 pounds boneless chicken
  breasts, skin-on, cut into
  2-inch pieces

2 cans (13.5 to 14 ounces each)
  coconut milk

¾ cup chicken broth or water

2 Tablespoons yellow
  curry powder

2 teaspoons ground cinnamon

2 large potatoes, peeled
  and quartered

1 cup cubed peeled carrots

1 cup green beans sliced into
  2-inch pieces

Pinch of salt

Pinch of ground black pepper

½ red bell pepper, seeded
  and sliced into strips

1 hard-boiled large egg, sliced

Accompaniments:

Steamed jasmine rice or naan

Deep-fried onion rings

Deep-fried eggplant slices

Raisins, pan-fried

Salted roasted peanuts

Mom's Mango Chutney
  (see following recipe)

Procedure

Heat the vegetable oil in a large saucepan over medium heat and
sauté the onions and garlic until soft in 1 to 2 minutes. Add the
chicken pieces and sear for 5 minutes, until slightly browned. Pour
in the coconut milk and broth or water, then stir in the curry powder and cinnamon. Once the coconut milk starts to boil, lower the
heat to a slow simmer. Stir every so often, so that the ingredients do
not stick to the bottom of the skillet.   *(continued)*

Continue cooking over a slow simmer. When chicken is nearly cooked, after about 25 minutes, add the potatoes, carrots and green beans. The chicken and vegetables should be tender in another 10 minutes (about 35 minutes total). Season with salt and pepper.

Transfer the curry to a serving bowl and garnish with bell pepper strips and hard–boiled egg slices. Serve the chicken curry with steamed jasmine rice or naan and side dishes of fried onion rings, eggplant slices, raisins, peanuts and a generous helping of mango chutney.

MOM'S MANGO CHUTNEY
Makes two 8-ounce jars

1½ cups brown sugar

½ cup white vinegar

1 teaspoon salt

2 large fully ripe mangoes, peeled, pitted and sliced into strips

1 cup water

1 large red bell pepper, seeded and sliced into strips

1 large green bell pepper, seeded and sliced into strips

1 Tablespoon paprika

1 Tablespoon minced garlic

1 large red onion, sliced thinly

1 teaspoon minced fresh ginger

1 red siling labuyo (bird's eye chile)

1 Tablespoon black peppercorns

2 large bay leaves

½ cup raisins

Mix together the brown sugar, vinegar and salt in a medium stockpot over medium heat and cook for about 8 minutes, until slightly thick like syrup.

Add the mangoes, water, red and green bell peppers paprika, garlic, onion, ginger, siling labuyo, peppercorns, bay leaves and raisins, and stir well. Bring the mixture to a boil, then lower the heat to a slow simmer and continue cooking for about 20 minutes, until the chutney takes on a thick, jam-like consistency. Keep stirring while cooking so that it does not burn.

Once the chutney has cooked, remove it from the stove and set aside to cool. Spoon into sterilized glass jars, cap and refrigerate. The chutney will keep 1 to 2 months in the refrigerator.

Cook's Comment: For best results, cook the mango chutney 1 to 2 days ahead so that the sweet flavors have time to set.

Sources

Abreu, José. "Ponciano Reyes, The Lawyer and Judge." *Philippine Law Review*, Volume 6 (1919): 75.

"Acts No. 4250." Attorneys of the Philippines, https://attorney.org.ph/acts/acts-no-4250.

Alcaraz, Ramon. "War diary of Ramon Alcaraz." The Philippine Diary Project, https://philippinediaryproject.wordpress.com/category/diary-of-ramon-a-alcaraz/.

Aquila, David. "A deeper level of hell." Historynet, https://www.historynet.com/a-deeper-level-of-hell/.

Argibay, Carmen M. "Sexual slavery and the comfort women of World War II." *Berkeley Journal of International Law*, v21 (2:2003). https://genderandsecurity.org/sites/default/files/Argibay_-_Sexual_Slavery_the_Comfort_W_of_WWII.pdf.

Benitez, Helena Z. "Girls in Blue." Our Own Voice, October 2002, https://oovrag.com/essays/essay2002c-4.shtml.

"Camp O'Donnell and Camp Cabanatuan." Center for Research: Allied POWs Under the Japanese, http://www.mansell.com/lindavdahl/omuta17/odonnell_cabanatuan.html.

Chen, C. Peter. "Ramon Magsaysay." World War II Database, https://ww2db.com/person_bio.php?person_id=906.

"Cinco nuevas candidatas para 'mujer mas popular'" *La Vanguardia* April 23, 1945, p 6. Last accessed November 2022; link no longer available.

Doeppers, Daniel F. *Feeding Manila in Peace and War, 1850–1945*. Madison: University of Wisconsin Press, 2016.

Dow, Robert Joseph. *Guest of His Imperial Highness.* Unpublished manuscript.

Gwekoh, Sol H. "The heroic martyrdom of Josefa Llanes Escoda." The Philippine Free Press Online, September 20, 1952, https://philippinesfreepress.wordpress.com/1952/09/20/the-heroic-martyrdom-of-josefa-llanes-escoda-september-20-1952/.

Hagar, George. "Lulu Reyes." *Extension,* v42, no.10. March 1948: 18–19, 53.

Hurley, John F. "Wartime Superior in the Philippines (when bombs fell on Manila)." Woodstock Letters, v98 (2: April 1, 1968), p 149–237, https://jesuitonlinelibrary.bc.edu/?a=d&d=wlet19690401-01.2.2&e=-------en-20--1--txt-txIN-------#.

Joven, Arnel. "Remembering Camp O'Donnell: from shared memories to public history in the Philippines." *The Asia-Pacific Journal: Japan Focus.,* v20, no11 (3: June 1, 2022), https://apjjf.org/2022/11/Joven.html.

Kerr, E. Bartlett. *Surrender and Survival: the Experience of American POWs in the Pacific, 1941–1945.* New York: W. Morrow, 1985.

Lopez, Salvador P. "Good evening, everyone everywhere." Voice of Freedom, April 9, 1942. Bataan-Corregidor Memorial Foundation of New Mexico, https://www.angelfire.com/nm/bcmfofnm/history/timeline/bataan_has_fallen.html.

Monaghan, Forbes J. *Under the Red Sun: a Letter from Manila.* New York: Declan X. McMullen, 1946.

Montgomery, Ben. *The Leper Spy: the Story of an Unlikely Hero of World War II.* Chicago: Chicago Review Press, 2017.

Peterson, Rick. "Back to Bataan: A Survivor's Story." Bataan Survivor, https://web.archive.org/web/20110912013120/http://www.bataansurvivor.com/content/introduction/1.php.

Quezon, Manuel L. "The Good Fight: the Autobiography of Manuel L. Quezon." Manuel L. Quezon III: The Explainer, https://www.quezon.ph/books-2/the-good-fight-the-autobiogrphy-of-manuel-l-quezon/.

"Regio desfile en que figuraran mas de setenta señoritas de la buena sociedad de Manila." *La Vanguardia.* February 3, 1934, 5, https://prensahistorica.mcu.es/es/catalogo_imagenes /grupo.do?path=1000380120&idImagen=1002949988&idBusqueda=190505&posicion=5&presentacion=pagina.

Ro Akeanon. 2020. "Dr. Simplicio Jugo Vidal (1901–1903)." Facebook, July 19, 2020, https://www.facebook.com/TheAkeanon /posts/dr-simplicio-jugo-vidal-1901-1903first-governor-of-the-provincial-government-of-/2792438280977901/.

Salm, Alma. "A brutally honest look inside Japan's largest WW2–era POW camp (Memoir #9)." Anastasia Harman, https://www .anastasiaharman.com/2020/05/02/cabanatuan-3-intro/.

Scroope, Chara. "Japanese culture: core concepts." Cultural Atlas https://culturalatlas.sbs.com.au/japanese-culture/japanese-culture-core-concepts.

Villarin, Mariano. *We Remember Bataan and Corregidor: The Story of the American and Filipino Defenders of Bataan and Corregidor and Their Captivity.* Baltimore: Gateway Press, 1990.

"Women made to be comfort women—Philippines." The Asian Women's Fund, https://www.awf.or.jp/e1/philippine-00.html.

Index

Page numbers in *italics* refer to notes; numbers in **bold** refer to recipes; numbers in ***bold italics*** are photos

Acknowledgments

My mother, Lulu Reyes Besa, taught me to always write a thank-you note to everyone and anyone who has given me a gift or did something nice for me. So, this is my THANK YOU note to all the wonderful people who urged me, inspired me, and helped me every step of the way to write this memoir.

I had a huge support team of amazing editors, book designers, readers, recipe testers, historians, culinarians, friends, family and dear ones.

A big thank you and a prayer for the late Corporal Robert J. Dow, of the American Army Air Forces, and former American POW during WWII in the Philippines, who was the catalyst of all these. It was his midnight phone call over 20 years ago that made me realize it was time to write my mother's story. It was Bob's stories about my mother Lulu's heroism during World War II that lit the fire in me to take pen to paper and to start my research of what life was for my parents and my home country, the Philippines, during the war in the Pacific.

I wouldn't be here today writing these stories had it not been for my brave family who came before me: my mom, Lulu, and my father, Gualberto Besa; my grandparents Luz "Nena" Jugo and Judge Ponciano Reyes Sr., my great grandparents Juana Serraller and Dr. Simplicio Jugo y Vidal; my uncles and aunts—Bobby J. Reyes, Willie and Helen Reyes, Poncy, Atang and Tessie Reyes. And to all sides of my Besa and Quirino families, and our extended families, the lessons learned from all of you have been invaluable.

To my publishing team: I am grateful to my manuscript editor, Tracey Paska, who held my hand, lifted my spirits and toiled with me till past the midnight hours, in different time zones, for endless days, months and nearly two years. She cracked the whip, mercilessly edited out my darlings and the result was a beautiful memoir.

To my copy editor Suzanne Fass, thanks for your patience and diligence. To my designer-formatter Barbara Scott-Goodman, thank you for making my words come alive in these pages. To Tim Quirino for designing the exquisitely unique book cover. To Constante G. Quirino, your sharp eye, keen insights and edits saved the day. Where would this book be without all of you?

A huge thank you to my beta readers and kitchen testers, for supporting me and patiently pointing out my flaws: Pinky Jacinto, Lena Mazanka, Jodi and Jay Ocampo, Juliet Abrantes, Marissa Q. Gonzalez, Janet Hizon, Sarah Burkly.

To those who keep inspiring me with their wisdom, prayers and unconditional friendship: Professor Caesar D'Mello, Monica Bhide, Bunny Arville, Marionette O. Martinez, Alex Castro, Claude Tayag.

To my childhood friends, here's to our second-generation friendships that began with our mothers' lifelong ties: Aurora Q. Avanceña and the entire Quezon-Avanceña family, Michael Kipping, Natasha Kosloff, Valerie Palou Erana and the Palou family, Maruja Paredes, Marianne Guidote Velez, Gigi Rodriguez, Pinky Pueo Francisco.

To the amazing authors I admire, who took time from their hectic schedules to read my manuscript, whose blurbs and reviews will never be forgotten by my grateful heart: Manuel L. Quezon III, Cecilia Gaerlan, Elena B. Mangahas, Desiree Benipayo, Ige Ramos, Bren Bataclan, Liren Baker, Joey L. Blanco, Jacqueline Chio-Lauri, Robyn Eckhardt, Ben Montgomery, Nancie McDermott, Grace Talusan, Edwin Lozada.

I believe everything that happened to me in the course of writing this book happened for a reason, and everyone in my life was sent to me for a purpose. Nothing was a coincidence in writing this memoir. To my sister, Isabel, a big hug and thanks for your prayers.

And to the most important people who are a precious part of my life, who have been there for me through thick and thin. To my husband, Elpi Quirino, my love, my calming presence, my strength and rock, I couldn't have done this without you. And to our children Tim and Chelsea and Constante, this story is yours to cherish, as much as it is mine. I wrote this for you. May we all find the strength and courage to face tomorrow with the same grace, gratitude, and faith that my brave mother taught us.

About the Author

Elizabeth Ann Besa-Quirino is a New Jersey–based award-winning journalist, food writer, cookbook author and memoirist. Previously a college professor and advertising creative director, Elizabeth develops recipes centered on Filipino home cooking on her website, TheQuirinoKitchen.com

Elizabeth Ann was born in the Philippines and raised in Tarlac, a province on the main island of Luzon that saw significant hardship during the Japanese occupation during WWII. Her writing is inspired by stories of her mother's courage and heroism in the face of insurmountable obstacles.

In her food writing, Elizabeth Ann is a contributor for Simply Recipes and a correspondent for the digital culture and lifestyle magazine Positively Filipino. Her work has also been featured on Books By Women, WriterCEO, FOOD Magazine, and Rustan's in-store publication, *Sans Rival*.

Elizabeth Ann is a member of the International Association of Culinary Professionals (IACP) and serves as a member of the Board of Advisors for the President Elpidio Quirino Foundation.